New Casebooks

THE DUCHESS OF MALFI

JOHN WEBSTER

EDITED BY DYMPNA CALLAGHAN

First published in Great Britain 2000 by
MACMILLAN PRESS LTD
Houndmills, Basingstoke, Hampshire RG21 6XS and London
Companies and representatives throughout the world

A catalogue record for this book is available from the British Library.

ISBN 0–333–61427–5 hardcover
ISBN 0–333–61428–3 paperback

First published in the United States of America 2000 by
ST. MARTIN'S PRESS, INC.,
Scholarly and Reference Division,
175 Fifth Avenue, New York, N.Y. 10010

ISBN 0–312–22861–9

Library of Congress Cataloging-in-Publication Data
The Duchess of Malfi : John Webster / edited by Dympna Callaghan.
p.   cm. — (New casebooks)
Includes bibliographical references and index.
ISBN 0–312–22861–9
1. Webster, John, 1580?–1625? Duchess of Malfi.   I. Callaghan, Dympna.
II. Series.

PR3184.D83 D83 2000
822'.3—dc21
                                99–045127

10   9   8   7   6   5   4   3   2   1
09 08 07 06 05 04 03 02 01 00

Printed in Hong Kong

New Casebooks

THE DUCHESS
OF MALFI

New Casebooks

POETRY

WILLIAM BLAKE Edited by David Punter
CHAUCER Edited by Valerie Allen and Ares Axiotis
COLERIDGE, KEATS AND SHELLEY Edited by Peter J. Kitson
JOHN DONNE Edited by Andrew Mousley
SEAMUS HEANEY Edited by Michael Allen
PHILIP LARKIN Edited by Stephen Regan
PARADISE LOST Edited by William Zunder
VICTORIAN WOMEN POETS Edited by Joseph Bristow
WORDSWORTH Edited by John Williams

NOVELS AND PROSE

AUSTEN: *Emma* Edited by David Monaghan
AUSTEN: *Mansfield Park* and *Persuasion* Edited by Judy Simons
AUSTEN: *Sense and Sensibility* and *Pride and Prejudice* Edited by Robert Clark
CHARLOTTE BRONTË: *Jane Eyre* Edited by Heather Glen
CHARLOTTE BRONTË: *Villette* Edited by Pauline Nestor
EMILY BRONTË: *Wuthering Heights* Edited by Patsy Stoneman
WILKIE COLLINS Edited by Lyn Pykett
JOSEPH CONRAD Edited by Elaine Jordan
DICKENS: *Bleak House* Edited by Jeremy Tambling
DICKENS: *David Copperfield* and *Hard Times* Edited by John Peck
DICKENS: *Great Expectations* Edited by Roger Sell
ELIOT: *Middlemarch* Edited by John Peck
E.M. FORSTER Edited by Jeremy Tambling
HARDY: *Jude the Obscure* Edited by Penny Boumelha
HARDY: *Tess of the D'Urbervilles* Edited by Peter Widdowson
JAMES: *Turn of the Screw* and *What Maisie Knew* Edited by Neil Cornwell and Maggie Malone
LAWRENCE: *Sons and Lovers* Edited by Rick Rylance
TONI MORRISON Edited by Linden Peach
GEORGE ORWELL Edited by Byran Loughrey
SHELLEY: *Frankenstein* Edited by Fred Botting
STOKER: *Dracula* Edited by Glennis Byron
STERNE: *Tristram Shandy* Edited byMelvyn New
WOOLF: *Mrs Dalloway* and *To the Lighthouse* Edited by Su Reid

DRAMA

BECKETT: *Waiting for Godot* and *Endgame* Edited by Steven Connor
APHRA BEHN Edited by Janet Todd
SHAKESPEARE: *Antony and Cleopatra* Edited by John Drakakis
SHAKESPEARE: *Hamlet* Edited by Martin Coyle
SHAKESPEARE: *King Lear* Edited by Kiernan Ryan
SHAKESPEARE: *Macbeth* Edited by Alan Sinfield
SHAKESPEARE: *The Merchant of Venice* Edited by Martin Coyle
SHAKESPEARE: *A Midsummer Night's Dream* Edited by Richard Dutton
SHAKESPEARE: *The Tempest* Edited by R. S. White
SHAKESPEARE: *Twelfth Night* Edited by R. S. White
SHAKESPEARE ON FILM Edited by Robert Shaughnessy
SHAKESPEARE'S HISTORY PLAYS Edited by Graham Holderness
SHAKESPEARE'S TRAGEDIES Edited by Susan Zimmerman
WEBSTER: *The Duchess of Malfi* Edited by Dympna Callaghan

GENERAL THEMES

FEMINIST THEATRE AND THEORY Edited by Helene Keyssar
POSTCOLONIAL LITERATURES Edited by Michael Parker and Roger Starkey

---

New Casebooks Series
Series Standing Order
ISBN 0-333-71702-3 hardcover
ISBN 0-333-69345-0 paperback
(outside North America only)

You can receive future titles in this series as they are published by placing a standing order.
Please contact your bookseller or, in case of difficulty, write to us at the address below
with your name and address, the title of the series and the ISBN quoted above.

Customer Services Department, Macmillan Distribution Ltd
Houndmills, Basingstoke, Hampshire RG21 6XS, England

Contents

Acknowledgements

The editor and publishers wish to thank the following for permission to use copyright material:

Karin S. Coddon, for 'The Duchess of Malfi: Tyranny and Spectacle in Jacobean Drama', in Madness in Drama: Themes in Drama, Vol. 15, ed. James Redmond (1993), pp. 1–17, by permission of the Cambridge University Press; Christy Desmet, for 'Neither Maid, Widow, nor Wife'; Rhetoric of the Woman Controversy in The Duchess of Malfi', in In Another Country: Feminist Perspectives on Renaissance Drama, ed. Dorothea Kehler and Susan Baker (1991), pp. 71–91, by permission of the Scarecrow Press; Andrea Henderson, for 'Death on Stage, Death of the Stage: The Antitheatricality of The Duchess of Malfi', Theatre Journal, 42 (1990), 194–207. Copyright © 1990 the Johns Hopkins University Press, by permission of the Johns Hopkins University Press; Theodora A. Jankowski, 'Defining/Confining the Duchess: Negotiating the Female Body in John Webster's The Duchess of Malfi', Studies in Philology, 87 (1990), 221–45. Copyright © 1990 by the University of North Carolina Press, by permission of the University of North Carolina Press; Kathleen McLuskie, for 'Drama and Sexual Politics: the Case of Webster's Duchess', in Drama, Sex and Politics: Themes in Drama, Vol. 7, ed. James Redmond (1985), pp. 77–91, by permission of the Cambridge University Press; Mary Beth Rose, for 'The Heroics of Marriage in Renaissance Tragedy', from 'The Expense of Spirit': Love and Sexuality in English Renaissance Drama by Mary Beth Rose (1988), pp. 155–77, by permission of Cornell University Press; Susan Wells, for 'Dominance of the Typical and The Duchess of Malfi', in The Dialectics of Representation by Susan Wells (1985), pp. 61–80, by permission of the Johns Hopkins University Press; Frank Whigham, for 'Sexual and Social Mobility in *The Duchess of Malfi*', *PMLA*, 100:2 (1985), 167–81, by permission of the Modern Language Association of America; R. S. White, for 'The Moral Design of *The Duchess of Malfi*', (1987) by permission of the author.

Every effort has been made to trace the copyright holders but if any have been inadvertently overlooked the publishers will be pleased to make the necessary arrangement at the first opportunity.

General Editors' Preface

The purpose of this series of New Casebooks is to reveal some of the ways in which contemporary criticism has changed our understanding of commonly studied texts and writers and, indeed, of the nature of criticism itself. Central to the series is a concern with modern critical theory and its effect on current approaches to the study of literature. Each New Casebook editor has been asked to select a sequence of essays which will introduce the reader to the new critical approaches to the text or texts being discussed in the volume and also illuminate the rich interchange between critical theory and critical practice that characterises so much current writing about literature.

In this focus on modern critical thinking and practice New Casebooks aim not only to inform but also to stimulate, with volumes seeking to reflect both the controversy and the excitement of current criticism. Because much of this criticism is difficult and often employs an unfamiliar critical language, editors have been asked to give the reader as much help as they feel is appropriate, but without simplifying the essays or the issues they raise. Again, editors have been asked to supply a list of further reading which will enable readers to follow up issues raised by the essays in the volume.

The project of New Casebooks, then, is to bring together in an illuminating way those critics who best illustrate the ways in which contemporary criticism has established new methods of analysing texts and who have reinvigorated the important debate about how we 'read' literature. The hope is, of course, that New Casebooks will not only open up this debate to a wider audience, but will also encourage students to extend their own ideas, and think afresh about their responses to the texts they are studying.

John Peck and Martin Coyle
University of Wales, Cardiff

Introduction

DYMPNA CALLAGHAN

I

When *The Duchess of Malfi* was published in 1623, the title page informed readers that the play had been 'Presented privately at the Blackfriars; and publiquely at the Globe, By the Kings Maiesties Servants', and names Richard Sharpe as the young actor who played the Duchess.[1] Since cast lists rarely indicated the names of players, that the identity of an actor who had played the Duchess is known to us provides an especially salutary reminder that the marvellous role of the Duchess was neither written for a woman nor ever peformed by one on the all-male Jacobean stage. The gender dissonance between the play's title role and the name of the actor who performed it is all the more striking because the tragic protagonist here *is* a woman.

In *The Duchess of Malfi*, Webster reworked the idea of a female tragic protagonist explored in his earlier and less well-received play, *The White Devil*. Yet, for much traditional criticism, female centrality has been the unacknowledged problem of *The Duchess of Malfi*, with issues of gender being displaced onto issues of structural distortion. Tellingly, Webster's insistence on female tragic centrality has been described as producing a world without a centre,[2] and while critics have consistently appreciated the wonderfully rich and dense imagery of Webster's language until relatively recently received opinion held that the 'fatal flaw' was not where it ought to be, allegedly in the struggling humanity of the tragic protagonist, but in the oddly decentred plot. The tragic predicament of the Duchess for

1

such historical critics both exemplifies and deviates from the struc-
turing principles of 'great man' tragedy, most thoroughly schema-
tised by the critic A. C. Bradley as the rise and fall of the man whose
greatness is marked by some fatal flaw.[3] The Duchess dies not in Act
V, like Lear or Othello, but in Act IV, well before the dénouement.
Critics have even suggested that in resorting to 'she-tragedy' Webster
demonstrates the demise of the genre itself. They have claimed
further that the tragic predicament was by this stage in the seventeenth century no longer concerned with the strength of human will
in the face of extreme adversity, but rather addressed itself to weakness as the ultimate human condition. Human fragility, it was
argued, was exemplified by woman as tragic hero, which the tragic
form would prove unable to sustain.[4] In contrast to this strain of humanist criticism, J. W. Lever and the cultural materialist critics who
followed him, took as their focus not the predicament of the individual but the play's power relations, or what Lever describes as 'the
tragedy of state'.[5] From this perspective, tragedy offers a radical critique of the existing political order: 'The court of Amalfi presents in
miniature the court of Whitehall, with its adventurers, its feverish
pulling of strings for office and promotion, its heedless and heartless
pursuit of privilege.'[6] If this criticism addressed questions of political
corruption and the power dynamics of court society, it failed to
address the question of why a Jacobean playwright would choose to
address these issues via a female tragic protagonist. That is to say,
such criticism still begged the question of tragic femininity, of the
problems of female sovereignty and the way in which female desire is
shown in the play to have the capacity to undermine, and ultimately
transform, the fabric of the state.

In contrast to the approaches outlined above, gender-conscious
criticism (the vein of enquiry represented by this volume) has emphasised the fact that Webster's play participates in a cultural
debate, not just about court corruption or politics in general, but
specifically and directly about the status of women. The historical
circumstance of the transvestite stage, from this perspective, makes
Webster's choice of tragic protagonist all the more remarkable.
Indeed, the phenomenon of cross-dressed boy actors underlines the
fact that *The Duchess of Malfi* is part of a cultural debate about
female sexuality, marriage, and especially widowhood, repeatedly
staged in Jacobean theatre. For example, in a play which offers a
parodic reflection on the concerns of *The Duchess of Malfi*, Lording
Barry's *Ram Alley*, Widow Taffeta avers: 'Widdowes are sildome

slow to put men to it.' She engages in bawdy banter with other women and judges men by the length of their codpieces and by the length of their noses. Widow Taffeta is thus a kind of pantomine dame, a figure in whom the sexual appetite imputed to widows becomes comically exaggerated. There is also a duchess widow in Middleton's *More Dissemblers Besides Women* (c.1619), and in his *No Wit, No Help Like a Woman's* (c.1611) Lady Goldenfleece constitutes the stereotype of the greedy lustful widow. By contrast, in Middleton and Fletcher's *The Widow* (1616), the character of Valeria offers a portrait of idealised widowhood. What Michael Shapiro has observed of *The Widow*, seems applicable also to Webster's play:

> It seems plausible to me, if unprovable, that the reflexive awareness of the male actors behind the ... heroines also heightened the spectators' awareness of the play-boy in the role of the duchess. Thus loosened from its mimetic moorings, the constructedness of the role both as a theatrical role and as a token in a cultural debate on widowhood would enable different spectators to interpret that role in radically different ways. To some, the duchess might indeed have seemed a corrective to negative stereotypes, while others could dismiss the same interpretation as a flattering concession to growing numbers of female spectators. To still others, she could be read as a satiric caricature of contemporary dowagers or as a parody of female stereotypes held by men.[7]

Webster's play echoes the cultural commonplaces about concupiscent widows in particular as well as about excesses of female sexual appetite in general.[8] Ferdinand reiterates these stereotypes by referring to his sister as 'lusty widow' (I.ii.259) and by claiming that 'women like that part, which, like the lamprey, / Hath nev'r a bone in't' (I.ii.255–6). In a parallel vein, Joseph Swetnam contends in his infamously misogynist tract, *The Arraignment of Lewde, idle, froward and unconstant women* (1615), that 'it is more easie for a young man or maid to forbeare carnall acts then it is for a widow'.[9]

However, Swetnam also argued that widows were simply more difficult to deal with than women who had never been married. Swetnam's diatribe enraged some of his female readers, and one, writing under the pseudonym Esther Sowernam, in a pamphlet entitled *Esther Hath Hang'd Haman; or, An answere to a lewd pamphlet entituled The Arraignment of Women* (London, 1617), argued that if maids were malleable and widows stubborn, it must follow that it was the experience of marriage that made them so: 'How cometh it then that this gentle and mild disposition [of the maid] is afterwards altered?'[10] Indeed, the social facts indicate that, if anything, women were reluctant rather than eager to remarry, and that despite the literary preoccupation with concupiscent widows, the incidence of remarriage was relatively low.[11] In fact, as Merry E. Weisner observes, 'studies indicate that women who could afford to resisted all pressure to remarry and so retained their independence'.[12] Although younger widows were more likely to remarry than older women, widows of all ages remarried with far less frequency than their male counterparts, who suffered from none of the cultural prohibitions that controlled women's patterns of remarriage following the death of a spouse.[13] There are many possible reasons for this, but the law of coverture might have been a disincentive to women to enter into a new conjugal union. Under this law all the woman's inheritance from her deceased spouse would become the property of a new husband, and she would lose that precious 'liberty to live after one's owne law'.[14] The wills of husbands may thus reflect a desire to protect their survivors' autonomy rather than a wish to prevent remarriage. Fenland yeoman John Pyne, in 1598, directed that 'my wiefe and my sonne ... shall remaine together with the encrease of their stockes and if my wife doe chaunce to mary then my will ys that my sons porcon [portion] shalbe putt in the handes [the hands] of [my overseer] ... to be put forth', and 'boundes [bonds] shalbe taken of the parties that shall have my childrens porcons'.[15] Another practice designed to evade the problem of coverture was that of granting a bequest for the lifetime of the widow. This gave widows maximum control over property while at the same time protecting it from any subsequent husband.[16]

By making the mad Ferdinand the primary mouthpiece for stereotypes about lecherous widows eager to remarry as soon as possible, *The Duchess of Malfi* distances its protagonist, the Duchess, from such notions, and does so in part by reminding the audience of the social reality of lives of many women upon the death of their spouses. In one of the most poignant domestic scenes in the play, we see the Duchess at her toilette, brushing her greying hair in an apt confirmation of what she earlier tells Antonio: ''Tis not the figure cut in Alabaster / Kneels at my husband's tomb' (I.i.444–5). She reminds the audience of the difference between representation and reality – between the effigies of living widows in wood and marble depicted praying for the souls of their departed husbands, and their continuing lived reality. More profoundly, the Duchess reminds us of the distinction between the quick and the dead. Yet, this reminder in the figure of the kneeling Duchess also connotes the very reason widows were so troubling: they were no longer in the position of subservience. Rather, in the play, this posture is echoed and inverted by Antonio's kneeling in a gesture of deference when the Duchess proposes marriage to him, and by her own gesture of stoic yet pious submission when she kneels for execution. Through the gesture of genuflection, the play mediates upon the power and autonomy that might fall to a woman upon her husband's death.

Women like the Duchess might well be still in the prime of life, or even very young, when their husbands died. While we in the twentieth century tend to connect widowhood with old age, this was far from being the case in Jacobean England, where it was quite possible for a woman both to become a widow at any age, and to find herself widowed more than once in a lifetime. Instead of returning to the household of her birth family, or being subsumed into the households of other male relatives (an unlikely event given that nuclear families were the norm), widows in early modern Europe became heads of households in their own right and were expected to support their dependants.[17] Widows were threatening because they were under the government neither of fathers nor of husbands, and, if they inherited wealth and property, they might remain outside the direct rule of men.

The status of the widow contrasted sharply with that of the married woman. A married woman was, to use the legal term for her condition, *feme covert*. That is, upon marriage all the woman's rights and property converted to her husband, and her very legal identity was subsumed by his. Once married, coverture (as the woman's status as *feme covert* was known) was a legal fiction that proposed that husband and wife were one person – on the biblical basis that in marriage the two become 'one flesh'. Furthermore, that one flesh belonged to the man. In practice, this meant that, as a wife, a woman could not, for example, sign a contract or obtain credit on her own behalf.[18] While such a system may seem at first glance to have women firmly in its rigid thrall, it is important to remember that, unlike today when most adult women in the population at any given time are married, most in early modern England were not – the majority were either unmarried or widowed. Additionally, although in theory also, primogeniture (the common law right of eldest sons to inherit their father's wealth) militated against widows inheriting, in practice, there were other forms of law – ecclesiastical and civil – that allowed for community property in marriage and partiality of inheritance (i.e. the right to divide inheritance up among surviving family members rather than bestowing everything to the eldest son).[19] More basically, however, male rule foundered upon the fact that men often died early, that only 60 per cent of marriages produced a son, and that, demographically, it was unlikely that a son would be of age at the time of his father's death. A son's inheritance thus often came into his mother's hands.[20]

Though set in Italy, this is precisely the Duchess's situation. Since Ferdinand is her twin brother, the Duchess must have inherited her sovereignty from her husband, their son being too young to inherit his father's dukedom. This seems to be corroborated by Ferdinand's outburst upon discovering that his sister has had children:

> **Ferdinand** Write to the Duke of Malfi, my young nephew
> She had by her first husband, and acquaint him
> With's mother's honesty.
>
> (III.iii.67–9)

At the end of the play, however, it is specifically Antonio's son, and not her son by her first husband, who is presented by Delio as the new heir, despite the fact that his nativity horoscope predicted short life and violent death:

> join all our force
> To establish this young hopeful gentleman
> In's mother's right.
>
> (V.v.111–12)

Whatever vagueness the play exhibits about the inheritance pattern by which the Duchess (and later, Antinio's son) inherits sovereignty, it is certainly the case that, as a widow, the Duchess has the potential she did not possess as a wife to wield power independently of a husband and to sever allegiances to other male kin.

II

It is not hard to see why a social system which placed such rigid restrictions on married women would find widows threatening.

Widows, like female sovereigns, brought together the apparently mutually exclusive categories of femininity and power and so constituted an anomalous but prominent category in early modern society. In some parts of Europe the law tried to avert the threat posed by widows by barring women from inheriting property on which public offices were entailed. (For instance, in France from 1464 onwards, Salic law prevented women from inheriting the French crown.[21]) But for the most part, widows presented an intractable problem for early modern patriarchy. Merry Weisner describes the difficulty as follows:

> They were still very disturbing to notions of male authority, however, both because they were economically independent and because they were sexually experienced women not under the tutelage of a man. Thus remarriage was often seen as the best solution to the problem of these women who were neither 'married or to be married'. Remarriage was also troubling, however, for this lessened a woman's allegiance to the family of her first husband and could have serious economic consequences for the children of her first marriage, and might also give a wealthy widow what was seen as an inappropriate amount of power over her spouse. Early modern laws regarding widows often reflect this ambivalence.[22]

The Italian setting of *The Duchess of Malfi* is significant in that some of the restrictions on women in Italy appear to have been greater than those elsewhere in Europe. One Italian text written by the Venetian Francesco Barbaro, *De re uxoria* (1416), which articulates Renaissance norms about the relation between the household and the state (ideas also recapitulated by Antonio at the beginning of *The Duchess of Malfi*) argues for controlling women's activities as a means of securing dynastic integrity. Barbaro, however, recognises the difficulty of control presented by widows: 'We can scarce with great ingeny [*sic*], elaborate industry, and singular care reduce widows, formed both to their own and other humors, to our own customes.'[23] Another Italian text, Giovanni Giorgio Trissino in his *Epistola del Trissino de la vita che dee tenere una donna vedova* (1542), describes a widow as 'a free woman: ... such may not be subject to a husband, or a father, or anyone else'. Surprisingly, Trissino argues, widows should consider themselves men. And indeed, unlike the English situation described above, in Italy widows, unlike wives, were entitled to appear in court, do business and deal in property. However, as Trissino points out, the widow's is 'a bitter liberty'. She may not, he specifically stipulates, interest herself in politics: 'to speak of what the Turk is up to in Constantinople, or the sultan of Egypt, or of what may be decided at the Diet of Augustus ... nothing is more inappropriate than to hear a woman speak of war and discuss statecraft.'[24]

The Duchess of Malfi thus combines one of the most threatening forms of domestic female power, namely widowhood, with the most threatening manifestation of all – sovereignty. Female government, or gynaecocracy, represents an exacerbated state of female autonomy and was in the Renaissance almost universally condemned. This presented something of a problem in early modern England which had two female monarchs in a short space of time and simultaneously a woman ruler in Scotland (James I's ill-fated mother, Mary Queen of Scots). Mary Tudor's accession to the English throne in 1553 shook the patriarchal foundations of English dynasticism. The problem that then presented itself was that if women were innately, biologically and ontologically inferior to men, how could female government ever be justified? It could not – at least according to John Knox's *The First Blast of the Trumpet against the Monstrous Regiment of Women* (1558):

> To promote a woman to bear rule, superiority, dominion or empire above any realm, nation, or city is repugnant to nature, contumely to God, a thing most contrarious to his revealed will and approved ordinance, and finally it is the subversion of good order, and all equity and justice ... I affirm the empire of a woman to be a thing repugnant to nature, I mean not only that God by the order of his creation hath spoiled women of authority and dominion, but also that man hath seen, proved and pronounced just causes why that it so should be. Man, I say, in many other cases blind, doth in this behalf see very clearly. For the causes be so manifest that they cannot be hid. For who can deny that it repugneth to nature, that the blind shall be appointed to lead and conduct such as do see? That the weak, the sick and the impotent persons shall nourish and keep the whole and strong, and finally, that the foolish, mad and frenetic shall govern the discreet, and give counsel to such as be sober of mind? And such be all women compared unto man, in bearing of authority. For their sight in civil regiment is but a blindness: their strength weakness: their counsel foolishness: and judgement frenzy, if it be rightly considered.[25]

In response, John Aylmer wrote his *Harborow for Faithful and Trewe Subjects* (1559). This tract urged obedience to the monarch regardless of sex, and attributed to female monarchs the same authority as male sovereigns. Knox's treatise, Aylmer argued, 'almost cracked the duty of true obedience'.[26] Knox's diatribe had been directed principally at the Catholic queens Mary Tudor and Mary Queen of Scots, but when the Protestant Elizabeth ascended the throne in the same year that Knox's tract was published, no amount of intricate ideological manoeuvring could undo the prevailing notion that the government of women, whether at the national or domestic level, contravened the natural order. Even the ultra-Protestant John Calvin, in Geneva, when consulted by Elizabeth's chief adviser, William Cecil, struck an equivocal note:

> Two years ago John Knox asked of me, in a private conversation, what I thought about the Government of Women. I candidly replied, that as it was a deviation from the original and proper order of nature, it was to be ranked, no less than slavery, among the punishments consequent upon the fall of man: but that there were occasionally women so endowed, that the singular good qualities which shone forth in them made it evident that they were raised up by Divine authority.[27]

Calvin is furiously backpedalling here, desperately trying to rationalise the reign of a Protestant female monarch, and, by way of a last ditch attempt at justification, he ultimately resorts to a singularly vague notion of divine authority.[28]

Elizabeth, of course, was the absolute manipulator of her anomalous status, turning her femininity to advantage in the myth of the Virgin Queen. To buttress this myth, a barrage of classical iconography was used to rationalise what might otherwise be construed as her unnatural and monstrous reign. She was identified with Diana, the goddess of Chastity, and with Astrea, the virgin from Virgil's fourth Eclogue who returns to re-establish the golden age. Paintings of Elizabeth sometimes depicted her with a sieve that holds water (a concept that was meant to represent her status as an unpenetrated virgin), but also with iconography that brings her a little closer to the values represented by Webster's Duchess, namely ears of corn, which were associated with Ceres, the goddess of fertility. In remaining unmarried, Elizabeth avoided the problem of the conflict between the sovereign's duty to govern the realm and the necessity that a wife submit to a husband. If a sovereign were married, her government would be effectively appropriated by her husband. In the Duchess's case, the realm may, upon her marriage, be effectively governed by her steward, who has after all, from the very beginning of the play, expressed very definite – and laudable – views about how the state should be run. On the other hand, the Duchess represents sovereignty not just in the state but also in the family household. Her class status cannot make it otherwise. One of the problems Aylmer had been most concerned to address was the knotty question of a married female ruler:

> Yea say you, God hath apoynted her to be subject to her husband ... [T]herefore she maye not be the heade. I graunte that, so farre as pertaineth to the bandes of marriage, and the office of a wife, she muste be a subjecte but as a magistrate she maye be her husband's head.[29]

This idea was indebted to the notion of the sovereign's two bodies – the mortal body and the body politic:

> [W]hen god chooseth himself by sending to a king, whose succession is ruled by inheritance and lineal descent, no heirs male: it is a plain argument that for some secret purpose he mindeth the female should reign and govern.[30]

A woman ruler, Aylmer claimed, was not a monstrosity but an anomaly, no more serious than those which occur in nature, such as twins or a man whose hair does not turn grey with age.

In a sense, what is most anomalous about the Duchess is that despite her clear legal claim to power, she cannot exercise it free of the control of her brothers. The Cardinal seeks dynastic sway, while the Duchess's twin, Ferdinand, is deranged by incestuous desire to control his sister's sexuality. He instructs Bosola:

>   observe the Duchess,
> To note all the particulars of her 'haviour:
> What suitors do solicit her for marriage
> And whom she best affects: she's a young widow,
> I would not have her marry again.
> **Bosola** No, sir?
> **Ferdinand** Do not you ask the reason: but be satisfied,
>   I say I would not.
>   (I.ii.173–8)

In these extraordinary circumstances, the Duchess, a pre-eminently public figure, is compelled to marry – that is, to undertake what should be a solemn and public undertaking – in the secrecy of an informal arrangement:

> **Duchess** If all my royal kindred
> Lay in my way into this marriage:
> I'd make them my low foot-steps. And even now,
> Even in this hate, as men in some great battles
> By apprehending danger, have achiev'd
> Almost impossible actions: I have heard soldiers say so,
> So I, through frights and threat'nings, will assay
> This dangerous venture. Let old wives report
> I winked, and chose a husband.
>
> (I.ii.260–8)

Marriage was a newly elevated condition in Protestant England where it was now defined as the mainstay of political order, 'a little commonwealth'.[31] Yet, marriage itself was not as clearly defined as we might expect, and this was a situation that both church and the state sought to rectify. Although certain property rights were contingent on a church wedding, and despite the fact that marriage was widely understood to be a formal public act that took place in church, there were aspects of what was known as 'the law of spousals' that led to conjugal irregularities of the type we find in Webster's plays.[32]

III

In Elizabethan and Jacobean England, an informal declaration was sufficient to create a valid and binding marriage even though the authorities strongly encouraged the principle that marriage should be formalised and sanctified by ecclesiastical solemnisation.[33] The complexities and confusion attending marriage were compounded by the fact that binding marriage contracts could be made in advance of public, church ritual. Martin Ingram observes:

> Among the less self-consciously pious sections of the population, moreover, the sheer inertia of social custom (especially in more conservative areas) was a powerful force which for a while helped to sustain the institution of spousals as a preliminary to marriage in church. Yet in the long term the custom was doomed to decline. Given the social and economic importance of marriage, it was desirable for all concerned that a single, incontrovertible act should signal entry into the married state; and the church ceremony, duly recorded in the parish registers, really made spousals redundant.[34]

The pitfalls of private, unofficial spousals are evident in numerous indictments of women for bastardy, some of whom, no doubt, had been led to believe that they were contracted in a binding way to their sexual partners. There were also many cases of breach of promise, where women sued men who had privately married them without benefit of solemnisation and then gone on to marry other women and beget children by them. In what represents, in a sense, the other side of the Duchess's clandestine nuptials, church courts were full of women who perceived themselves to have been deceived and defrauded. Consolidation of the nuclear family required formal, legal, sanctification of marriage in an indisputable way, and the struggle to arrive at this state of things is what we see in the late sixteenth and early seventeenth centuries. Nonetheless, authorities were obliged to uphold informal contracts and legal and moral ambiguity inevitably ensued from these unregulated unions:[35]

> A marriage ceremony was regarded as 'clandestine' when it neglected one or more of the canonical regulations governing the solemnisation of matrimony. After 1604 this meant a marriage without the three-fold publication of the banns or the issue of a valid licence, a ceremony conducted outside the diocese in which the couple dwelt, or a marriage performed during certain prohibited seasons or outside certain set hours, or in any circumstances save within a lawful church or chapel and in the presence of a properly constituted minister of the church of England.[36]

Crucially, what defined marriage – clandestine or solemnised – was the mutual consent of the couple. Thus there was a tradition of freedom of consent, regardless of the wishes of parents or the dynastic ambitions of families. The problem of freedom of choice in selecting a marriage partner was a trans-European phenomenon, and in England there had been an attempt to address it in the reign of Edward VI in what is known as the *Reformatio legum*. This legislation would have made all marriages invalid that took place without the consent of parents or 'governors'. (The Duchess's brothers would, of course, have fallen into the latter category.) This legislation was aborted at the convocation of 1597 despite strong support for its measures. In the demise of this proposal the principle of mutual consent was reasserted: 'consent in marriage is the matter specially to be regarded, and credit of kindred, honour, wealth, contentment and pleasure of friends be rather matters of conveniency than necessity in matrimony.'[37] The problem of family interests remained, however, and family pressure versus individual choice in marriage was the cause of litigation in more than half the spousal cases brought before the ecclesiastical courts, and was especially the case where wealth and property were involved.[38] Kindred objected particularly to marriages where there was a class discrepancy between the two parties. And here, despite its foreign and aristocratic setting, the Duchess's marriage bears a resemblance to somewhat lowlier English cases, such as that of Katherine Imber, who wished 'that she might be gone away from her father's house for that she was weary to be kept as she was', and succumbed to an ardent manservant.[39]

It must be emphasised that in the heated debates about freedom of choice in marriage in this period, there was a widespread belief that familial consent was necessary, if not to the legality of the marriage, at least to its social acceptability and viability. The defiance of children over parents in choice of marriage partner met with strong disapproval. *The Duchess of Malfi*, in a sense, recasts this controversy by making the issue not one of parents versus children but one of familial interests versus female autonomy. As a widow, the Duchess is clearly not suffering from an adolescent infatuation like that of Romeo and Juliet, which might well attract disapprobation. While the Duchess's clandestine contract indeed marks her transgression, it is obviously one pitched to attract the sympathy of the audience. Ferdinand and the Cardinal are so manifestly manipulative and corrupt that her secret contract with Antonio is presented as a necessary exigency. The opening of the play certainly recapitulates a very tense struggle about the contest between individual and family interests. Crucially, however, the play focuses on woman's interest, woman's erotic choice, and Antonio as the object of that choice is by far the more passive party in the transaction.

What constituted a marriage in essence, then, was not a church ceremony, but a contract or 'spousals', also known as 'making sure' or 'handfasting' – that is the act by which the couple bound *themselves* without the intervention of clergy or relatives – to one another.[40] The presence of other parties, priest and family, was not essential to the act of conjugal union, but rather merely its formal ratification. The couple could not be married by anyone else – they could, in effect, only themselves marry one another in a deliberate act of volition and choice. This was the fundamental and abiding principle of Canon (i.e. Church) law.

The kind of marriage the Duchess and Antonio undergo conforms to these specifications for a contract *per verba de praesenti* – that is, a verbal contract using words of the present tense, binding from that moment forth; it is the performative utterance of the couple to one another that constitutes the marriage:

> I have heard lawyers say, a contract in a chamber,
> *Per verba de presenti*, is absolute marriage.
> Bless, Heaven, this sacred Gordian, which let violence
> Never untwine.
>
> (I.ii.391–4)

The Duchess's 'I have heard lawyers say' perhaps indicates the unusual nature of such a practice and the necessity of providing some explanation of a rather unorthodox, albeit legally binding arrangement, to the audience. Even though the two clearly take hands, as we can discern from Antonio's words about 'loving palms', in a visual image onstage of conjugal unity much like that to be found in emblem books, it is rather difficult to discern exactly which words exchanged between the couple would actually constitute the conjugal contract:

> That we may imitate the loving palms,
> Best emblem of a peaceful marriage
> That nev'r bore fruit divided.
> **Duchess**   What can the Church force more?
>
> (I.ii.338–401)

The words of contract are not self-evident here, and there is no unequivocal nuptial event. The earlier exchange of rings, for instance, occurred at the moment when the Duchess announced her intention to marry Antonio and clearly did not constitute the marriage itself. Again, when the Duchess pronounces: 'We are now man and wife, and tis the Church / That must but echo this', it is not obvious in exactly what earlier declaration they became so. There is certainly no echo of the unambiguous wording prescribed by the Book of Common Prayer. Moreover, the Duchess appears to signal that the marriage will be solemnised by the church at some future date – though there is no evidence in the text that this ever occurs.

Clandestine marriages, like that of the Duchess and Antonio, which combined passion and subterfuge, were made for the stage.

In real life, such contracts caused confusion and dispute in the church courts. For instance, a contact to marry *per verba de futuro* (a promise to marry someone) could be superseded by a *de praesenti contract* (a private contract) with someone else.[41] Further, present and future contracts were often confused, although widespread uncertainty about what constituted a marriage contract had greatly diminished by the reign of Elizabeth.[42] Given the sharp decline in spousal litigation, it would seem that the Protestant state, in contrast to the Catholic, Italian state in which Webster's play is set, had succeeded in its efforts to regulate marriage despite the intractable anomalies of Canon law. Somehow – by dint of prevailing ideology as much as by the conduct of ecclesiastical judges – the state had inculcated the notion that only solemnisation in church or chapel in the presence of a minister satisfactorily constituted matrimony.[43]

IV

What is unique about *The Duchess of Malfi* is that here a private contract is intended to be perpetually clandestine, never to become public. Most couples who married privately, usually to evade the wishes of family, would make their union public after they were married. It is the prolonged secrecy of the Duchess's situation that gives it its dramatic quality and reflects the real life historical events on which the story Webster borrowed was based.[44] The problem faced by plaintiffs in ecclesiastical courts was that of proving that they were in fact married. The Duchess seems to solve this problem by bringing Cariola in as a witness – though, in practice, single witnesses were of little use if marriages came to litigation.[45] Moreover, ecclesiastical judges also urged that such marriages which had not been solemnised should be publicised.[46] On this count, the marriage of the Duchess to Antonio falls far short.

The Duchess's marriage, in fact, bears an alarming resemblance to some of those English marriages that came to litigation, as Ingram notes. In 1583, for example:

> an Amesbury servant called Christian Veriat paid a surprise visit to her lover, Thomas Sharpe, a weaver dwelling with his master at Durrington. That night, as Sharpe and his master were walking her home, Christian allegedly took it into her head to become contracted immediately. The older man advised that 'the matter required no

such haste but might be done afterward some time when she had made her friends privy thereunto and by their consents'. But Christian would brook no such delay, and according to Thomas Sharpe's story, they were contracted on the spot, 'on the road between Durrington and Amesbury'.[47]

In England, in Church courts, which claimed growing jurisdiction over marriage, and increasingly in the society generally, a solemnised church ceremony alone was regarded as a definitive union. As it did so, concern about clandestine marriages grew.

Though *The Duchess of Malfi* is often read as a valorisation of marriage as a private phenomenon, separable from issues of state power, the circumstances in which this marriage occurs are highly questionable to say the least. What finally betrays the Duchess's clandestine marriage to her subjects is her pregnant body – the somatic marker of her femininity. The way in which the contradictions of female government are brought to a head is exemplified not just by her maternal concern for her children at her death or by some depiction of an abstract concept of motherhood, but by the fact that we see her through the processes of labour and childbirth. These facts of sexually active femininity were also what proved most difficult to hide from the world. That Webster shows us the Duchess on stage and pregnant is a factor of the utmost significance, since woman's sexuality constituted in the Renaissance the single and most intransigent obstacles to any argument which countered the belief in innate female inferiority. Constance Jordan summarises the case:

> Woman, it is generally agreed, is not as strong physically as man and, more important, is vulnerable sexually as he is not. Not only because pregnancy and lactation make her dependent on other persons, although this physical dependence is clearly important, but because her sexual activity, in contrast to his, can result in scandal and disgrace. Her body can and commonly does signify that she is sexually active whether or not she wishes the fact to be known. Maternity, unlike paternity, is not a discretionary matter, to be acknowledged or not, at will. These biological facts underlie arguments for restricting all woman's activities, particularly those that take her into the public arena. Misogynists tend to perceive her inability to control the effects of her sexuality – pregnancy – as an indication of an inherent moral debility.[48]

In this scheme of things a woman's chastity was not merely an abstract construct but a means of securing dynastic integrity: 'it was the foundation upon which patriarchal society rested.'[49] The business of determining whether a woman – married or not – was pregnant, then, was invested with weighty public and social significance. Medical manuals and popular handbooks of the period detailed 'the signs to know whether a woman be with child or no' and 'the tokens and signs whereby ye may perceive whether the time of labour be near'.[50] Some women were taken by surprise and gave birth without knowing they were pregnant, like Lady Anne Effingham in 1602 who went into labour during a game of shuttlecock and 'was brought to bed of a child without a midwife, she never suspecting that she had been with child'.[51] Unusual incidents such as this suggested the alarming possibility that a woman (albeit a less chaste one than Lady Anne) might hide the signs of her licentiousness from the world. Although the apricots applied by Bosola to get proof of the Duchess's pregnancy were not commonly known to accelerate delivery, a number of herbs contained properties that were believed to do so: stinking gladdon (a variety of iris), dragonwort, and cyclamen were all known as purgatives which 'scoureth and cleanseth [the womb] mightily'.[52] What endows Bosola's pregnancy test with an even more sinister cast is that its application could potentially operate as an abortifacient. The apricots thus fall into the category of these herbals about which the author of the period's definitive treatise on midwifery, Nicholas Culpeper, warned: 'give not any of these to any that is with child, lest you turn murderers.'[53]

When the Duchess goes into premature labour, Antonio, like a good husband, follows the advice of William Gouge by providing 'such things as are needful for (the woman's) travail and lying in childbed'.[54] But in his case, what is most 'needful' is that he maintain the secret of his wife's childbearing. The most famous instance of clandestine pregnancy in the Renaissance was that of Pope Joan, recorded in one of the most prominent books of the Italian Renaissance, Boccaccio's *De mulieribus claris* (c.1380). Allegedly a book of famous women, it is essentially a catalogue of notorious members of the sex, including Joan, who, in male disguise, advances in the church hierarchy until she is elected pope. God, however, intervenes:

> pitying his people from on high, did not permit a woman to occupy such a high place [as the papacy] ... Advised by the devil ... elected to the supreme office of the papacy, [Joan] was overcome with a burning lust [*ardor libidinis*] ... She found one who mounted [*de-*

fricere] her in secret (she, the successor of Peter!) and thus allayed her flaming prurience.[55]

Joan becomes pregnant and gives birth ignominiously in public. That is, the labour of Pope Joan exemplifies the scandal of commingling the otherwise discrete categories of private femininity and public power. The achievement of Webster's play is that it makes public the 'feminine' secrets of domestic and family life in a way that exonerates its heroine and casts a shadow on a public world, whose exclusion both of women and of personal happiness is the sign of its absolute corruption.

V

The essays in this volume not only acknowledge but also foreground the question of gender in *The Duchess of Malfi*, and in this they represent an intervention in a critical tradition which has deflected issues of gender and sexuality by focusing instead on alleged structural flaws, decadence, and amorality. In contrast, many of the critical inquiries included in this volume are avowedly motivated by feminism, and by an endeavour to see how the general cultural predicament of Jacobean women might have become plausible or even exemplary as a subject for Webster's tragedy. A further characteristic of the essays which follow is that, unlike traditional criticism, they do not measure Webster's tragedy against either some mythic standard of artistic wholeness, or against the aesthetic pinnacles of Shakespearean tragedy. Instead, the critics in this volume situate Webster on the cusp of modernity and trace the ways in which he anticipates new models of political and social being.

Karin S. Coddon's '*The Duchess of Malfi*: Tyranny and Spectacle in Jacobean Drama' (essay 1) addresses the trope of madness, which, in nascent modernity, functions not as the sign of internal chaos as it does now, but instead mainly functions in the drama of the period as a means of disguise or, alternatively, as a spectacle. In Webster's play, Coddon argues, the emergent ideology of rational individualism becomes visible at the point where madness appears and is identified with the corrupt public world. Sanity, in contrast, is identified with the private world that madness encroaches upon. In this opposition, we can see the beginnings of a new model of subjectivity, which valorises the rational individual. For Coddon, Webster's play anticipates fundamental dimensions of emergent modernity, especially in the primacy of private over public life. Furthermore, by rendering authority 'unreasonable' (mad), Coddon suggests that the play anticipates the rationalisations which would lead later in the century to the decapitation of Charles I. The essay, then, helps to situate the play's concern with public and private life in a larger political and social context.

In '"Neither Maid, Widow, nor Wife": Rhetoric of the Woman Controversy in *The Duchess of Malfi*' (essay 2), Christy Desmet engages a different context, by taking up the series of paradoxes about women from the *querrelle des femmes*, the controversy about women, which raged through the period. In part, Desmet argues, these paradoxes must be seen as a component of a highly stylised rhetorical game which took women as its subject. The structure of this rhetoric, Desmet contends, as much as its content, constitutes the means and method of women's subordination. As with much recent criticism, Desmet thus focuses on the significant role language plays in shaping and controlling the human subject.

Like Karin Coddon, Andrea Henderson (essay 3) sees Webster's play as anticipating the tumultuous events later in the century, specifically in this case the closing of the theatres in 1642. In 'Death on Stage, Death of the Stage: The Antitheatricality of *The Duchess of Malfi*' she argues that the Duchess represents emergent bourgeois values, while her brothers represent aristocratic values of decadent self-display. In a sense, then, the Duchess represents not just the private sphere as the arena of family affections, but also the realm beyond theatrical representation, in particular, the closed-off domestic space of the family withheld from the public gaze. The play, Henderson argues, is the product of ideological transition, of the change from the world of court to that of the family, one that, despite itself predicts the demise of the drama altogether.

Theodora Jankowski's 'Defining / Confining the Duchess: Negotiating the Female Body in John Webster's *The Duchess of Malfi*' (essay 4) argues that even though Webster's Duchess represents, if not the inherent impossibility of female sovereignty, then the insurmountable obstacles that face it, she also challenges typical Jacobean views about female sexuality and the female body by demonstrating the slippery distinctions between the body politic and the body natural in the case of a female ruler. In choosing to marry her social inferior, Jankowski argues, the Duchess selects a man who will support her as a woman rather than a consort who will help her uphold her political office. The Duchess's struggle becomes one of maintaining the distinction between her public and private roles which, paradoxically, her reign only serves to elide. Like Andrea Henderson, Jankowski thus sees the play shifting between contradictory discourses about woman and politics.

The sense that Webster in some sense looked beyond the historical moment in which he was writing precisely by dramatising some of the most compelling contradictions of that moment is taken up again in Kathleen McLuskie's 'Drama and Sexual Politics: the Case of Webster's Duchess' (essay 5) which focuses, like Henderson, on the politics of theatre. Using the full range of theatrical forms available to him, she argues, Webster draws attention to crucial contemporary issues of politics and sexuality. Attempts to give *The Duchess of Malfi* a false sense of coherence in theatre production thus work to deprive the play of some of its most radical attributes. McLuskie offers as an example the 1981 production at the Manchester Royal Exchange, which cut the dumb show where the Cardinal dons military regalia before banishing the Duchess. This cut in the production, McLuskie argues, worked to undermine the import of the play, which is not merely about the plight of a woman in her search for personal happiness (a twentieth-century theme) but about the way political and military forces combine to discipline the Duchess's sexuality. As with earlier essays in the volume, McLuskie's essay focuses on the radical potential of the play in its critique of the social and cultural forces that seek to contain the Duchess.

Mary Beth Rose's essay (6), 'The Heroics of Marriage in Renaissance Tragedy', argues that the Duchess is an appropriate emblem for the new Protestant conception of marriage and serves to unite private and public life by stressing marriage as a field of heroic endeavour. When the Duchess enters into her class-transgressive marriage with Antonio, her use of the temporary freedoms of widowhood becomes analogous to that of the cross-dressed heroine of the comedies whose disguise confers upon her the freedom of the green world until she finds her true mate. While Webster recognised the radical potential of female heroism, Rose shows that because the Duchess embodies the play's major conflicts she has to be removed from their resolution and therefore suffers the same fate as other female tragic victims, such as Desdemona, who are dispatched before the tragic hero makes his exit. Rose's argument is thus at once about both the play's tragic structure but also its relationship to contemporary politics. Indeed, perhaps the most significant shift in the criticism of the last few years has been towards a recognition of the need to situate all readings both in a wider cultural context and a specific historical context. In turn, this provides a dynamic for recent criticism, particularly recent gender criticism as we come to see how texts are constructed in a complex web of ideas.

Written in the mid-eighties, Susan Wells's essay, 'Dominance of the Typical and *The Duchess of Malfi*' (essay 7), is concerned, as many critics were at that time, to offer not just a reading of the play, but a densely theorised understanding of how it offers a specific instance of the more general problems about the nature of representation. Wells sets up a theoretical framework for her reading which distinguishes between two types or registers of representation: the 'typical' and the 'indeterminate'. The typical register, the one operating in Webster's play, determines the problems that occupy a text, while its obverse is the dark and obscure 'indeterminate' register, in this case the world of the Duchess's brothers. The 'typical register' of *The Duchess of Malfi*, Wells argues, is one that was not typical for its time in its focus on the family and private life rather than on the state and public life, the downfall of great men and kings, which constituted the more usual objects of tragedy. The Duchess's own body, pregnant, vomiting, ageing, is the emblematic focus of this new emphasis in the representation of tragedy. Although students may find this one of the more difficult essays included in this volume, the effort required to engage its arguments is rewarded by the light Wells throws on the significance of the play's representation, on how Webster was writing in a world before the instantiation of private life as we know it. The world he presents to us in *The Duchess* staked out new territory, and yet, paradoxically, this is the world which has become our own.

Frank Whigham's 'Sexual and Social Mobility in *The Duchess of Malfi*' (essay 8) addresses the play as a site of contradictions 'between the dominant social order and emergent pressures toward social change'. This tension, argues Whigham, is especially to be found in the issues of incest and the social mobility of servants as the places where rigid social hierarchy can be seen to be torqued by the pressures of emergent modernity. Webster's play, he argues, focuses deliberately on 'womanish eccentricity' and in so doing takes a radical and oppositional perspective on Jacobean society. In common with other essays in this volume, then, Whigham repositions the play in its social and historical moment. Like other essays, too, his reading is inflected in part by Marxist ideas, in part by feminist thinking. It is this conjunction that has allowed recent criticism to come to terms with Webster's play in a more productive way than traditional criticism.

Finally, R. S. White's essay, 'The Moral Design of *The Duchess of Malfi*' (essay 9) offers an explicit critique of traditional criticism of the play by arguing that we should take seriously the Renaissance belief that literature was intended to 'teach and delight'. Webster's play, White argues, promulgates in vivid and dynamic ways distinct moral and political positions, rather than the amorality and fragmentation that critics so often find there. For White, the play offers a series or moral awakenings, none more poignant than that of the onstage strangulation of the Duchess, through which Webster condemns the destructive manipulations of the society around her.

All these essays point to the importance of historical context, and see Webster's tragedy as offering a dynamic interaction with its audience. Crucially, as the essays included here demonstrate, the play speaks to us today because it succeeds in being at the very centre of political and social changes, changes which were most vividly, poignantly but also necessarily embodied in the figure of a female tragic protagonist.

NOTES

1. Elizabeth M. Brennan (ed.), *The Duchess of Malfi* (New York, 1993), p. xxxii.

2. Gunnar Boklund, *The Sources of 'The White Devil'* (New York, 1993), p. 179.

3. For an account of Bradley's view of tragedy, see Dympna Callaghan, *Woman and Gender in Renaissance Tragedy* (Brighton, 1989), p. 2.

4. See Norman Rabkin (ed.), *Twentieth Century Interpretations of 'The Duchess of Malfi'* (Englewood Cliffs, NJ, 1968), p. 2.

5. J. W. Lever, *The Tragedy of State: A Study of Jacobean Drama*, with an introduction by Jonathan Dollimore (New York, 1987), p. 95.

6. Ibid., p. xiii.

7. Michael Shapiro, *Gender in Play on the Shakespearean Stage: Boy Heroines and Female Pages* (Ann Arbor, MI, 1996), pp. 60–1.

8. See Lisa Jardine, *Still Harping on Daughters: Women and Drama in the Age of Shakespeare* (New York, 1983), pp. 68–102.

9. K. Usher Henderson and B. MacManus, *Half Humankind: Contexts and Texts of the Controversy about Women in England 1540–1640* (Urbana, IL, 1985), p. 239.

10. Ibid.

11. Amy Louise Erickson, *Women and Property in Early Modern England* (New York, 1993), p. 166.

12. Merry E. Weisner, *Woman and Gender in Early Modern Europe* (Cambridge, 1993), p. 166.

13. Ibid., p. 75.

14. Erickson, *Women and Property*, p. 164.

15. Ibid., p. 168.

16. Ibid., p. 169.

17. Weisner, *Woman and Gender*, pp. 73–4.

18. Erickson, *Women and Property*, p. 3.

19. Ibid., p. 6.

20. Ibid., p. 9.

21. Constance Jordan, *Renaissance Feminism: Literary Texts and Political Models* (Ithaca, NY, 1990), p. 95.

22. Weisner, *Woman and Gender*, p. 41.

23. Ibid., p. 46.

24. Ibid., pp. 71, 72.

25. Katte Aughterson (ed.), *Renaissance Woman: Constructions of Femininity in England* (New York, 1995), p. 138.

26. Ibid., p. 140.

27. Philippa Berry, *Of Chastity and Power: Elizabethan Literature and the Unmarried Queen* (London, 1989), p. 69.

28. Ibid.

29. Aughterson, *Renaissance Woman*, p. 141.

30. Ibid.

31. The family–state analogy is pervasive in this period. For numerous examples of it, see Callagham, *Woman and Gender*, pp. 14–27.

32. Martin Ingram, *Church Courts: Sex and Marriages in England 1570–1640* (Cambridge, 1987), p. 133.

33. Ibid., p. 132.

34. Ibid., p. 133.

35. Ibid.

36. Ibid., p. 213.

37. Quoted ibid., p. 135.

38. Ibid., pp. 200–1.

39. Ibid., p. 204.

40. Ibid., p. 189.

41. Ibid., p. 90.

42. Ibid., p. 92.

43. Ibid., p. 193.

44. Brennan, *The Duchess of Malfi*, pp. xvii–xx.

45. Ingram, *Church Courts*, p. 196.

46. Ibid., p. 195.

47. Ibid., pp. 196–7.

48. Jordan, *Renaissance Feminism*, p. 29.

49. Ibid.

50. David Cressy, *Birth, Marriage, and Death: Ritual, Religion, and the Life-Cycle in Tudor and Stuart England* (Oxford, 1997), p. 4.

51. Quoted ibid., p. 42.

52. Ibid., p. 50.

53. Quoted ibid., p. 49.

54. Quoted ibid., p. 44.

55. Quoted Jordan, *Renaissance Feminism*, pp. 39–40.

1

The Duchess of Malfi: Tyranny and Spectacle in Jacobean Drama

KARIN S. CODDON

The untenability of the mad tragic subject in early seventeenth-century English drama suggests a significant rift between interiority and unreason. For while Jacobean drama is noteworthy for its ubiquitous lunatics, the disordered *subjectivity* that so marks the later Elizabethan and early Jacobean tragic hero tends to be eclipsed, if not outright effaced, by representations of madness almost impenetrable in their exteriority, their theatricality.[1] The corruption of the courts in which tragic madmen move is duplicated rather than opposed in the morbid declamations of the melancholy malcontent who is at once emblem and effect of his disordered world. The contamination of subjectivity by an exterior-ised mad discourse heralds the exhaustion of the trope of madness, as the problematic subject of absolutist authority gives way to an increasingly rational and privatised subjectivity enabled by operations of authority less and less centred in the power of sovereignty.

The individual – and individuated – mad tragic subject is displaced by emblematic madmen whose 'out of fashion melancholy' no longer signifies internalised contradictions in a disruptive dialogue between subject and authority: it now signifies the external, manifestly public effects of that disruption. No Jacobean melancholic is more vituperative and morbid than Tourneur's Vindice – nor less individuated, as his morality-play name suggests.[2] The ostensible content of his madness – corrupt power, lechery, physical decay – is also the content of Hamlet's and Lear's tirades, but with a significant difference: Vindice's speeches have a strikingly literal, even reportorial quality whose excesses are matched, even subsumed, by the material circumstances of the play-world. Vindice's melancholy is engaged in these very material circumstances, not unlike the macabre but eminently *functional* prop of Gloriana's skull. In *The Revenger's Tragedy* as in *The Duchess of Malfi*, madness's alignment with representation becomes its explicit function: madness is emphatically identified with outwardness, with costume, disguise, playing. Like the spectacular body,[3] the exteriority of madness in Jacobean tragedy marks a disjunction between inwardness and materiality. If madness can be excluded from inwardness, its externalisation enables confinement if not containment; the notion of a wholly 'private' self necessarily excludes the unreason that traverses indistinct boundaries between inward and outward, psychic and political. The privatisation of subjectivity, then, depoliticises as well as stabilises the interior space.

If Elizabethan madness serves at once to subversively demystify the myths of absolutism and to contain such interrogations within the marginality of unreason, the relentless Jacobean deflation of absolutist mythology effaces the transgressive space from which madness speaks.

> Surely, we're all mad people and they
> Whom we think are, are not – we mistake those;
> 'Tis we are mad in sense, they but in clothes

comments Vindice (III.v.78–81),[4] and to an extent he articulates the structural reformulation of madness in Jacobean tragedy. Disclaiming any authority to speak that within which passes show, madness is no longer the medium of disordered, potentially transgressive subjectivity. Madness is confined, almost literally, to mere playing, 'seeming', spectacle. The concentration of madness in the spectacular body enables its objectification as a pathological phenomenon; madness is thus something that is observed in a clinical, proto-empirical sense as well as in the realm of theatricality. And, as I have argued elsewhere in reference to *Macbeth*,[5] from such observation madness enters into the discursive order of diagnosis, wherein the language of reason may define, dissect, and silence that of unreason. If its 'wild and whirling words' are madness's excess that evades the containment – the discipline and / or punishment – imposed on the lunatic's body, the literal objectification of madness (i.e., its constitution as an *object* of discourse and knowledge) is bound up in the erasure of any possible or liminal position from which madness might speak. The displacement of the mad subject from the tragic centre in Jacobean drama is, then, no less politically interested a narrative restructuration than the shift in the late 1590s from king to tragic subject.[6]

Thus in such plays as *The Revenger's Tragedy* and *The Duchess of Malfi*, madness neither defers nor mediates the disclosure of subjectivity. The madness of Hamlet or of Marston's Antonio speaks the contradictions of early modern subjectivity, the conflict between post-Reformation inwardness and the microcosmic subject of sovereign power. But the madness of Macbeth or Vindice, Bosola or Flamineo, is more mirror than mask, its object the spectacle itself. The exteriority of such madness recalls but is not necessarily a throwback to the sensational Senecan fury in which excessive passion is nonetheless accommodated within narrativity. Rather, Jacobean madness is inscribed almost haphazardly among a variety of characters and theatrical effects; so the dramas become themselves strangely useless, forgoing even the perfunctory claim to edification or affirmation of 'moral order'. Jacobean tragedy is distinctive, however, not only for the pervasive and explicit ethical anarchy that misrules the plays of Tourneur and Webster, but also for its almost self-parodic theatricality, what Francis Barker has called 'the innocent foregrounding of [the theatre's] own device'.[7] The 'theatricality of this theatre'[8] is perhaps nowhere better exemplified than in *The Duchess of Malfi*, with its pageant of Bedlamites, mutilated wax figures that 'plague in art', and overt plot manipulations (e.g., the dropped horoscope, the Cardinal's bizarre instructions that his cries for help be ignored). It is as if the notion of inwardness is beginning to retire from the publicity of the spectacle, the mutilated bodies that bloody the Jacobean stage suggestive of the violent unreason that will be exiled from the realm of a private and unseen 'self'. This disciplining and displacement of the violence within is a necessary condition for the emergence of the reasoned resistance that will make revolution – and regicide – feasible in seventeenth-century England. Yet the tragic madman of late Elizabethan and early Jacobean tragedy comes to the representational foreground touched by emergent as well as residual cultural elements.[9] The mad tragic hero articulates and embodies untenable contradictions in an anachronistic ideology, not the over-throw of 'subjectification' but rather a tacit perception of the inade-quacy of the dominant in fashioning subjects.[10] But if madness speaks the breakdown of the relation of inwardness to its enabling authority, it posits no alternative discourse. The inchoate construc-tion of an alternative – the private, rational subjectivity – signifies the tragic madness's obsolescence. To some extent, however, tragic madness has been engaged in the production of the reasonable indi-vidualist subjectivity that will exclude unreason from the discourse of contestation. By exposing the conflicts between inwardness and authority, and in the spectacular medium wherein power was not only represented but *reproduced* (i.e., proliferated), tragic madness plays both a liminal and a productive role in the crucial reformation of the seventeenth-century English subject.[11]

But the melancholy malcontent is less frequently the tragic hero of Jacobean drama than he is a kind of embodied emblem, an overt stage device.[12] Such figures as Flamineo and Bosola in Webster's plays are narratively as well as socially marginalised, serving a nar-rative structure as ruthless and unaccommodating as the courtly power structure it represents. Instrumentalised and contaminated by this narrative / political structure, they are ultimately contained by it as well. 'We are merely the stars' tennis-balls, struck and bandied which way pleases them', Bosola surmises (V.iv.54–5)[13] in a play in which coincidence, accident, and apparently inexplicable plot manipulations dominate tragic action. Moreover, the Jacobean emphasis on the material, economic conditions of the malcontent's melancholy is not only topical,[14] but also allows for the construc-tion of inwardness outside of melancholy, which is represented as a political guise rather than a 'private' and subjective malaise. In *The Duchess of Malfi* Bosola's melancholy is chiefly emblematic and instrumental, bound to visible strategies of corrupt political practices.[15] But this overt appropriation of madness by the author-ity to which it is ostensibly antagonistic does not structurally efface the space of transgression. Rather, it opens up a different, but significant, site for contestation as well as for subjectivity: the private and domestic sphere that the resolutely sane Duchess and Antonio strive to occupy.

Indeed, in *The Duchess of Malfi* madness is an instrument and metonymy of the public, spectacular world that constantly encroaches upon the private, the subjective, the sane. No longer located in the equivocal, ambiguous space between interiority and exteriority, subjectivity and subversion, madness *seems* rather than *is*; it is explicitly but an action that a man might play. Like political power in the play, madness is as fragmented itself as it is fragmenting, dispersed among the dramatis personae.[16] But rather than destabilising subjectivity, madness itself is unstable, a habit or livery that aptly is put on. Thus Bosola deflates Ferdinand's boast that

> He that can compass me, and know my drifts,
> May say he hath put a girdle 'bout the world,
> And sounded all her quicksands
> (III.i.84–6)

by advising the Duke 'That you / Are your own chronicle too much, and grossly / Flatter yourself (ll. 87–9). Like Bosola's own melancholy, Ferdinand's unfathomable distraction functions chiefly as a mode of self-representation equivalent to the part he plays. In a similar fashion Antonio will debunk the authenticity of Bosola's melancholy, identifying it with a manifestly political strategy:

> Because you would not seem to appear to the world
> Puffed up with your preferment, you continue
> This out-of-fashion melancholy
> (II.i.91–3)

Mechanistic and depersonalised, madness in the play becomes a material instrument of an equally disordered power; as Bosola and the Bedlamites are to the perverse will of Ferdinand, so all are the 'creatures' of a spectacle that overtly disclaims any other dramatic or didactic purpose than to 'plague in art'.

The world of *The Duchess of Malfi* is one in which the macro-microcosmic mythology of order, centred in the body and blood of the monarch, is honoured only in the breach. Where *King Lear* dramatises the degeneration of the sovereign's mystical body into the naked and battered body of unaccommodated man, *The Duchess* takes as its points of departure the vacuity of the organic paradigm.[17] The mystical political body which incorporates immutable sovereign authority is displaced by 'a rotten and dead body [that] we delight / To hide ... in rich tissue'. Antonio's early speech in the first act gives lip-service to the conventional ideal of the body politic, but only as it points up the discrepancy between a distant political ideal and an immediate political reality. He admires the French court because

> In seeking to reduce both state and people
> To a fixed order, their judicious king
> Begins at home, quits first his royal palace
> Of flattering sycophants, of dissolute
> And infamous persons, which he sweetly terms
> His master's masterpiece, the work of Heaven,
> Considering duly that a prince's court
> Is like a common fountain, whence should flow
> Pure silver drops in general, but if't chance
> Some cursed example poison't near the head,
> Death and disease through the whole land spread.
>   (I.i.5–15)

The possibility of a topical reference to the actual state of things in France is less significant than the location of order well outside the realm in which the dramatic action takes place. As has been often noted, not only the troubled court of Malfi but the equally troubled court of James is none too subtly evoked in Antonio's speech. James's penchant for 'flattering sycophants' and 'dissolute and infamous persons', of which Robert Carr and George Villiers were two of the more notorious, was a character flaw far more typical of the King of England than of either of the fictive dukes of Malfi.[18] Indeed, the speech seems almost pointedly addressed to the courtly world outside rather than within the play. As J. W. Lever has remarked,

> At the time when [*The Duchess of Malfi*] was being written, James I had dispensed with … chief minister Cecil, and placed the entire control of the state in the hands of his young favourite Robert Carr. The Privy Council had become a mere rubber stamp for arbitrary personal rule. Honours were openly bought and sold; marriages and divorces were steps to political influence.[19]

The ideal body politic is thus markedly excluded from the spectacle, as distant from the court of James as from the court of Malfi. Significantly, the spectacle cannot *show* the ideal but only narrates it, for representation is itself implicated in the corrupt world of dissembling but opaque appearance.

Accordingly, then, Antonio becomes as good as a chorus, providing the gloss for each of the emblematic actors who appear onstage to people the court of Malfi. The lofty speech on the French court is negatively punctuated by the immediate appearance of the malcontent Bosola vainly suing the Cardinal for advancement. Notably, both authority and malcontent are characterised by the idiom of poison and disease; in fact, Antonio's description of the Cardinal is more evocative of the conventional idiom of treasonous melancholy than is his description of Bosola. Of Bosola, Antonio comments, 'This foul melancholy / Will poison all his goodness' (ll. 77–8), suggesting a faint tension between an essentialist 'self' and the politically inscribed suite of woe. Antonio's remarks about the Cardinal are far more damning:

> observe his inward character: he is a melancholy churchman; the spring in his face is nothing but the engendering of toads; where he is as jealous of any man, he lays worse plots for him than ever was imposed on Hercules, for he strews in his way flatterers, panders, intelligences, atheists, and a thousand such political monsters.
>
> (ll. 166–72)

For the Elizabethans it was usually the melancholy subject, the malcontent, who was 'a brocher of dangerous Matchiavellisme, and inventor of strategems, quirkes, and policies';[20] here the malcontent is almost literally but the extension of a corrupt and corrupting distraction inscribed in authority itself. If the Cardinal is especially sinister for his identification with the anti-Christ papist church, Ferdinand, possessed of a 'most perverse and turbulent nature' (l. 179), is even more the embodiment of the mad *actor*; the Duchess's twin, he also doubles the Cardinal and Bosola in opaque dissemblence: 'What appears in him is merely outside' (l. 180).

Hence, the play seems to question any significant distinction between princely authority and politic disorder. However, the tragedy does posit an alternative, in the person of the Duchess. Antonio praises her in terms of her personal, 'essential' qualities, and the opposition of the highly individuated, virtuous subject to impenetrably mad and theatrical authority comprises a major conflict in the drama. The conflation of prince and traitor indicts a power structure here exposed as degenerate and unable to sustain its enabling distinctions; the constitution of opposition in the space of the private and individual opens up a different structural possibility that obviates the function of the mad subject. Thus the ruler and the malcontent are crudely aligned against inwardness.

Ferdinand commissions Bosola to infiltrate the Duchess's privacy, to 'live i' th' court here, and observe the duchess; / To note all the particulars of her havior' (ll. 261–2). The task that Ferdinand requests is more than a little voyeuristic, as it involves the visual penetration of a private, female space. But Ferdinand's interest in the government and constraint of the Duchess's sexuality cannot be taken as normative, patriarchal self-assertion, for it is deeply implicated in incest and madness. But again, it is a madness externalised, delegated in fact to Bosola. Bosola apparently recognises as much: 'It seems you would create me / One of your familiars' (ll. 267–8), he comments, adding shortly afterwards, 'I am your creature' (l. 297). The notion that authority enables the subject's agency is parodied and literalised in the compact; Bosola becomes the instrument of corrupt though legitimate authority.

Similarly, melancholy becomes an actual guise, a role, in the service of princely authority attempting to disrupt the construction of the private. Ferdinand bids Bosola to

> Be yourself;
> Keep your old garb of melancholy; 'twill express
> You envy those that stand above your reach,
> Yet strive not to come near 'em: this will gain
> Access to private lodgings.
>
> (ll. 287–91)

Specifically aligned against rather than with inwardness, melancholy is explicitly ideological, even its conventional association with thwarted ambition engaged in the performance of the very political power it ostensibly threatens. The malcontent is indeed the prince's creature. Webster's relentless exploration of the instrumentalisation of identity is historically rather than humanistically informed; in Jacobean England the wholesale commercialisation of social status persisted in blatant disregard of the fixed social hierarchy of contemporary propaganda.[21] The notorious title-mongering of the Jacobean court, in divorcing blood and social status, would ultimately work against the interests of those who most profited from the sale of titles in the short run. Ironically, it is the purity of royal bloodlines that ostensibly impels Ferdinand's outrageous response to the Duchess's marriage, but this complicity in the debasement of blood as a basis for nobility is signified not only by his madness but also by his perversion of patronage. 'Say, then, my corruption /

Grew out of horse-dung', Bosola sardonically concludes (ll. 296–7); the prince's bounty degenerates into a mutually contaminating transaction.

Significantly, the compact is followed shortly by another trans- action, though one of markedly contrasting variety. The audience is given a window into the 'private lodgings' of the Duchess yet to be penetrated by the 'politic dormouse' Bosola. That the Duchess summons Antonio under the premise that she is 'making [her] will' (I.ii.84) is more than a portent of the violent end to which her mar- riage dooms her. Perhaps more than any other legal document, the will is a token of *individualism*, a literal inscription of the subject as a possessor and distributor of objects that, conversely, constitute his or her *self*-possession.[22] Here, the unorthodox self-assertion of the Duchess's courtship of her steward further underscores the pun of her 'will'. Certainly, according to common contemporary notions of social hierarchy, the Duchess is transgressing natural order, not only as a woman courting a man, but a prince courting a com- moner.[23] However, to assume, as many critics have, that the Duchess is thus 'responsible' for her tragic fate is to overlook Webster's explicit identification of the social values and political practices of the dominant with dissemblance, corruption, even madness. Disorder in the play is overly aligned with those figures who embody and articulate strict enforcement of hierarchy and degree – Ferdinand and the Cardinal. Christopher Hill has gone so far as to argue that 'Webster clearly approves of the Duchess of Malfi's marriage beneath her, though it horrifies her court'; Hill contends that Webster, like Middleton, had a strong allegiance to so-called 'city values'.[24] Whether or not the play actively endorses the Duchess's marriage is, I believe, deliberately ambiguous; what is clear is that the ideology by which her deed is constituted as trans- gressive is virtually indistinguishable from a madman's perverse ob- session. Antonio may initially demur from the Duchess's proposal with a solemn invocation of hierarchy and degree, but given the contamination of these by their intersection with madness, his conservative position seems more nostalgic than prescriptive. Just as his early speech of Act I, scene i pays self-conscious homage to a conventional icon – the idealised body politic – that is travestied both in the text and context of the play. Antonio's response to the Duchess's overtures articulates the conventional, indeed, the 'official' position on ambition and madness that has just been thrown into confusion in the previous scene between Ferdinand and Bosola:

> Ambition, madam, is a great man's madness,
> That is not kept in chains and close-pent rooms,
> But in fair lightsome lodgings, and is girt
> With the wild noise of prattling visitants,
> Which makes it lunatic beyond all cure.
> (ll. 125–9)

But ambition in the play is *not* 'a great man's madness'; for the madness of Ferdinand, the most flamboyant and obvious distraction in the drama, is bound up in authority and punishment, not in the excessive ambition that is so typically their object.

Thus, the Duchess counters with a notion of desert that is resolutely private and individualistic. She discards her public role as freely as an actor stepping out of character, subordinating 'representation' to the 'authenticity' of a privileged essentialist subjectivity:

> What is't distracts you? This is flesh and blood, sir;
> 'Tis not the figure cut in alabaster
> Kneels at my husband's tomb. Awake, awake, man!
> I do here put off all vain ceremony,
> And only do appear to you a young widow
> That claims you for her husband, and, like a widow,
> I use but half a blush in 't.
> (ll. 157–63)

The Duchess's 'will' to discard the values of an ideology centred in public ceremony and fixed hierarchy in favour of values centred in individual merit and desire is yet premature; Ferdinand, of course, does succeed in imposing by violence the tyranny of blood upon his would-be bourgeois individualist sister. But the Duchess's very articulation of subjectivity based on markedly 'private' criteria points up the decadence of the 'public' values of Malfi. Similarly, her playful invocation of *legalese* in securing Antonio's acquiescence to marriage anticipates the crucial movement in early modern England to a contractual society rather than one centred in the body and blood of the monarch, a movement whose culmination enables the execution of a king in the name of the very state the sovereign was once purported to incarnate. So the Duchess's clandestine marriage to Antonio resonates with implications beyond the realm of the purely domestic: in the world of Ferdinand and the Cardinal, it is a patently subversive act. The Duchess explicitly privileges the private negotiation over the institutional sanction: 'We now are man and wife, and 'tis the Church / That must but echo this' (ll. 192–3). If the gesture of rebellion against 'the [Roman Catholic] Church' accords with Anglican as well as Puritan marriage theory, the exclusion of institutional authority from the realm of subjectivity rests at the heart of the English Revolution as well as the Reformation.

Alan Sinfield has remarked that '[the Duchess] asserts her own will, but she seeks merely domestic happiness'.[25] But I would suggest that the domestic context of the Duchess's defiance of her brothers' wishes does not efface its subversive implications. Nor should Cariola's commentary at the scene's end be taken as authoritative. As in Antonio's conventional rhetoric of ambition, Cariola offers a self-consciously facile identification of madness with social transgression:

> Whether the spirit of greatness or of woman
> Reign most in her, I know not, but it shows
> A fearful madness; I owe her much of pity.
> (ll. 204–6)

As a kind of summary statement, Cariola's speech is rather incongruous, for the behaviour to which it refers manifestly does *not* show 'a fearful madness'. Indeed, as the audience has just witnessed, the Duchess has conducted her courtship of Antonio with an air of legalistic calm and practicality. Her love for Antonio is plainly not the distracted passion of amorous melancholy nor the frivolous and irrational affection identified with 'spirit ... of woman', as the Homily on Marriage (1547) describes it:

> the woman is a weak creature not endued with ... strength and constancy of mind; therefore they be the sooner disquieted, and they be the more prone to all weak affections and dispositions of the mind, more than men be, and lighter they be, and more vain in their phantasies and opinions.[26]

Cariola's declaration puts forth a parodically simplistic formula – the Duchess transgresses authority, *ergo* the Duchess is mad (and 'fearfully', at that). Implicit in Antonio's speech about ambition, explicit in Cariola's comments, the referent of 'madness' is clearly at odds with its sign. Again, the possibility of contestation that is *not madness* at once heralds the emergence of oppositional individualism and the deterioration of the sign of madness into but a sign. In *The Duchess of Malfi* madness participates in a maze of semiotic and spectacular confusion, about which Franco Moretti has remarked:

> In Webster, meaning does not deceive, but rather dissolves: into appearance ('methinks'), indeterminacy ('a thing'), and inexplicable detail ('arm'd with a rake'). Nor is the problem how to interpret such signs, but, more basically, to determine whether or not they are in fact signs.[27]

The madness that Cariola and Antonio invoke is, like the organic sovereign body of Act I, scene i, a trope invested in a symbology fallen into incoherence in the world of the play.

Thus madness and contestation serve as mighty opposites, the former contiguous with the tyrannical power that has produced it, the latter bound up in an individualistic self-assertion that cannot be contained by the discourses of madness. This opposition is metaphorised by two antithetical images of the body – one emblematic, spectacular, and semiotically dissembling, the other the site of private contracts, essentialism, secrecy. Bosola's morbid denunciation of the 'outward form of man' is not only a conventional, overtly theatrical set-piece; it is a 'meditation' (II.i.52) whose referentiality is wholly circumscribed, confined to the public and spectacular, deflected and contradicted by the private and individuated body of the Duchess:

> What thing is this outward form of man
> To be beloved? We account it ominous,
> If nature do produce a colt, or lamb,
> A fawn, or goat, in any limb resembling
> A man, and fly from 't as a prodigy:
> Man stands amazed to see his deformity
> In any other creatures but himself.
> But in our own flesh, though we bear diseases
> Which have their true names only ta'en from beasts –
> As the most ulcerous wolf and swinish measle –
> Though we are eaten up of lice and worms,
> And though continually we bear about us
> A rotten and dead body, we delight
> To hide it in rich tissue: all our fear
> Nay, all our terror, is lest our physician
> Should put us in the ground to be made sweet.
> (ll. 53–68)

This corrupt, grossly material yet essentially specious body will become literally the body of representation, prefiguring not only the mutilated wax dummies of Antonio and his children, but also the metamorphosis of Ferdinand into an 'ulcerous wolf', mad with lycanthropia. In a sense, Bosola's speech formulates a response to Antonio's idealised but absent body politic, the malcontent's version of the *Realpolitik* of the court of Malfi borne out by the spectacle itself. But if the 'rotten and dead body' of Bosola's speech contradicts the healthy body politic of Antonio's paean to France, it is itself contradicted by the Duchess's body, the 'rich tissue' of her 'loose-bodied gown' concealing not corruption but fecundity. As Bosola turns his attention to the Duchess's body and the possibility of her pregnancy, he necessarily undermines his own 'meditation' on the sterility and morbidity of the flesh. The Duchess's condition thus deflates any ostensible claim to inwardness put forth in Bosola's bitter discourse; the speech becomes but another piece of self-conscious theatricality, at jarring odds with any narrative referent. The Duchess's body, while concealed, is nonetheless the site of essentialist authenticity; the body whose 'outward form' is impenetrable – the spectacular body as well as the body in which madness is inscribed – is a sign whose referent is almost literally nothing.

Similarly, Bosola's comment that the Duchess's gown is 'contrary to our Italian fashion' (l. 75) points up the degree to which her disregard for 'outward form' is engaged in her particular transgression. She bids the ever-orthodox Antonio to keep his hat on before her, noting that

> 'Tis
> Ceremony more than duty that consists
> In the removing of a piece of felt.
> (ll. 131–3)

It is important to note that it is not 'duty' but 'ceremony' that the Duchess is questioning; she is more a proponent of Protestant individualism than of egalitarianism. She is not challenging hierarchy per se, only its ceremonial, public model. For it is, after all, Antonio, not Bosola, whom she urges to disregard courtly protocol, and by virtue of their secret marriage, he is *her* lord. That the observation of public hierarchy conflicts with 'duty' to a private, domestic hierarchy heralds the displacement of the macro-microcosmic model of social relations by a significant stratification for seventeenth-century England. As Jean Elshtain has observed,

> *All* social ties and relations suffer as the split between public and private widens into a gap and then a chasm. Within the domain of *Realpolitik* intractable terms like 'power, force, coercion, violence' structure political action and consciousness. On the other side of the chasm, softness, compassion, forgiveness, and emotionality are allowable insofar as they do not intervene with the public imperative. The private world is called upon to 'make up' for the cold (but necessary) inhumanity of the public.[28]

In *The Duchess of Malfi* the private and domestic has yet to 'intervene with the public imperative'; but their tension nevertheless anticipates the full emergence of the 'public/private' dichotomy by which early modern European capitalism will be constructed and sustained.

The spectacular but ultimately specious function of madness in the play is exemplified in the double-torture that Ferdinand contrives for the Duchess: the mutilated wax figures of Antonio and the children, and the pageant of Bedlamites. In both instances, opaque theatricality serves Ferdinand's madness precisely as the melancholy Bosola does. All three – the waxen corpses, the Bedlamites, and the malcontent – literally embody Ferdinand's corrupt power; their materiality gives his madness local habitation and a name, but, significantly, displaces inwardness as the site of distraction. Like Bosola, the artificial corpses and the madmen are crudely instrumental devices designed to break down the pales and forts of the Duchess's inward resolve, her subjectivity. 'Her melancholy seems to be fortified. With a strange disdain', Ferdinand observes (IV.i.11–12); not even physical confinement is sufficient to disrupt her *self-possession*, indeed, her 'will'. The Duchess's sanity is even enabled by the spectacles of madness Ferdinand imposes upon her. Briefly, however, Ferdinand's perverse ploy seems to achieve its end, when the Duchess, devastated though deceived by 'the sad spectacle' of the waxen corpses, weakly grants theatricality the tyrannical efficacy with which the duke – if not the playwright – wishes to invest it: 'I account this world a tedious theatre, For I do play a part in 't 'against my will' (ll. 80–1). The subordination of agency ('will') to power's spectacle comprises one important foundation on which pageants of power rested in Elizabethan and Jacobean England. But Webster's play demonstrates this structure primarily to interrogate and parody it. By the end of the play it is Bosola, the self-identified 'creature' of a mad tyrant, who invokes the 'world-as-stage' topos to account for his subjection to lunatic authority, referring to himself as 'an action in the main of all, / Much 'gainst my good nature' (V.v.87–8). Theatricality comes to trope – and demystify – the determination of the subject by an absolute power unable to sustain the coherence of its own illusions.

Ferdinand's anticipation that his sister will 'needs be mad' (l. 123) because of his deceptive spectacle assumes, like Hamlet's faith in playing to 'make mad the guilty and appall the free', a dramatic effectivity that much of late Elizabethan and early Jacobean tragedy calls into question. Thus the Duchess may nonetheless assert, 'I am not mad yet' (IV.ii.22); in fact, it will be the very 'tyranny' (l. 3) of the madmen's masque that will 'Keep [her] in [her] right wits' (l. 6). The Duchess's recognition that her sanity is deeply engaged in the constitution of an *external* madness counters Ferdinand's attempt to impose his 'tyranny' (here, literally identified with madness) wholly upon the world of the play, to distort the boundaries between spectacle and subjectivity, public and private. The Duchess's resistance not only deflects madness, but situates it in a maze of antic self-reflexivity on the margins of subjectivity's discourse. Her madness may be the material instrument of power, but the Duchess's response (or lack thereof) points ahead to the emergence of *reason*'s sovereignty that will relegate unreason to a distant realm of otherness against which the rational will construct and define itself. In many ways *The Duchess of Malfi* is a consummately Jacobean play, but Foucault's commentary on madness in 'the classical age' (not coincidentally, *l'âge du raison*) seems almost uncannily appropriate to Ferdinand's perverse stagecraft – and to Webster's:

> Thus madness is no longer considered in its tragic reality, in the absolute laceration that gives it access to the other world, but only in the irony of its illusions. It is not a real punishment, but only the image of punishment, thus a pretence; it can be linked only to the appearance of a crime or to the illusion of a death ... Madness is deprived of its dramatic seriousness; it is punishment or despair only in the dimension of error.[29]

So the appearance of the Bedlamites represents playing at its most purposeless, madness literally in the employ of a power that yet cannot secure a stable ideological effect. As Frederick Kiefer has noted, the Bedlamites serve no 'readily discernible purpose: the dancers' appearance before the Duchess is completely unexpected; it fails to advance the plot; and it seems to reveal little, if anything, about the characters onstage'.[30] Precisely; but rather than to seek a covert rationale for the lunatics' pageant, it is more useful, I think, to attend to its very narrative inutility. Stephen Orgel has remarked that '[m]asques are the expressions of the monarch's will, the mirrors of his mind';[31] the masque of madmen, commissioned by Ferdinand, travesties the ideological investment of the spectacle. The madmen embody tragic representation at its most ineffective and irrational, the furthest point possible from the didactic *de casibus* model of early Elizabethan tragic theory. Collective rather than individuated, spectacular rather than interior, the madness of the Bedlamites is manifestly *not tragic*. A testimonial to the unintelligibility of spectacular representation, the madmen are but poor players who perform their 'dismal kind of music' before a subjectivity 'chained to endure [their] tyranny'[32] but notably indifferent to it. The Duchess ostensibly observes the grotesque pageant,[33] but there is no direct interaction between her and the madmen. Their several but undistinguished mad speeches have markedly no reference to her particular situation – or to that of the play. Nor is there any suggestion that madness contaminates the Duchess's subjectivity: 'I am the Duchess of Malfi still' (l. 142). The resilience of her self-possession emphasises the estrangement of madness and subjectivity; if there is any bridge between the two it is Bosola, whose participation in the antic disguise of the pageant reiterates the subordination of his 'good nature' to the irrationality of a spectacle determined and contaminated by corrupt power. His assumption of the role of Death augments the scene's parody of tragic form itself. 'The end is death and madness', Hieronymo proclaims in *The Spanish Tragedy*; the achievement of this 'end' in *The Duchess of Malfi* is self-consciously theatrically contrived. The externalisation of both madness and death, that they may all but literally vanquish the subject, is reminiscent of the emblematic *ars moriendi* tradition,[34] but its anachronism is offset by the refusal to naturalise the represented event – the Duchess's murder is no morality play allegory but a deed expressly ordered by a mad tyrant.

The swiftly ensuing estrangement of the instruments of the Duchess's death – Ferdinand and Bosola – from their agency in her murder metaphorises the estrangement of tragic form and tragic purpose. Unlike Hamlet or Lear, Bosola and Ferdinand may act, but their wills and fates do so contrary run. Both explicitly disclaim any authority for what has occurred, openly disavowing its enactment. There is no reason in madness because it has been displaced by a yet deeper polarity, a division of agents from their actions; will, or subjectivity, becomes wholly irrelevant to the deed's performance and effects. Bosola's apparent inability to allow his compassion for the Duchess to impede his complicity in her torture and murder, Ferdinand's castigation of Bosola, his 'creature', for obeying him ('By what authority didst thou execute / This bloody sentence?' [IV.ii.296–7]), are not simply refusals to accept moral responsibility for the deed. Rather, these self-contradictions work to deflate any illusion of subjectivity that has been at least metonymically suggested by the one's madness, the other's melancholy. The sole representational possibility that the play has offered for coherent subjectivity has been the Duchess; with her extinction, the space of inwardness is wholly effaced by brutal theatricality, the very spectacular violence that has executed her. The structural homology between the tragedy and public executions[35] is parodied as the spectacle becomes almost the literal means of the heroine's torture and death. The proposition that Webster seems to be implying is striking: if theatre is but one public manifestation (executions would be another) of the violence monopolised by tyrannical power, to what extent is the play itself a 'creature', a crude instrument, of tyranny?

So the fifth act of the play is virtually given over to theatricality that can do little more than call parodic attention to itself. The onset of Ferdinand's lycanthropia is sensationalistic, more reminiscent of the bestial furor of Hieronymo and Titus than of the madnesses of Hamlet and Lear. The burlesque business with the Cardinal and his instructions that his cries for help be ignored is as self-consciously contrived as the 'echo' that warns Antonio of his wife's death. And, perhaps most memorably, Bosola accidentally slays Antonio, as an overt plot manipulation mocks and engulfs his professed will. As Moretti has noted, 'At the heart of Jacobean tragedy we find a consciousness devoid of autonomy, an agency devoid of freedom'.[36] Indeed, the tragic is violently displaced by 'accidental judgements and casual slaughters', by 'purposes mistook / Fallen on th' inventors' heads'. In fact, the plot summary so glaringly inadequate to closure in *Hamlet* could quite accurately serve as epilogue for *The Duchess of Malfi*. This is not, however, to suggest that Webster's tragedy is an anachronistic reversion to the less equivocal madness and mayhem of the theatre of the 1580s.

What is most equivocal – and most Jacobean – about *The Duchess* is that its conviction of the estrangement between spectacle and signification is rigorously articulated in the very medium whose authority it disclaims. For the authority of spectacle is contaminated by a madness and tyranny that are mutually indistinguishable; hence contestation may be constructed only in a space outside the publicity of the spectacle. The Duchess's murder *by* the spectacle as much as *within* it effectively removes subjectivity and its contestatory possibilities from the stage. But the exclusion of the transgressive subject pointedly does not simultaneously exclude madness; rather, the tragic spectacle itself degenerates into the semiotic opacity of unreason. For Hamlet or Lear, madness cannot be recuperated or effaced: it can only be silenced. In *The Duchess of Malfi*, the purpose of playing itself is given over to madness, as if in anticipation of a forthcoming silence. The figuration of authority rather than subjectivity as irrational suggests the conditions under which opposition is generated and legitimised – that is, rendered *reasonable*. The realisation of these conditions in Jacobean and Caroline England testifies to the drama's productive role in pre-Revolutionary as well as post-Reformation English society.

From *Madness in Drama: Themes in Drama*, Vol. 15, ed. James Redmond (Cambridge, 1993), pp. 1–17.

NOTES

[Karin Coddon's essay takes up the themes of power, spectacle, and surveillance, which have become vitally important in early modern cultural studies. Power is emphasised in the work of the French philosopher, Michel Foucault, while spectacle – especially the idea of woman as the subject of the male gaze – has been the focus of feminist film theory. Coddon takes these theoretical paradigms and analyses them in relation to gender differentiated space – the public and the private – which is, of course, the cause of the play's tragic catastrophe. Ed.]

1. On the interplay of the disordered subjectivity and the unruly political subject, see Karin S. Coddon, '"Suche Strange Desygns": Madness, Subjectivity and Treason in *Hamlet* and Elizabethan Culture', *Renaissance Drama*, 20 (1989), 51–76.

2. Cf. Catherine Belsey, *The Subject of Tragedy* (London, 1985), pp. 31–3.

3. I refer, of course, to Francis Barker's still provocative *The Tremulous Private Body: Essays on Subjection* (London, 1984).

4. I am citing the New Mermaid's Edition of *The Revenger's Tragedy*, ed. Brian Gibbons (New York, 1967, 1989). Compelling discussions of Tourneur's play may be found in C. Belsey, *The Subject of Tragedy*, pp. 31–3; Jonathan Dollimore, *Radical Tragedy* (Chicago, 1984), pp. 139–50.

5. Karin S. Coddon, 'Unreal Mockery: Unreason and the Problem of Spectacle in *Macbeth*', ELH, 56 (1989), 485–501; 498.

6. Franco Moretti, *Signs Taken for Wonders*, trans. Susan Fischer, David Forgacs and David Miller (London, 1983), p. 74.

7. Barker, *Tremulous Private Body*, p. 18. Cf. Dollimore, *Radical Tragedy*, p. 65.

8. Barker, *Tremulous Private Body*, p. 17.

9. I use the terms 'dominant', 'residual', and 'emergent' with indebtedness to Raymond Williams's enlightening discussion of the 'dynamic interrelations' of cultural processes in *Marxism and Literature* (New York, 1977), pp. 121–7.

10. For a concise definition of 'subjectification', see Michel Foucault, 'The Subject and Power', *Critical Inquiry*, 8 (Summer 1982), 777–81; 781.

11. As Louis Montrose remarks, 'To speak, then, of the social production of "literature" or of any particular text is to signify not only that it is socially produced but that it is socially productive – that it is the product of work and that it performs work in the process of being written, enacted, or read' ('Renaissance Literary Studies and the Subject of History', *ELR*, 16:1 [Winter 1986], 5–12; 8–9).

12. Belsey considers the emblematic tradition as it pertains to *The Duchess* in her fine essay 'Emblem and Antithesis in *The Duchess of Malfi*', *Renaissance Drama*, 11 (1989), 115–34.

13. All references are to the AHF Crofts Classic Series Edition of *The Duchess of Malfi*, ed. Fred B. Millett (Arlington Heights, IL, 1953).

14. See Frank Whigham's essay 'Sexual and Social Mobility in *The Duchess of Malfi*', *PMLA*, 100 (March 1985), 167–86. [Reprinted in this volume – Ed.]

15. Ibid.

16. Charles and Elaine Hallett assert that 'Webster has transferred the madness from the hero-revenger to the villain [both Bosola and Ferdinand]' (*The Revenger's Madness* [Lincoln, NE, 1980], p. 291), but do not account for the passing identification of the Duchess and Antonio with madness (see I.ii.125 and I.ii.204–6).

17. Irving Ribner characterises Webster as 'a dramatist who can no longer accept without question the postulates of order and degree so dear to the Elizabethans' (in *The White Devil and The Duchess of Malfi*, ed. R. V. Holdsworth [London, 1985], p. 118). While I have reservations about *which* Elizabethans Ribner believes were so enamoured of 'order and degree', his observation about Webster is acute.

18. M. C. Bradbrook comments extensively on the possible significance of the Robert Carr–Frances Howard scandal for Webster's artistic development in *Artist and Society in Shakespeare's England* (Brighton, 1982), pp. 56–7.

19. J. W. Lever, *The Tragedy of State* (London, 1971), p. 87.

20. The description of the malcontent is that of minister Thomas Walkington (quoted in Lawrence Babb, *The Elizabethan Malady* [East Lansing, MI, 1951], p. 80).

21. Stone, *The Crisis of Aristocracy* (New York, 1967), pp. 37–61.

22. On the evolution of the will from spiritual to secular (and individualistic) document, see Philippe Ariès, *The Hour of Our Death*, trans. Helen Weaver (New York, 1981), pp. 188–201. Inga-Stina Ekenblad also notes the pun on 'will', 'playing, of course, on the two senses of "testament" and "carnal desire"' (*John Webster: A Critical Anthology*, ed. G. K. and S. K. Hunter [Harmondsworth, 1969], pp. 220–1).

23. According to James Calderwood, for example, the Duchess's courtship of Antonio demonstrates her 'reckless inattention to social degree' (Hunter [ed.], *John Webster*, pp. 266–80).

24. Christopher Hill, *Collected Essays, Volume One: Writing and Revolution in Seventeenth Century England* (Brighton, 1985), p. 7.

25. Alan Sinfield, *Literature in Protestant England 1560–1660* (London, 1983), p. 103.

26. Quoted in Doris Stenton, *The English Woman in History* (New York, 1977), p. 105.

27. Moretti, *Signs Taken for Wonders*, p. 80.

28. Jean Elshtain, *Public Man, Private Woman: Women in Social and Political Thought* (Princeton, NJ, 1984), p. 99.

29. Michel Foucault, *Madness and Civilisation*, trans. Richard Howard (London, 1967), pp. 32–3.

30. Frederick Kiefer, 'The Dance of the Madmen in *The Duchess of Malfi*', *Journal of Medieval and Renaissance Studies*, 17:2 (1987), 211–33.

31. Stephen Orgel, *The Illusion of Power* (Berkeley and Los Angeles, CA, 1975), p. 45.

32. Ibid., p. 58.

33. Kiefer identifies the Duchess's apparently impassive response to the madmen with the medieval iconographic tradition of Dame World witnessing the dance of the Seven Deadly Sins ('The Dance of the Madmen', pp. 211–33).

34. '*The Duchess of Malfi* ... is a play poised, formally as well as historically, between the emblematic tradition of the medieval stage and the increasing commitment to realism of the post-Reformation theatre' (Belsey, 'Emblem and Antithesis', p. 115).

35. For examinations of the peculiar, spectacular relation between theatrical scaffolds and the scaffold of punishment, see Karin S. Coddon, 'Unreal Mockery: Unreason and the Problem of Spectacle in *Macbeth*', *ELH*, 56 (1989), 485–501; Steven Mullaney, 'Lying Like Truth: Riddle, Representation and Treason in Renaissance England', *ELH*, 47 (1980), 32–7; Leonard Tennenhouse, *Power on Display* (London and New York, 1986).

36. Moretti, *Signs Taken for Wonders*, p. 79.

2

'Neither Maid, Widow, nor Wife': Rhetoric of the Woman Controversy in *The Duchess of Malfi*

CHRISTY DESMET

I

Despite a taste for extravagant displays of good and evil, Jacobean drama also celebrates women who cross conventional lines between virtue and vice. Among the most controversial of these heroines are Isabella from Shakespeare's *Measure for Measure*, the aspiring nun who chooses chastity over charity, and the Duchess of Malfi, the Italian 'prince' who compromises the 'greatness' of her position by marrying her steward.[1] The Renaissance Woman Controversy, attacks on and defences of women that become particularly popular between 1600 and 1630, records misogynistic commonplaces that are relevant to criticisms levelled against these heroines; more important, the battle between woman's defenders and detractors models a process in which rhetoric is used to deny women any possibility of virtue and therefore of power. The drama also exploits rhetoric in this way. In *Measure for Measure* and *The Duchess of Malfi*, men who blame their own crisis of identity on the women resort to stereotypes of female vice; but the misogynistic reading of woman gains a wider currency by the end of both plays, when Isabella, Mariana, and the Duchess undergo trials of the spirit, en-

46

during the kinds of verbal abuse promulgated regularly by antifeminist writers. I will argue that these pieces of staged invective, which force the heroines to enact commonplaces about woman's inconstancy and monstrosity, literally put in their place women who transcend conventional roles – who, like *Measure for Measure*'s Mariana, are neither maid, widow, nor wife. Thus the drama affirms traditional hierarchies through rhetorical play.[2]

Rhetoric is crucial to the Woman Controversy, both in polemic and drama. Linda Woodbridge suggests that the controversy is partly an exercise in gamesmanship, a ritual rehearsal of 'woman's virtues and vices; defences and attacks, sometimes by the same author, were written in the same format and with the same voice... '.[3]

II

While *Measure for Measure* explores the supposed fluidity of feminine identity – woman's deceit and sexual inconstancy – *The Duchess of Malfi* examines a woman who is barred from normal feminine experiences by her political position. Much recent criticism on the Duchess concentrates on her private life, particularly on the problematics of widowhood and remarriage.[4] William Painter's *Palace of Pleasure*, the play's source, clearly treats the Duchess as a lusty widow of noble blood. Painter links her with Semiramis, Pasiphaë, and other exempla of lust in high places, but only once – when the brothers' minions attempt to lure her from the safety of Ancona – is allusion made to the fact that she actually rules the Duchy of Malfi.[5] Characters within Webster's play also attempt to define the Duchess as a woman rather than a prince by resorting to feminine stereotypes. To her brothers, she has the vices typical of widows. In a studied duet warning their sister against remarriage, Ferdinand and the Cardinal build their argument on a litany of common female faults: because women are all driven by lust, widows who remarry are not far removed from whores. Naturally shameless, women also neglect their reputation; and weak in both mind and will, they succumb easily to amorous advances and smooth tales of courtship. Antonio, with the admiring eyes of a faithful officer, describes the Duchess as an aristocratic paragon. His encomium on the Duchess, based on Guazzo's *Civile Conversazione*, exaggerates the Duchess's sexual allure; her discourse is full of 'rapture' and her looks, so divine that they 'cut off all lascivious and vain hope', nevertheless have the power to inspire a man lying in a 'dead palsy' to dance a sexually suggestive galliard. At the same time, Antonio's Duchess is more severely ascetic than Guazzo's lady; not only does Malfi's Duchess work assiduously for virtue during the day, she has such innocent nights that even her dreams are as chaste as other women's 'shrifts' (I.ii.115–33).[6]

The categorisation of women as angels or devils is familiar from Swetnam's *Arraignment*, but in Webster's play, the Duchess's character and her brothers' revulsion against her are complicated by the fact that she is a female 'prince'. Webster, unlike Painter, dwells on the paradox of female rule and so looks at the 'woman problem' from a perspective unlike that of either Swetnam or Shakespeare. John Knox's *First Blast of the Trumpet Against the Monstrous Regiment of Women*, although written substantially before the *Duchess of Malfi*, is the only major work within the controversy to apply traditional arguments about the relationship of female vice and virtue to the specific case of a woman ruler. Knox's *First Blast* precedes, *The Duchess of Malfi* postdates, Elizabeth's reign. Marie Axton has documented the unique relationship between Elizabeth I's two bodies, the incorporation of her body politic into the body natural, which was subject to 'infancy, infirmity, error and old age'.[7] Leonard Tennenhouse, distinguishing Jacobean from Elizabethan use of the body natural as a theatrical metaphor, says that under Elizabeth, 'as the church came to house the secular emblems of state, the queen's sexual body acquired the power of a religious image'.[8] In the Jacobean period, however, there appears a second notion of the body politic, which represents 'the female body – ... specifically that of the aristocratic female – as the symbol and point of access to legitimate authority, thus as the potential substitute for blood and a basis for counterfeit power'.[9] Under these circumstances, female sexuality threatens the integrity of the body politic. Certainly Ferdinand regards his sister's body natural in this way when he declares that her body, 'while that my blood ran pure in't, was more worth / Than that which thou wouldst comfort, call'd a soul' (IV.i.120–1). But as Ralph Berry has noted, *The Duchess of Malfi* was 'distinctly old-fashioned' at the time of its appearance.[10] Although the relationship between the Duchess's body natural and body politic is one of the play's concerns, it is the specific obsession of its villains; the conflict between the body domestic and body politic is also present, and diffused more widely throughout the play.[11]

In his *First Blast of the Trumpet*, Knox attacks the Catholic reign of Mary Tudor with an argument based on gender; although her religion is the focus of Knox's vituperation, he frames his attack in terms of the Woman Controversy, arguing that 'to promote a woman to beare rule, superioritie, dominion or empire above any realme, nation, or citie, is repugnant to nature, contumelie to God, a thing most contrarious to his reveled will and approved ordinance, and finallie it is the subversion of good order, of all equitie and justice'.[12] Knox bases his attack on the domestic relation between men and women. Drawing equally from the Bible and from Aristotle, he argues woman's inferiority both from her natural imperfections and from an analogy between man and woman. At her best, woman is a 'tendre creature, flexible, soft and pitifull', made fit for nursing children by her soft nature (p. 25). But she is also foolhardy, rash, and consumed by a covetousness insatiable as 'the goulf of hell'; her subordination to man is made necessary by the wildness of her natural character. For the natural analogy between man and woman that makes female rule illogical, Knox draws on a traditionally antifeminist text, 1 Corinthians 11:3, which he paraphrases as 'man is head to the woman, even as Christ is heade to all man' (p. 28). He also cites 1 Timothy 2:12, which forbids women to teach, or to usurp authority over men. Knox's argument is resolutely conventional and monotonously single-minded: that a female ruler is monstrous is his repeated thesis, because God has forbidden women to have dominion over men.

In the *First Blast*'s final section, Knox addresses the problem of those Old Testament women, among them Debora, who apparently governed with God's blessing. Counterexamples do not disprove the law, he insists: Debora is an anomaly, exempted by God from the 'common malediction geven to women' and against nature made 'prudent in counsel, strong in courage, happie in regiment, and a blessed mother and deliverer to his people' (p. 40). Knox does not praise Debora as a good *woman*; he simply says that God raises her above her sex. Because the good woman never seeks dominion over men, the woman who rules is by definition a sexual monster: thus, Mary Tudor is pictured as a Jezebel, who 'may for a time slepe quietlie in the bed of her fornication and hoordome, she may teache and deceive for a season: but nether shall she preserve her selfe, nether yet her adulterous children frome great affliction, and

frome the sworde of Goddes vengeance, whiche shall shortlie apprehend suche workers of iniquitie' (p. 37).

While Swetnam revels in paradox, Knox relies on an enthymeme,
or implicit syllogism dealing with non-mathematical content:
because God has forbidden women to have dominion over men,
Mary, who is undeniably a woman, is not a true ruler. By extension, because she attempts to usurp the male prerogative of rule,
Mary is no better than a whore. The aftermath of Knox's *First Blast*
underscores the inflexibility of his rhetorical method. Mary died
before the *First Blast* was published; and since the attack against
women rulers fits Elizabeth as well as her Catholic sister, Knox was
forced to apologise. His first apology, which praises Elizabeth as a
second Debora – a woman raised by God above her sex – and concludes with fatherly counsel to Elizabeth, was so tepid that he had
to issue a second retraction; and as Katherine Rogers notes, even
defenders of female rule depicted women as weak, if not completely
frail and frivolous.[13]

The rigidity of Knox's argument, plus his contention that
womanhood and sovereignty are logically incompatible, can shed
light on the fate of Webster's Duchess. Although the men in her life
see the Duchess as either angel or devil, the play also emphasises
her position as *Duchess* of Malfi. It opens with a political metaphor
praising the French King, who recognises that his court is a
common fountain dispensing 'pure silver-drops', unless some
'curs'd example', namely the king himself, 'poison't near the head',
spreading death and disease throughout the land. Knox himself uses
the fountain to emblematise the dire results of Mary's reign.[14] Thus,
the fountain symbolises the Duchess's position as ruler; the implied
comparison between her and the French King also raises questions
about the propriety of female rule. The dumbshow representing the
Duchess's banishment from Ancona, a superfluous piece of dramatic exposition, also stresses that the Duchess, unjustly banished
at her brother's instigation, remains a 'prince'. Therefore, the controversy over her virtue or vice takes place within the particular argument over female rule.

Lisa Jardine, who reads the Duchess's progress toward repentance and death as a masculine wish fulfilment directed at the
theatre audience, sees her as metamorphosing from a 'strong
woman', the threatening *hic mulier*, to a comfortably passive figure
of female suffering.[15] The pathos of the Duchess's fate, however,
comes less from her loss of masculine will than from the fact that

both sovereignty and respectable female roles – as wife and mother – are systematically denied to her. Ferdinand and the Cardinal, who see the female ruler as Knox sees her, 'prove' their sister unfit for rule by stressing her sexuality. The Duchess herself explores another consequence of the logical argument against female rule: according to Knox, the female ruler is not a ruler; according to the Duchess, the woman prince is not fully a woman. Preparing to woo Antonio, she arms herself as a soldier, for battle and 'dangerous venture' (I.ii.271–3). But when Antonio responds fearfully, the pathos behind her martial rhetoric becomes manifest. Despite the fact that she exerts pressure on him, the Duchess is bound rhetorically by the terms in which Antonio interprets her marriage offer, those of political and economic ambition. Sophistry and truth meet in the Duchess's lament that in wooing a husband she must act like a tyrant who equivocates his words and masks violent passions in riddles; the undeniable reality of her public role forces her to be aggressive.

When Bosola and Ferdinand subject the Duchess to torture and death, their masque dramatises self-contradictions inherent in the notion of a female ruler. Bosola piously represents the trials which the Duchess endures – looking at the wax tableau of her supposedly dead family, kissing a dead man's hand in the dark, entertaining the masque of madmen, and finally, facing her tombmaker and ex-ecutioners – as an exercise in contrition, meant to bring her by degrees to mortification. Ferdinand wants only to drive her to despair. Critics have discussed how the pageant reflects Ferdinand's own motivation, but few have considered the masque as a rhetor-ical production, intended to persuade the Duchess to adopt Ferdinand's debased image of her by playing on her intellect and her emotions.[16] What the trials inflicted on the Duchess represent are commonplaces about feminine frailty, much like those the brothers sought earlier to impress on her. According to Ian Maclean, antifeminist accounts of woman based on the scholastic tradition often argue either that woman differs from man by nature or that she represents an imperfect or corrupted version of man.[17] The tortures Ferdinand prepares for his sister centre also on the notion that woman is an inferior version of man, derived from Adam's left side. Bosola, in his powerful set piece concerning the nature of man and woman, has already introduced the idea that woman's vices are linked to man's; his ludicrous accusation that the old midwife 'paints' with cosmetics and the grotesque image of a woman who flays her scarred face until she resembles an 'abortive hedgehog' is followed, without clear narrative logic, by a version of Hamlet's diatribe against mankind in general, who hide 'a rotten and dead body' in 'rich tissue' (II.i.28–68). With this non sequitur, Bosola suggests that while masculine nature defines the feminine, woman's vices mar man.

Like Knox, who blames England's state on Mary, Bosola lays the blame for man's disorders at woman's door.[18] Knox, in his exordium, also provides an appropriate gloss on Ferdinand's masque. Insisting that feminine rule is repugnant to both nature and God, Knox appeals to his readers with a series of rhetorical questions: 'For who can denie but it repugneth to nature, that the blind shal be appointed to leade and conduct such as do see? That the weake, the sicke, and impotent persones shall norishe and kepe the hole and strong, and finallie, that the foolishe, madde, and phrenetike shal governe the discrete, and give counsel to such as be sober of mind? And such be al women, compared unto man in bearing of authoritie.'[19] The dead man's hand the Duchess accepts in 'blind' darkness, and more obviously, her mad companions, dramatise the supposed 'blindness' and 'madness' of woman; not only is female sexuality a prominent topic of their conversation, but the madmen themselves have a feminine dimension, since the English tailor is crazed by his assiduous study of new fashions, while the doctor has forfeited his wits by jealousy.[20] None of these flaws is exclusively feminine; in Jacobean drama, Othello and Leontes are familiar exemplars of male jealousy, while the *Haec Vir* and *Hic Mulier* pamphlets chastise men and women alike for wearing outlandish clothing. The Duchess, however, does respond to her trial as an assault on her political identity through her femininity. When confronted by Ferdinand in her bedchamber, she asserts her right to be both wife and prince, asking, 'Why should I, / Of all the other princes in the world, / Be cas'd up like a holy relic?' (III.ii.137–9). Even at the point of death, although humbly seeking to cast off her 'last woman's fault' (IV.ii.230), she insists that she is 'Duchess of Malfi still' (IV.ii.147).

With his grotesque masque, Ferdinand forces the Duchess to see and experience all those vices which should make her, as a female governor, unfit to rule her dukedom and her fortune. In this sense, the Duchess's trial and death resembles that of Julia, who is poisoned for her curiosity, another notorious female vice. Ferdinand's allegory of woman's proverbial madness, vanity, and impiety is therefore an exercise in identity manipulation; demonstrating through association that the Duchess shares the vices common to all women, he seeks to prove that she is not, properly speaking, a female prince. Joyce Peterson, in an interesting comparison between the Duchess's execution and Mary Stuart's, notes that Elizabeth's counsellors purposefully kept quiet the proceedings of Mary Stuart's execution: 'One purpose of all these precautions was that there be no demonstration of public mourning that would dignify Mary's death as that of a queen. Another was that there be no publicity, no account of the courageous and Christian manner in which Mary met her death. The world was not to see Mary's death as Mary herself had come to anticipate it, as a Christian martyrdom.'[21] Like Ferdinand, Elizabeth and her counsellors knew the value of a private execution; they knew also the power of final scenes in establishing a Queen's moral identity.

By emphasising his sister's femininity, Ferdinand seeks to deprive her not only of her life and political title, but of her very identity. The Duchess defends herself against Ferdinand's stereotypes with stoic exemplars of her own, choosing to die like Brutus's faithful wife Portia. Lee Bliss, who considers the malignant effect of politics on private aspiration in *The Duchess of Malfi*, argues that the Duchess tries to shut out the political world to which she belongs and 'establish a private sphere, a world of intimate relationships and family concerns to which she can devote herself as private individual'.[22] Bliss's point is well taken, since the Duchess insistently represents herself as a tender mother who makes provision for her child's cough syrup, and as Antonio's wife. When Bosola gives her false news of Antonio's death, the Duchess asks only that he bind her to Antonio's lifeless trunk, evoking an image used in emblems by Alciati and Whitney to symbolise ill-matched marriages.[23] The Duchess wants to die as a wife and mother, even as a disgraced wife and mother. But she also recognises the centrality of her political title to her identity when at Bosola's entrance she remarks that 'Fortune's wheel is over-charg'd with princes, / The weight makes it move swift' (III.v.93–4). Even though the Duchess may die with a martyr's passive acquiescence, her tragedy has less to do with her moral nature than with the logical dilemma surrounding female rule.

Governed by the kind of relentless logic found in Knox's *First Blast*, *The Duchess of Malfi* lacks *Measure for Measure*'s happy resolution of the woman question. Bosola's masque accomplishes nothing. As Susan Baker argues, the Duchess is a static figure who passes through her trials unchanged: she 'does not develop, or grow, or learn anything significant from her experiences'.[24] Having taken a stand, she defends the integrity of her identity for the duration of the play, even returning after death to counsel Antonio through an echo. Echo, however, is a liminal figure, defined by her simultaneous absence and presence. She is the persistently faithful lover, who mourns Narcissus eternally; but in the Duchess's case she also represents the individual's absorption into a tragic role, condemned to eternal mourning.[25] The Duchess, like Echo, is both present and absent. She remains a prince until her death and is succeeded by her son; but since 'female prince' is an empty category in the language of the Woman Controversy, her existence is also a logical impossibility. The Duchess's continued sense of alienation can be measured by the persistence of masculine imagery in her self-representations. Even as she struggles to define her death in feminine terms, she represents her plight in rough masculine terms, imagining the life she leaves behind as the galley slave's suffering at his oar (IV.ii.28–9). The Duchess, a second Bosola, stands outside society's boundaries. As a woman, she cannot properly be a prince. As a 'prince', she is 'neither maid, widow, nor wife' in a more profound sense than *Measure for Measure* admits. Ferdinand, like Lucio, chooses a simple answer for the riddle of woman's nature: to him, the Duchess is merely a whore. But for the Duchess, to be neither maid, widow, wife, nor prince means to be nothing.

In *The Duchess of Malfi*, potential paradoxes – the female ruler, the widowed bride, and the princely mother – dissolve into incoherence. The Duchess, in the end, has not many identities but none. Frank Whigham, focusing on problems of masculine identity in *The Duchess of Malfi*, argues that Ferdinand, facing social challenges from Antonio and Bosola, destroys the sister whose marriage threatens the integrity of his identity as an aristocrat.[26] In such a reading, the drama occurs between Bosola and Antonio, the economic upstarts, and the Duchess's brothers; she is the battlefield over which these social forces fight. Yet reducing the Duchess to the occasion for her brothers' fantasies and her husband's ambition does not falsify her character, since reading the play from the perspective of the controversy over women underscores the fact that a patriarchal culture seeks to define the female ruler out of existence. Only Bosola, the outsider, believes strongly enough in the Duchess's regal identity to die for her.

III

In 'The Philosophy of Literary Form', Kenneth Burke writes that 'critical and imaginative works are answers to questions posed by the situation in which they arose. They are not merely answers, they are *strategic* answers, *stylised* answers.'[27] In approaching *Measure for Measure* and *The Duchess of Malfi* through the rhetoric of the Renaissance Woman Controversy, I have been treating both critical and imaginative works as stylised answers to questions about gender relations. The 'mere act of naming an object or situation decrees that it is to be singled out as such-and-such rather than as something-other', Burke continues.[28] In limiting my focus to the rhetoric of gender, I have therefore 'sized up' the plays in a particular way, to uncover strategies that control women by demonstrating the improbability of female virtue or the logical impossibility of female rule. Because the controversy is highly conventionalised, we can expect a certain amount of overlap among situations that pose the questions answered by critical and imaginative works; in other words, despite differences in genre and chronology, the works I have discussed, as symbolic action, share a family resemblance. Significantly, the two different strategies I have described – the use of stylistic amplification (particularly paradox) and of rhetorical logic (enthymemes) – produce a common result; both subjugate women to patriarchal authority by excluding them from the realm of moral agency with rhetorical sleight-of-hand.

Feminist critics have long noted that Renaissance drama and polemic both draw on misogynistic stereotypes. In the Woman Controversy, however, method often seems more powerful than evidence. Writers manipulate authority and exempla of virtue and vice at will: figures such as Judith, Debora, or even Eve may appear as witnesses for either the prosecution or the defence; biblical citations are handled with equal insouciance. When women begin to write in self-defence, they attack the style and logic of their detractors. Constantia Munda, one of Swetnam's respondents, mocks the way he writes: 'by heaping together the scraps, fragments, and reversions of diverse English phrases, by scraping together the glanders and offals of abusive terms and the refuse of idle-headed Authors and making a mingle-mangle gallimaufry of them'.[29] Ester Sowernam notes that although Swetnam steals his meagre material from lighter works such as Lyly's *Euphues*, he makes no reference to the weightier, classical antifeminist writers. In attacking the learning and the language of misogynist writers, female defenders of women are sensible of the limitations imposed on them by their own education; Constantia Munda, for instance, suspects that Swetnam attacks women because they lack the rhetorical tools to defend themselves:

> If your currish disposition had dealt with men, you were afraid that *Lex talionis* [the law of retaliation] would meet with you; wherefore you surmised that, inveighing against poor illiterate women, we might fret and bite the lip at you, we might repine to see ourselves baited and tossed in a blanket, but never durst in open view of the vulgar either disclose your blasphemous and derogative slanders or maintain the untainted purity of our glorious sex.[30]

Walter Ong has argued that Latin language education, the environment that kept classical rhetoric alive during the Renaissance, initiated boys into an exclusively male world.[31] Although this is a simplification, women as a group lacked access to the verbal play that characterises Swetnam's *Arraignment* and to the rhetorical syllogisms found in Knox's *First Blast*. The presence of classical rhetoric, the property of men in the Renaissance educational system, therefore makes the game of attacking and defending women coercive, since woman's worth is measured by male arts of language.

Constantia Munda expresses eloquently her frustration at being manipulated by writers like Swetnam: 'Nay, you'll put gags in our mouths and conjure us all to silence; you will first abuse us, then bind us to the peace. We must be tongue-tied, lest in starting up to find fault we prove ourselves guilty of those horrible accusations.'[32] What she objects to more than Swetnam's invective is the way his rhetoric exiles her from the continuing conversation of the Woman Question. When commonplaces from the controversy appear in the drama, they have the same rhetorical force that they do in polemical pamphlets; they are not 'images' defining female characters, but exercises in definition. Linda Woodbridge and Lisa Jardine have shown the pertinence of the Woman Controversy to characterisation in Renaissance literature, but I would suggest that the rhetorical strategies employed in the controversy have a wider relevance to the drama, since the controversy depends on habits of mind and on structures of language that are deeply embedded in Renaissance culture. The Woman Controversy works, in drama as in polemic, by encompassing women with a game that excludes them.

From *In Another Country: Feminist Perspectives on Renaissance Drama*, ed. Dorothea Kehler and Susan Baker (Metuchen, NJ and London, 1991), pp. 71–91.

NOTES

[Christy Desmet's essay indicates why the feminist paradigm for reading Webster has been so powerful. 'Woman' in the Renaissance is demonstrably a series of discursive categories – widow, maid, wife – a series of states defined by women's relation to men. The Renaissance controversy about woman, then, at times approximates something like a language game. Yet this game, this wordplay, this endless rhetoric, has immeasurable material impact on the lives of real women. Ed.]

1. For a summary of the charges brought against Isabella and Mariana, see Susan Moore, 'Virtue and Power in *Measure for Measure*', *English Studies*, 63 (1982), 308–17; and Darryl F. Gless, '*Measure for Measure*', *the Law, and the Convent* (Princeton, NJ, 1979), pp. 177–213. For the Duchess, see Alexander W. Allison, 'Ethical Themes in *The Duchess of Malfi*', *Studies in English Literature*, 4 (1964), 263–73; and Bob Hodge, 'Mine Eyes Dazzle: False Consciousness in Webster's Plays', in *Literature, Language, and Society in England, 1580–1680*, ed. David Aers, Bob Hodge, and Gunther Kress (Totowa, NJ, 1981), pp. 100–21.

2. For a comparable account of how antifeminist polemical works attempt to control women readers, see Susan Schibanoff's analysis of Christine de Pisan's *Booke of the City of Women*, 'Taking the Gold Out of Egypt: The Art of Reading as a Woman', in *Gender and Reading: Essays on Readers, Texts, and Contexts*, ed. Elizabeth A. Flynn and Patrocino P. Schweickart (Baltimore, MD, 1986), pp. 83–106. For a more wide-ranging discussion of how rhetoric, as an instrument of social order, reinforces existing hierarchies, including hierarchies of gender, see Patricia Parker, 'Motivated Rhetorics: Gender, Order, and Rule', in *Literary Fat Ladies: Rhetoric, Gender, Property* (London, 1987), pp. 97–125.

3. Linda Woodbridge, *Women and the English Renaissance: Literature and the Nature of Womankind, 1540–1620* (Urbana, IL, 1984), pp. 1–6.

4. On the Duchess's status as a widow who remarries, see Frank W. Wadsworth, 'Webster's *Duchess of Malfi* in the Light of Some Contemporary Ideas of Marriage and Remarriage', *Philological Quarterly*, 35 (1956), 394–407; Margaret Lael Mikesell, 'Catholic and Protestant Widows in *The Duchess of Malfi*', *Renaissance and*

Reformation, 19 (1983), 265–79. For a recent analysis of *The Duchess of Malfi* that examines the conflict between the Duchess's anomalous social position and the Protestant notion that marriage can successfully unite public and private life, see Mary Beth Rose, *'The Expense of Spirit': Love and Sexuality in English Renaissance Drama* (Ithaca, NY, 1988), pp. 155–77. [Reprinted in this volume – Ed.]

5. William Painter, *The Palace of Pleasure*, ed. Joseph Jacobs, 3 vols (1890; rpt. New York, 1966), vol. 3, p. 35.

6. See R. W. Dent, *John Webster's Borrowing* (Berkeley, CA, 1960), p. 184. All references to *The Duchess of Malfi* come from *The Selected Plays of John Webster*, ed. Jonathan Dollimore and Alan Sinfield (Cambridge, 1983).

7. Marie Axton, *The Queen's Two Bodies: Drama and the Elizabethan Succession* (London, 1977), p. 12; quoted in Leonard Tennenhouse, *Power on Display: The Politics of Shakespeare's Genres* (London, 1986), p. 102.

8. Tennenhouse, *Power on Display*, p. 103. See also Louis Adrian Montrose, '"Shaping Fantasies": Figurations of Gender and Power in Elizabethan Culture', *Representations*, 2 (1983), 61–94; rpt. in *Representing the English Renaissance*, ed. Stephen Greenblatt (Berkeley, CA, 1988), pp. 31–64.

9. Tennenhouse, *Power on Display*, pp. 113–14.

10. Ralph Berry, *The Art of John Webster* (Oxford, 1972), p. 6.

11. On the subject of the body domestic/body politic conflict, see Joyce E. Peterson, *Curs'd Example: 'The Duchess of Malfi' and Commonweal Tragedy* (Columbia, MO, 1978). Peterson makes useful comparisons between Malfi's Duchess and Mary Stuart, arguing that the Duchess, 'by placing her private desires above her public responsibility', has 'forced herself into positions that have caused her to forfeit first order and decorum, then reputation, and finally, freedom. By the end of Act III, she has lost out as woman and as duchess; she is separated from husband and son and is a prisoner in the land she formerly ruled' (p. 78). Peterson also touches on Knox's relevance to Webster's play.

12. John Knox, *The First Blast of the Trumpet, Against the Monstrous Regiment of Women, 1558*, ed. Edward Arber, English Scholar's Library, vol. 1, no. 2 (1878; rpt. New York, 1967), p. 11. For discussion of Knox's *First Blast*, see Arber, pp. ix–xviii; Suzanne W. Hull, *Chaste, Silent, and Obedient: English Books for Women, 1475–1640* (San Marino, CA, 1982), pp. 108–9; and Katherine M. Rogers, *The Troublesome Helpmate: A History of Misogyny in Literature* (Seattle, WA, 1966), p. 137. For an overview of the continuing debate over woman's rule, see Constance Jordan, 'Woman's Rule in Sixteenth-

Century British Political Thought', *Renaissance Quarterly*, 40 (1987), 421–51.

13. Rogers, *The Troublesome Helpmate*, p. 137.

14. Dent, *John Webster's Borrowing*, pp. 175–6; and Knox, *First Blast*, p. 48.

15. Lisa Jardine, *Still Harping on Daughters: Women and Drama in the Age of Shakespeare* (Brighton, 1983), p. 91.

16. For interpretations of Ferdinand's motives, see Bettie Anne Doebler, 'Continuity in the Art of Dying: *The Duchess of Malfi*', *Comparative Drama*, 14 (1980–1), 203–15; Lee Bliss, *The World's Perspective: John Webster and the Jacobean Drama* (New Brunswick, NJ, 1983), p. 152; and Inga-Stina Ekeblad, 'The "Impure Art" of John Webster', *Review of English Studies*, 9 (1958), 253–67.

17. Ian Maclean, *The Renaissance Notion of Woman: A Study in the Fortunes of Scholasticism and Medical Science in European Intellectual Life* (Cambridge, 1980), pp. 8–9 and 31–3.

18. Bosola, like Knox, also uses misogyny to serve political motives. As Peter Stallybrass points out, Bosola, marginalised by aristocratic privilege, reviles the old lady to displace 'his own abjection onto a person even more marginal and vulnerable' ('Patriarchal Territories: The Body Enclosed', in *Rewriting the Renaissance: The Discourses of Sexual Difference in Early Modern Europe*, ed. Margaret W. Ferguson, Maureen Quilligan, and Nancy J. Vichers [Chicago, 1986], p. 134).

19. Knox, *First Blast*, pp. 11–12.

20. Dale Randall demonstrates how some symbols in the play, such as the poniard, dead man's hand, and apricots, are used by the Duchess's adversaries to define her as a 'woman of pleasure' and to stress the unsavoury nature of woman's sexuality. Dale B. J. Randall, 'The Rank and Earthy Background of Certain Physical Symbols in *The Duchess of Malfi*', *Renaissance Drama*, 18 (1987), 171–203.

21. Peterson, *Curs'd Example*, p. 99.

22. Bliss, *The World's Perspective*, p. 146.

23. Dent, *John Webster's Borrowing*, p. 231.

24. Susan C. Baker, 'The Static Protagonist in *The Duchess of Malfi*', *Texas Studies in Literature and Language*, 22 (1980), 343.

25. See Jonathan Goldberg, *Voice Terminal Echo: Postmodernism and English Renaissance Texts* (New York, 1986): 'To attend critically to echo – to the *figure* of echo – one marks a *tacti* and reverbatory middle, a between' (p. 11).

26. Frank Whigham, 'Sexual and Social Mobility in *The Duchess of Malfi*', *PMLA*, 100 (1985), 167–86. [Reprinted in this volume – Ed.]

27. Kenneth Burke, *The Philosophy of Literary Form: Studies in Symbolic Action* (Berkeley, CA, 1973), p. 1.

28. Ibid., p. 4.

29. Constantia Munda, *The Worming of a Mad Dogge: A Soppe for Cerberus the Jaylor of Hell*, in Katherine Usher Henderson and Barbara F. McManus, *Half Humankind; Contexts and Texts of the Controversy about Women in England, 1540–1640* (Urbana and Chicago, 1985), p. 255; feminist objections to the antifeminists' logic and style are discussed on pp. 37–8.

30. Ibid., p. 253.

31. Walter J. Ong, SJ, 'Latin Language Study as a Renaissance Puberty Rite', in *Rhetoric, Romance, and Technology: Studies in the Interactions of Expression and Culture* (Ithaca, NY, 1971), pp. 113–41. See also Lawrence Stone, *The Family, Sex, and Marriage in England, 1500–1800* (New York, 1977): 'Although the mid-sixteenth century saw the emergence of a number of highly educated noblewomen, in general access both to sacred truth and to new learning was monopolised by men, thus increasing their prestige and influence and reducing that of women' (p. 158).

32. Munda, *The Worming of a Mad Dogge*, p. 253.

3

Death on Stage, Death of the Stage: The Antitheatricality of *The Duchess of Malfi*

ANDREA HENDERSON

> And Fortune seems only to have her eyesight,
> To behold my tragedy.
>
> (IV.ii.35–6)[1]

As Frank Whigham puts it, 'most readings of *The Duchess of Malfi* apply two categories of analysis: psychological inquiry ... and moral evaluation'.[2] Whigham asks 'prior questions' – why are these characters here at all? – in an effort to understand the play in terms of its historical social context. By asking a 'prior question' of another sort – why does this play represent theatricality the way it does? – we can better understand the play both in terms of its historical context and its internal workings. We will find that *The Duchess of Malfi* is preoccupied not only with reality and illusion and the effects of observation, but also with a growing sense of the theatrical nature of personal identity and the difficulty of locating a meaningful action which can be represented on stage.[3] We will see that ultimately the play can only confusedly point beyond itself, toward a new, textually oriented middle-class culture which will, for a time at least, prohibit theatrical display altogether.

I

We can broach the matter of the representation of theatricality within *The Duchess of Malfi* by noting that theatricality takes two different forms as it is experienced by two types of characters. For the sake of convenience, I label these types *aristocratic* and *bourgeois*, but whether a character belongs in one group or the other depends not on his or her class but on what he or she values. Thus, I consider the Duchess a bourgeois figure although I consider her brothers aristocratic ones. My reasons for labelling particular characters the way I do should become clear as I discuss their relation to theatricality.

Ferdinand and the Cardinal are the play's representative aristocrats, and we can begin an investigation of theatricality in their lives by noting that both are actor figures. We are only minutes into the play when Antonio alerts us to a division between both Ferdinand's and the Cardinal's inner and outer selves: he says of Ferdinand that, 'what appears in him mirth, is merely outside' (I.ii.95), and of the Cardinal that 'Some flashes superficially hang on him, for form: but observe his inward character: he is a melancholy churchman' (I.ii.80–2). When she is finally able to speak after her brothers have taken turns warning her not to remarry, the Duchess says 'I think this speech between you both was studied, / It came so roundly off' (I.ii.251–2). Not only do these comments imply that the brothers are like actors with prepared scripts, but in context they also imply an equivalence between successful performance and domination. The Cardinal and Ferdinand are consummate showmen whose shows oppress their audience.

When they are not forcing others to play the role of passive spectator, the brothers require them to *participate* in their shows, to speak according to their scripts; that is, they function as playwright figures. We see this function particularly in their manipulation of Bosola, and in Ferdinand's orchestration of the shows in the fourth act: the wax figures, the masque of madmen, the presentation of Bosola as a tomb-maker, and so forth. As Ferdinand says to his courtiers, 'Methinks you that are courtiers should be my touchwood, take fire when I give fire; that is, laugh when I laugh ...' (I.ii.43–5). Whether or not he says this jokingly, we know that he believes it. And as the fire metaphor makes clear, Ferdinand's insistence that those around him merely serve as actors of his own will not only denies them independent action, it also consumes them, destroys them.

The theatricality of the Aragonian brothers, then, is not only deceitful, but is also destructive of the development or expression of selfhood in those around them.[4] We suspect, however, that the use of this kind of expansive and dominating theatricality is not simply the product of the unusual personalities of Ferdinand and the Cardinal. Although at the beginning of the play Antonio describes the French court as uncorrupted and free of flatterers, the play as a whole morbidly dwells on the tendency of all court life to become theatrical. As Bosola says to Castruchio, if one is to be a successful courtier, it is taken for granted that one will speak 'in a set speech' (II.i.7), and it is recommended that one put on deceitful shows like Ferdinand's: 'When you come to be a president in criminal causes, if you smile upon a prisoner, hang him, but if you frown upon him, and threaten him, let him be sure to scape the gallows' (II.i.9–12). This theatricality, moreover, is not simply the incidental product of a struggle for power, but is an intrinsic part of the lives of those in the ruling classes. As the dumb-show of the investiture of the Cardinal makes clear, theatricality is fundamental to aristocratic life.[5]

The play's representation of aristocratic display as hollow and repressive rather than meaningful and socially unifying is best understood in its seventeenth-century context. It signals on the one hand a problem in the determination of identity and personal merit *at court* – what Whigham describes as a proliferation of mutual observations which had become a cliché, and a 'predicament', by this time.[6] But the theatricality of court life was part of a larger arena of theatrical relations; as Jean-Christophe Agnew demonstrates, theatricality came to seem a metaphor for and a symptom of uncontrolled social mobility, and the disguises and travesties of the marketplace were perceived as infiltrating every aspect of social life. Aristocratic theatricality comes under attack, then, not just for being antiquated and aristocratic but also because theatricality generally, with the growth of the mercantile economy, has come to seem a threatening sign of the instability of social hierarchies. The model for identity which was developed by the bourgeoisie in response to this theatricality, and which I will return to later, was a depth model which privileged self-definition and self-scrutiny. In a world where identity is understood to be the product of one's own labour, a ruler's insistence that his subjects passively accept identity from him becomes not only pointless, but a violation. The antitheatrical prejudice that we see here, then, is a sign of resistance to the extension of market relations at the same time that it reflects the ascendancy of a market-based model of identity. Absorption in the theatrical is dangerous for all, but those still devoted to the ways of the old order make the particularly dangerous mistake of failing to recognise that (in a market economy) one must always look beneath or beyond the shows one sees.

Not surprisingly, in *The Duchess of Malfi* aristocratic display not only inhibits the development and expression of identity in its viewers but also discourages self-understanding in its practitioners. Ferdinand, in projecting his will outwards onto others, and in feeling free to 'act' however he likes, fails to recognise his own 'acting', his own artifice. Unlike the bourgeois characters, who take it for granted that they must continually monitor themselves in order to keep track of who they really are, Ferdinand mistakenly believes he can understand himself simply by watching the shows he produces around him. In the early part of the play, when the Cardinal tells Ferdinand to control his anger at the Duchess, he sarcastically responds: 'So, I will only study to seem / The thing I am not' (II.v.63–4) – he refuses to be an actor, unaware that he already is one. Throughout the first half of the play, Ferdinand experiences the role-playing that Antonio sees in him as freely willed self-expression, only to discover in the second half that he has no idea what that self is.

As the volume of criticism directed at the problem of Ferdinand's character and motivation attests, the question of who he 'really' is is no simple matter. He shows signs of knowing that he is not simply what he seems, but his sense of his own complexity is tied up with his tendency toward self-projection and self-aggrandisement: 'He that can compass me, and know my drifts, / May say he hath put a girdle 'bout the world, / And sounded all her quicksands' (III.i.84–6). That Ferdinand accepts Bosola's response to this line, 'you ... grossly / Flatter yourself' (III.i.87–9) may indicate a fundamental confidence in his own knowability. By the fifth act, however, it is clear that Ferdinand's tendency toward self-projection rather than self-reflection has rendered him incapable of understanding his own motives and desires, of seeing behind his own masks. He is unable to relate the show of the Duchess's murder, which he directed, to his deeper feelings about her. He is now incoherent, insane:

> **Ferdinand** Eagles commonly fly alone. They are crows, daws, and
>   starlings that flock together. Look, what's that follows me?
> **Malateste** Nothing, my lord.

Ferdinand Yes.
Malateste 'Tis your shadow.
Ferdinand Stay it; let it not haunt me.
(*Throws himself upon his shadow.*)
(V.ii.30–8)

Not only do these lines reflect Ferdinand's desire to escape a part of himself, but they also reflect his discovery of his own doubleness. Where once he enjoyed company merely as a further extension of his (one) self, he now discovers that even when literally alone he is not truly alone. That 'shadow' was sometimes used to mean 'actor' during the Renaissance shows the extent to which Ferdinand is now haunted by his own theatricality, his own masks. In throwing himself on his shadow he is not only trying to destroy a haunting part of himself but is also trying to reunify himself.

Appropriately, both the Cardinal and Ferdinand are 'punished' for their abuse of theatricality by becoming victims of their own fictions and shows. Ferdinand orders the masque of madmen for the Duchess with the ostensible aim of making her sane but with the true aim of making her insane, and yet it is he and not she who becomes mad. When the doctor suggests a similar cure for him he rebukes him and shows him that strange behaviour in others will only exacerbate his condition – another sign of his difficulty in distinguishing himself from the shows around him. Similarly, the Cardinal's fiction that he may cause a commotion in the palace to which no one should respond, turns on him when he does call out for help and no one heeds him in time. As Pearson says, 'by his attempt to manipulate fictions the Cardinal dooms himself, and his death provides ... an exact judgement upon him'.[7] What we see in *The Duchess of Malfi* then, is an intense concern, not only with reality and illusion, but with the boundaries and meaning of personal identity. Subjects can no longer glean identity from their rulers because they must establish their own identities, and all identities, including that of the ruler, are radically unstable. Ferdinand, though he represents an older order, has the same problem with the establishment of identity that the 'bourgeois' characters have: identity is no longer supplied by one's social role but must be generated from within.

The essential difference between the aristocratic and bourgeois characters is encapsulated in Bosola's description of Antonio's speech: 'Both his virtue and form deserv'd a far better fortune: / His discourse rather delighted to judge itself, than show itself'

(III.ii.254–5). Antonio's speech serves the function of introspection rather than display. For this second group of characters, language is put in the service of self-understanding and private self-definition. As Agnew argues, the growth of the market economy and the power of the bourgeoisie during the Renaissance were paralleled by an increase in the tendency to locate meaning and agency in the human subject – a subject which was conceived as unified but at some deep point in the psyche.[8] At the same time, it was understood that on the surface, people, like merchants, wore masks and were potentially deceitful. One of the Duchess's speeches from the 'wooing' scene could serve as a textbook example of the interrelations of the expanding market economy, theatricality, and the bourgeois notion of the self:

> **Duchess**   You were ill to *sell* yourself;
> This dark'ning of your worth is not like that
> Which tradesmen use i'th' city; their *false lights*
> Are to rid bad wares off: and I must tell you
> If you will know where breathes a complete man.
> (I speak it without flattery), turn your eyes,
> And *progress through yourself*.
> (I.ii.351–7, my emphasis)

The connection drawn here, between the market economy and the conception of people as salesmen of themselves who must continually be stripping off their own masks and plunging deep within to find their 'true' selves, is clear. Here the display and theatricality of the royal progress function not as an external and socially useful pageant, but are turned inside to every man's private realm, the self.[9]

Not surprisingly, the bourgeois characters, unlike Ferdinand and the Cardinal, try to separate themselves from, rather than lose themselves in, the shows they witness. It is fitting that the masque, the world of which serves as an extension of the ruler's realm and is continuous with it, should be Ferdinand's preferred form of drama. But whereas he provides his masque of madmen to the Duchess ''cause she'll needs be mad' (IV.i.124), she says it will save her from madness precisely because she will divorce herself from it: 'Indeed I thank him: nothing but noise, and folly / Can keep me in my right wits, whereas reason / And silence make me stark mad' (IV.ii.5–7). Interestingly, the Duchess's preferred form of theatre is tragedy, and again, she enjoys it through separation of herself from it:

Duchess Discourse to me some dismal tragedy.
Cariola O 'twill increase your melancholy.
Duchess Thou art deceiv'd;
   To hear of greater grief would lessen mine.

(IV.ii.8–10)

Theatre for the Duchess is not something to lose oneself in or be defined by; rather, it provides a touchstone, an outer border against which the realm of oneself and one's own concerns can be understood.

In spite of her effort to dissociate herself from the theatrical, the Duchess is herself an actor figure. If one understands the masque of madmen as functioning for her as an antimasque,[10] the implications for the theatrical quality of the Duchess's own life are clear: when the masque proper begins, members of the court rather than professional actors will take to the 'stage'. The madmen exit, Bosola enters costumed as an old man to prepare the Duchess for death, and she finally says: 'I account this world a tedious theatre, / For I do play a part in't 'gainst my will' (IV.i.83–4). Like her brothers then, the Duchess is an actor, but unlike them, she both recognises the theatricality of her life and she experiences it not as pleasurable self-extension but as painful self-concealment. As she tells Antonio:

The misery of us, that are born great,
We are forc'd to woo, because none dare woo us:
And as a tyrant doubles with his words.
And fearfully equivocates: so we
Are forc'd to express our violent passions
In riddles, and in dreams, and leave the path
Of simple virtue, which was never made
To seem the thing it is not.

(I.ii.360–7)

What the play teaches us, however, is that it is not just 'the great' who are forced to play roles against their will. In fact, Antonio and Bosola have even more trouble than the Duchess in finding proper roles for themselves. As a steward, Antonio has a fairly comfortable social role. But in taking advantage of the new opportunities for social mobility based on merit, in choosing to leave the world of granted positions for the world of achieved jobs, he suddenly finds himself without a stable role at all. Whigham provocatively suggests that although he is a trustworthy spokesman at the beginning of the play, Antonio becomes disappointingly self-involved later because he feels torn between two roles in his relation to the Duchess, 'bound both to the traditional hierarchy of rank, which enjoins his submission, and to the traditional gender hierarchy, which enjoins him to dominate'.[11] That is, Antonio ceases to be able to function because he has no one clear role. I would suggest in addition that by tapping the potential for mobility, which is perceived as permitting people to change roles in theatrical fashion, Antonio becomes dysfunctional.[12] In agreeing to become an *actor* in the drama of Malfi rather than a passive observer, he finds himself in a system where all roles are unstable. This transition begins the moment the Duchess convinces him to marry her; he says: 'These words should be mine, / And all the parts you have spoke' (I.ii.390–1). From now on, Antonio will live the life of an actor. At best, this makes him 'a lord of mis-rule' (III.ii.7) as the Duchess teasingly calls him – a fitting name for a figure who has enjoyed a carnivalesque change of status. But for the most part, the new-found theatricality of Antonio's life is painful. As he says at one point: 'How I do play the fool with mine own danger!' (II.ii.68). He is horrified by and ashamed of his own theatricality: '*The great are like the base; nay, they are the same, / When they seek shameful ways to avoid shame*' (II.iii.51–2). By the end of the play, he has realised that the deceitful life is not worth living: 'to live thus, is not indeed to live: / It is a mockery, and abuse of life' (V.iii.46–7).

Ironically, Antonio's failure in the world of actors and action is due to the fact that his inability to find a stable role prevents his becoming anything more than a spectator. In the bedroom scene, for instance, he listens in hiding while Ferdinand threatens his wife, but takes no action to protect her. After Ferdinand leaves, he says he wishes that 'this terrible thing would come again, / That, standing on my guard, I might relate / My warrantable love' (III.ii.147–9), but responds to a knock at the door with 'How now? Who knocks? More earthquakes?' (III.ii.155). Now that he is involved in the plot of the play, Antonio's inability to find a role for himself in it renders him helpless. More unfortunate than the Duchess in this respect, Antonio is forced to play a part against his will which is so unstable as to be hardly a part at all. It is important to recognise, however, that Antonio's part is unstable not just because it is torn by conflicting allegiances and operates in a socially mobile and therefore unstable world, but also because it was never formally and ceremonially recognised. Antonio cannot step in and defend the Duchess's honour by claiming to be her husband in part because, in the absence of a public marriage ceremony, he hardly seems to be her husband at all. The play thus presents a world in a double-bind. Ceremony and public shows seem invariably to be empty rituals which deceive both their viewers and their participants, but defining one's identity and social role in the absence of ceremony and a fixed social structure is a terribly difficult task.

Bosola is, of course, the supreme representative of a person without a role. From the beginning, he is presented as an actor figure under the direction of the Aragonian brothers: 'I fell into the galleys in your service, where, for two years together, I wore two towels instead of a shirt, with a knot on the shoulder, after the fashion of a Roman mantle' (I.i.35–8). Bosola puts on roles, costume and all, for the aristocrats. It is not, then, just that Bosola will play a part, act a role, but he will play the part of the person who plays a part; that is, he will try to define himself as an actor. It is little wonder, then, that his 'true nature' is so radically ambiguous. Throughout the play other characters prize or chide him for his acting. Ferdinand tells him: 'Be yourself: / Keep your old *garb* of melancholy ... This will gain / Access to private lodgings' (I.ii.201–5), my emphasis); and Antonio says 'Because you would not seem to appear to th'world / Puff'd up with your preferment, you continue / This *out of fashion* melancholy; leave it, leave it' (II.i.88–90, my emphasis). Typically, Ferdinand enjoins theatricality for the sake of extending one's boundaries, and conceives of it as self-expression, whereas Antonio wants Bosola to discard all masks as far as possible.

In trying to establish himself through acting, Bosola involves himself in a vicious cycle: the more he tries to play his role, the less he understands himself. He ends up dividing himself in two, becoming both actor and spectator, and observing himself as a mere actor in moments of crisis. In the Duchess's execution scene we see him at his most 'actorly'. He arrives dressed as an old man, and his roles change so often as to be almost comic: he seems at first to be simply a spiritual guide of some sort, admonishing the Duchess to remember that death will come; then he insists that he literally is a tomb-maker; and finally he calls himself 'the common bellman' (IV.ii.172). Significantly, the language he uses at this point ('I am the common bellman, / That usually is sent to condemn'd persons, / The night before they suffer' [IV.ii.172–4]) emphasises the foreign and impersonal quality of his own role, as well as its theatrical construction. That is, in calling himself '*the* common bellman' rather than 'a common bellman' Bosola establishes himself as a sign for, rather than simply a member of, a group.

II

Given that all the principal characters of *The Duchess of Malfi* are actor figures, and that the sense of life as theatre is remarkably pervasive in this play, it is significant that *The Duchess of Malfi* presents a world which is stagnant. Ferdinand's early comment, 'when shall we leave this sportive action, and fall to action indeed?' (I.ii.9–10) becomes one of the major questions of the play as a whole. Catherine Belsey notes that it takes a remarkably long time for the 'action' of the play to begin and it is not until the final scene that Bosola says 'Thus it lightens into action' (V.v.10).[13]

Again, this problem of stagnation is closely related to the newfound necessity of individual establishment of identity and the concomitant reduction of the social usefulness of public display. As Bosola says: 'He [the Cardinal] and his brother are like plum trees, that grow crooked over *standing pools*, they are rich, and o'erladen with fruit, but none but crows, pies, and caterpillars feed on them' (I.i.49–52, my emphasis). Although Bosola is primarily concerned with money here, his description can easily be seen as a criticism of the severed link between ruler and ruled which traditionally provided both goods and identity to the latter. The newly dispersed social body, because it cannot act as a whole, and because its social displays are now perceived as devoid of honest signification, is unable to discover an action that is socially meaningful. It is practically impossible for the people of Malfi to 'fall to action indeed'. But if aristocratic, public display seems hollow and meaningless, where else might the play find a suitable action for representation? A possible answer is embedded in the context of Ferdinand's comment on action:

> **Ferdinand** Who took the ring oft'nest?
> **Silvio** Antonio Bologna, my lord.
> **Ferdinand** Our sister Duchess' great master of her
>   household? Give him the jewel: when shall we leave
>   this sportive action, and fall to action indeed?
>
>   (I.ii.6–10)

As many critics have noted, Antonio's capture of the ring with his lance foreshadows his marriage to the Duchess. On one level then, the 'action indeed' which is to replace the 'sportive action' is not battle but marriage and its consummation. But to what extent can marriage and consummation be considered 'action', and, more specifically, action fit for the stage?

Catherine Belsey calls *The Duchess of Malfi* 'the perfect table of emergent liberalism', pointing not only to its focus on the bourgeois subject, but also to its reflection of the new dichotomy between public and private life.[14] The play 'celebrates the family, identifying it as a private realm of warmth and fruitfulness separate from the turbulent world of politics, though vulnerable to it.'[15] Ferdinand and the Cardinal, although they resist this distinction between the two realms, nevertheless concede its existence in their very language: Ferdinand warns that 'your *privat'st* thoughts, / Will come to light', and the Cardinal adds, 'You may flatter yourself, / And take your own choice: *privately* be married / Under the eaves of night –' (I.ii.238–41, my emphasis). The bourgeois characters honour the distinction. This is of course most apparent in the way the Duchess perceives her married life as private business, and it is even encapsulated in a single statement of Cariola's:

> Duchess   To thy known secrecy I have given up
>   More than my life, my fame,
> Cariola   Both shall be safe:
>   For I'll conceal this secret from the world
>   As warily as those that trade in poison,
>   Keep poison from their children.
>   (I.ii.262–6)

Cariola will safeguard the Duchess's public life by keeping it separate from her private life, just as others safeguard their private life by keeping it separate from the public.

But the historical movement to a world where public life is 'devalued by contrast with the true fulfilment available within the enclave of the family' has important repercussions for the theatre.[16] When the Duchess tells Antonio that their private life is their business alone, she puts it this way; 'Do not think of them [my brothers]: / All discord, without this circumference, / Is only to be pitied, and not fear'd' (I.ii.386–8). As Wayne Rebhorn suggests,

> although the Duchess' reference to circumference is usually glossed as meaning the couple's embracing bodies or arms, there is no reason why the word could not be taken as a more general reference, accompanied by a sweeping gesture, to the room and hence the palace in

which the couple are presently located. As a result, the empty Elizabethan stage, which is identified so often as a room or courtyard in the Duchess' palace and which significantly projects forward creating an enclosed space in the midst of the audience (at least in the public theatres), thus becomes itself a final extension of the ring or circle image, separating the protected, sacred sphere of the Duchess' world even from the profane, 'real' world of the audience.[17]

The implications of this reading clearly extend beyond the matter of imagery. How is the private life which the play values to be represented on stage without thereby confusing it with the public and violating its very nature? Significantly, the real 'marriage', the consummation, takes place offstage – the Duchess and Antonio walk off as she says that his bosom is to be 'the treasury of all my *secrets*' (I.ii.419, my emphasis). Rebhorn provides an extensive account of the way ring images in the play, including hugs, rooms, buildings, and so on, are established as a defence against penetration of various kinds – a penetration which nevertheless occurs. Moreover, these 'rings' which were intended for protection become traps, and as the play progresses one gets an ever stronger feeling of claustrophobia.

The problems that the presentation of the private life poses suggest two very good reasons why these rings become traps. First of all, it is likely that the play cannot present the private life at this point because it has not yet been fully ideologically constructed – what should be a three-dimensional sphere is never completely filled out. Secondly, this entrapment reflects on some level the inability of the play to represent the depth of the world within the 'ring' if one can only see into it by puncturing it. In an *avant la lettre* demonstration of the Heisenberg uncertainty principle, the play reflects the impossibility of presenting the private publicly – the viewer changes it, flattens it, by his presence.[18] The room that could be the centre of a fulfilling life for the Duchess and Antonio becomes merely a trap when invaded by others. As Agnew notes, 'as early as the seventeenth century ... one can see the formative conventions of literary realism already presuming a social world (or a portion of that world) from which the reader was made to feel at once excluded and privy.'[19] This was ultimately to lead to what Bakhtin called the '"alcove realism" of private life, a realism of eavesdropping and peeping'.[20] Clearly, *The Duchess of Malfi* is pointing in this direction, but it has not yet naturalised this voyeurism. In scene after scene, the play presents the audience with representatives of itself in the form of characters hiding on stage for the purpose of peeping. With the possible exception of Cariola's hiding as a witness to the marriage of the Duchess and Antonio, this looking-on seems to be a rather sneaky, disreputable business[21] – it is significant that Ferdinand and the Cardinal are its greatest practitioners.

III

In *The Duchess of Malfi*, then, not only is life a 'tedious theatre' but the theatre itself hardly seems capable of representing the things it values. The bloody confusion of the final act proves to be the only meaningful action which the play can comfortably present. The ultimate answer to Ferdinand's question 'When shall we fall to action indeed?' lies not, then, in the marriage suggested by its context but in the violence that ends the play. As Bosola says before killing the Cardinal: 'Thus it lightens into action' (V.v.10). In a world where the private life cannot be shown and the shows of public life are meaningless, it is only in the conflict between the two that one finds a form of action that is both honest and presentable. That the spectacular and violent fifth act should constitute an alternate climax in the play is thus not terribly surprising.[22]

Francis Barker argues that Jacobean theatre was spectacularly bodily and bloody because it reflected a transitional period wherein bodies and the visual were still important but were being cleared away for a new textually-oriented bourgeois order where the body was to be effaced.[23] *The Duchess of Malfi* can indeed be understood as enacting a ritualistic purging of the bodily, but it can more broadly be seen as enacting the purging of the theatrical. Within the play, the closest the characters come to discovering their 'true' selves is in the moment before they die, and only in death itself can they finally escape from theatricality. Antonio's answer to Bosola's 'What art thou?' (V.iv.47) after being struck by him is 'A most wretched thing / That only have the benefit in death, / To appear myself' (V.iv.47–9). The Cardinal, Ferdinand, and Bosola, although their final statements may not 'sum up' their character in some affirmative way,[24] at least are finally willing to confront and express the horror of what they have been and done. Desperate to leave the stage of life, the Duchess finds death the 'Best gift' (IV.ii.225), and says 'I know death hath ten thousand several doors / For men to take their exits ... any way, for heaven sake, / So I were out of your whispering' (IV.ii.219–23).

The death of the characters, then, represents the death of the body and the death of the theatricality of their lives, but it also ends the play. The death of theatricality within the play is thus continuous with the death of the theatricality which constitutes the play itself. As Rebhorn notes, the play's 'trapped characters found their release only in death; the audience will find its only when it finally escapes the confines of the theatre'.[25] *The Duchess of Malfi* deploys a full range of theatrical forms and techniques,[26] ultimately only to kill the theatre in itself. Just as Antonio's marriage would have had less purely private significance if performed publicly and yet hardly seemed a real marriage without that publicity, the play appears to recognise that its only tools for understanding its characters are theatrical, and yet what is meaningful about the characters cannot be reached through theatrical means. Theatricality can finally only be managed through its destruction. An ideologically transitional period may not only afford a new freedom through the looseness of its categories, it may also leave people with no place to locate meaning at all.[27]

The play ends, the stage littered with corpses, with the standard tragic reassertion of social continuity through the announcement of an heir to power. Since this heir is to be Antonio's son, this announcement could be viewed as the play's effort to reconcile aristocratic and bourgeois orders. In light of what has gone before, however, the hopefulness of the future seems tenuous at best (recall Antonio's dying wish that his son fly the courts of princes, and the prophecy that this child would die an early and violent death).[28] The last words of the play are Delio's adage, '*Integrity of life is fame's best friend, / Which nobly, beyond death, shall crown the end*' (V.v.120–1) – an aggressively insufficient effort to sum things up. It is as if the play is struggling to make sense of itself but can do so only by glossing over its own uncentredness.[29] Significantly, it closes by pointing to the problem of integrity – suggesting not only the importance of leading an upright life, but also the necessity for personal integration, coherence.

That this play, for all its spectacular qualities, is in fact antitheatrical and reflects a movement toward a literary culture which privileges private reading is suggested not only within the play but also in the quarto in which it was preserved. The title page of the quarto claims to offer 'The perfect and exact Coppy, *with diverse /*

things Printed, that the length of the Play would / not beare in the Presentment' (my emphasis). This is not simply the record of a performance, a sort of substitute, but a text which caters to the private reader. That this play was written not only to be performed but also to serve as a specifically *textual* monument is clear from the dedicatory letters. John Ford addresses his letter 'To the *reader* of the author' and speaks of the characters taking life from Webster's 'clear *pen*' – not from their actors on stage.[30] The production of this text becomes a self-defining act for a Webster who himself lived in an age of self-definition through work – as Thomas Middleton puts it: 'thou by this work of fame, / Hast well provided for thy living name.'[31] Tellingly, 'all the evidence points to Webster's active participation in the production of the Quartos'.[32] Webster's concern with his self-defining textual product can even be seen in minor matters such as the marginal note by the song in Act III, scene v that 'The Author disclaims this Ditty to be his'. Ironically, even while extolling 'plainness', Middleton's dedication reflects the pervasiveness of the contemporary conception of man as a self-fashioned art object: 'for every worthy man / Is his own marble; and his merit can / Cut him to any figure'.[33]

What we have in *The Duchess of Malfi* is a truly transitional play, a play which presents an older order which is no longer meaningful, but which can only tentatively look toward the new order that will replace it. Remarkable for its early celebration of bourgeois values, it nevertheless cannot fully apprehend them, and struggles desperately to manage the sense of pervasive theatricality that grew in strength with the bourgeoisie. *The Duchess of Malfi* finds itself unable to valorise old forms of display but without a way to naturalise the public presentation of the private life, so that, finally, it can only find its proper subject matter in its own destruction. Although itself a play, *The Duchess of Malfi* anticipates the closing of the theatres in 1642, the definitive effort to put an end to theatricality.

From *Theatre Journal*, 42 (1990), 194–207.

NOTES

[Andrea Henderson's essay takes up the relation between representation and the real, specifically the representation of death in tragedy and the demise of theatricality. Once again, as with Coddon's essay, this essay is indebted to

Foucauldian ideas about the spectacle of power being the enactment of power itself. That is to say, power is understood to reside within the spectacle itself rather than standing behind the spectacle as its guarantee. Ed.]

1. John Webster, *Three Plays*, ed. D. C. Gunby (New York, 1972). All subsequent references to the play will be to this edition.

2. Frank Whigham, 'Sexual and Social Mobility in *The Duchess of Malfi*', *PMLA*, 100 (1985), 167. [Reprinted in this volume – Ed.]

3. For a treatment of the role of illusion in the play, see Susan McCloskey, 'The Price of Misinterpretation in *The Duchess of Malfi*', in *From Renaissance to Restoration: Metamorphoses of the Drama*, ed. Robert Markley (Cleveland, OH, 1984), pp. 34–55; on the problems of observation see Anat Feinberg, 'Observation and Theatricality in Webster's *The Duchess of Malfi*', *Theater Research*, 6 (1980), 36–43.

4. I mean 'subject' and 'self' in the specific sense in which it is used by such critics as, for instance, Jean-Christophe Agnew in *Worlds Apart: The Market and the Theater in Anglo-American Thought, 1550–1750* (Cambridge, 1986); Francis Barker in *The Tremulous Private Body* (New York, 1984); and Catherine Belsey in *The Subject of Tragedy* (New York, 1984). I will discuss this particular model of subjectivity in some detail later in the article.

5. As Leonard Tennenhouse argues in *Power on Display* (New York, 1986), the theatre itself was an important vehicle for the display of aristocratic and particularly royal power. It is somewhat surprising, then, that he does not discuss the way a play like *The Duchess of Malfi* criticises such display.

6. Frank Whigham, 'Interpretation at Court: Courtesy and the Performer–Audience Dialectic', *New Literary History*, 14 (1983), 629.

7. Jacqueline Pearson, *Tragedy and Tragicomedy in the Plays of John Webster* (Totowa, NJ, 1980), p. 91.

8. William B. Worthen, in *The Idea of the Actor* (Princeton, NJ, 1984), provides an excellent account of problems of theatricality in *The Duchess*, points to the way acting can 'blur the priorities of social degree' (p. 57), and connects both these issues to the imagery of plague and disease in the play. My account of the play differs from his primarily in that he tends to treat the play's representation of identity and subjectivity as that of a norm under pressure rather than a social product undergoing laborious construction.

9. For the reading of 'progress' as a royal progress see Kathleen McLuskie, 'Drama and Sexual Politics: The Case of Webster's Duchess', in *Drama, Sex, and Politics*, ed. James Redmond (New York, 1985), p. 79. [Reprinted in this volume – Ed.]

10. See Feinberg, 'Observation', p. 41.

11. Whigham, 'Mobility', p. 176.

12. Although he probably doesn't intend the pun, William Archer fittingly refers to Antonio as a '*shadowy* character', in '*The Duchess of Malfi*', in *Twentieth-Century Interpretations of 'The Duchess of Malfi*', ed. Norman Rabkin (Englewood Cliffs, NJ, 1968), p. 18, my emphasis.

13. See Catherine Belsey, 'Emblem and Antithesis in *The Duchess of Malfi*', in *Renaissance Drama*, 11 (1980), 118–21.

14. Belsey, *The Subject of Tragedy*, p. 197.

15. Ibid., p. 198.

16. Ibid., p. 199. Many critics have wondered at the significance of the play's having a heroine instead of a hero. Norman Rabkin suggests that Webster 'signifies the final helplessness of his tragic protagonists by making them women' ('Introduction', in *Twentieth-Century Interpretations*, 4). Others suggest that the Duchess's very female-ness indicates that she falls something short of the stature of the traditional tragic hero. In fact, however, it makes perfect sense that a woman should be the hero of this play; it is, after all, a play about the private life, a life which, as it became a recognisable category, was simultaneously being associated with women. If the Duchess seems a different kind of tragic hero, it is not because she is less intrinsically heroic, but because she is a middle-class hero, as much as we may think of the title as oxymoronic.

17. Wayne Rebhorn, 'Circle, Sword, and the Futile Quest: The Nightmare World of Webster's *Duchess of Malfi*', *Cahiers Elisabéthains*, 27 (1985), 54.

18. Interestingly, Bosola, the principal actor figure, the 'actor in the main of all' (V.v.85), is the guilty exposer of private matters.

19. Agnew, *Worlds Apart*, p. 67.

20. Ibid.

21. Significantly, looking on in *public* scenes is not represented as bad; recall for example Antonio and Delio's observation of the court in the first scene. But at the same time, these public scenes only present us with hollow displays and corruption.

22. Critics have long struggled with the 'problem' of the heroine's death in the fourth act; see for instance Archer, '*Duchess*', p. 19.

23. Barker, *The Tremulous Private Body*, pp. 14–21. What we have here is something like an early form of the analysis and channelling into discourse of the desires of the body that Foucault describes as develop-

ing at that other moment that marks a leap forward in the development of capitalism and bourgeois power – the Industrial and French Revolutions (Michel Foucault, *The History of Sexuality* [New York, 1980]). It is also worth noting that many writers of the early nineteenth century, and especially detractors of the French Revolution considered the period an age of paper; see W. J. T. Mitchell, *Iconology: Image, Text, Ideology* (Chicago, 1986), pp. 143, 23n.

24. For a standard treatment of this problem, see Ralph Berry, *The Art of John Webster* (Oxford, 1972), p. 52.

25. Rebhorn, 'Nightmare World', p. 63.

26. See McLuskie, 'Drama and Sexual Politics', p. 78.

27. I am thinking here of Catherine Belsey's suggestion that 'the contest for meaning of the family which took place in the sixteenth and seventeenth centuries disrupted sexual difference' and that new possibilities of being emerged in the gap between the old and new meanings of the family ('Disrupting Sexual Difference: Meaning and Gender in the Comedies', in *Alternative Shakespeares*, ed. John Drakakis [New York, 1985], p. 178). It seems to me that in this case, for whatever reason, the gap between ideologies or meanings has generated a crisis of meaning, a merely horrifying void. As Mulryne puts it, the play 'is written in the service of no identifiable absolute, whether political, moral, or religious' (quoted in Joyce Peterson, *Curs'd Example: 'The Duchess of Malfi' and Commonweal Tragedy* [Columbia, MO, 1978], p. 8).

28. For an intelligent discussion of the ironies in the last act and the ending itself see Pearson, *Tragedy*, pp. 89–95.

29. Catherine Belsey uses *The Duchess* as an example of a Renaissance play which combines both new techniques of realism and the old medieval techniques of emblem and antithesis (Belsey, 'Emblem'). The question she never asks is why a play written around 1614 should make more use of medieval techniques than do many earlier Renaissance plays. It may do so in part to give a safely traditional look to a relatively progressive play. In addition, I would suggest that the play is struggling to contain and manage the indeterminacy of identity and the difficulty of locating meaning by providing us with the conventions of an older and more stable order – sententiae, emblematic scenes, long set pieces, antithetical characters, and so forth. The play is trying to put the reins on a too-threatening realism. This effort is only partially successful, however; the sententiae, for example, seem so insufficient, so forced, that few commentators have located the play's meaning in them.

30. Webster, *Three Plays*, p. 173, line 17, my emphasis.

31. Ibid., p. 172, ll. 6–7.

32. Ibid., p. 31.

33. Ibid., p. 172, ll. 15, 10–12. On the issue of the development of the notion of individual authorship, its relation to printing, and its frequent opposition to theatricality, see Peter Stallybrass and Allon White, *The Politics and Poetics of Transgression* (New York, 1986), esp. chapter 1, 'The Fair, the Pig, Authorship'.

4

Defining/Confining the Duchess: Negotiating the Female Body in John Webster's *The Duchess of Malfi*

THEODORA A. JANKOWSKI

The relatively rapid appearance in mid-sixteenth-century Britain of three reigning female monarchs severely taxed existing early modern political theory. The rich discourse that explored the various ramifications of the nature of authority and male rulership had been remarkably silent about both the potential for and the nature of possible female rule. Thus, the presence of Mary Tudor and Mary Stuart on British thrones served to point out – to political theorists especially – that no language existed for describing the nature of female rule. That a large discourse did exist for describing married women – one that showed them to be subservient to their husband – did not make the task of creating a political discourse for women any easier. In fact, the existence of such a powerful mode of describing married women as subject to their husbands prompted John Knox to argue in 1558 that the nature of female rule was 'un-natural'.[1] Whether this pronouncement was universally accepted or not is not important. What is important is that various 'disastrous' events in the reigns of the two Marys served to cast severe doubt upon the nature of female rule itself, especially given the fact that

monarchs *had* to marry to produce heirs. So strong was the traditional belief in women as subservient beings that John Aylmer had
some difficulty in supporting the concept of a female monarch. His
not very convincing argument was that a woman ruler could be
'subject to' her husband as he was her husband and yet 'rule over'
him as she was his magistrate. While Aylmer's solution was, at best,
'tricky', his basic aversion to female rule on principle did not help
his argument carry the day.[2] Elizabeth I clearly did not find his solution helpful, since she avoided the problem altogether by remaining 'virgin'. But despite Elizabeth's avoidance of matrimony, the
vexed question of a female sovereign's marriage does surface in a
number of early modern plays, notably John Webster's *The
Duchess of Malfi*, where it becomes a central issue.

The *Duchess of Malfi* is an unusual play not only because it explores questions of rulership as they relate to a female sovereign,
but also because it explores these questions as regards the sovereign's marriage. The play thus participates in the discursive construction of women in the early modern period and helps to reveal
the contradictions in the notion of a female ruler. These contradictions are explored in the ways in which the Duchess is represented
as using her body natural and her body politic.[3] Webster's Duchess
of Malfi establishes a system of rule in which she fails to consider
her body's potential either as a means to power or as a means by
which she can lose power. This widow attempts to secure herself
politically by divorcing her natural body from her political one by
creating a private second marriage that exists simultaneously with –
but hidden from – her public life as a ruler. In this double position
of wife and ruler, then, the Duchess becomes an uneasy and threatening figure. I will argue, therefore, that, despite the character's
failure to create a successful means by which she can rule as a
woman sovereign, she challenges Jacobean society's views regarding
the representation of the female body and woman's sexuality.

Critics have rarely considered the Duchess of Malfi as a political
character despite the fact that she rules Malfi as Regent for her son,
the minor heir to the Duke of Malfi, her dead husband. Given her
role as sovereign ruler, the Duchess needs also to be viewed as a political figure. Yet Kathleen McLuskie observes that the critical
history of *The Duchess of Malfi* reflects an 'unease with a woman
character who so impertinently pursues self-determination'.[4] This
'unease' has led to a criticism that focuses primarily on the
Duchess's private roles of wife, mother, unruly widow, or

victimised woman and slights consideration of her public role as ruler. The only sustained political reading of the play is presented by Joyce E. Peterson who argues that the Duchess improperly sets the private claims of her body natural above the public claims of her body politic. As a result of her 'anarchic will', Webster's character places her private desire to marry Antonio above her public responsibility as a ruler, an action that identifies her with her corrupt brothers. Peterson also suggests that the 'generic expectations ... insist inexorably on her culpability as a ruler, on her responsibility for her own fate, and, worse, for the disruption of her duchy'.[5]

While I agree that much of the tension of The Duchess of Malfi derives from the conflicting claims of the Duchess's bodies natural and politic, I do feel that Peterson's judgement of the Duchess as a 'bad' ruler fails to take account of how Renaissance gender ideologies are made. Her harsh reading of the Duchess may be based upon what she rightly perceives to be an action directly subversive of prevailing ideologies, but which she does not examine as such. It seems to me, then, that Peterson's failure to consider the overall implications of early modern sexual, social, and political attitudes toward women leads to her reading of this play as a simple lesson in bad rulership. By not discussing why the Duchess's marriage is so threatening and by reproducing oppressive gender ideologies in an unqualified way, Peterson blunts her argument and simplifies the very complex nature of the representation of 'woman' – especially 'woman as ruler' – displayed in this play.

The Duchess of Malfi is a play that is clearly concerned with questions of gender ideology, but its employment of various, often contradictory, literary and social discourses regarding gender relations makes it difficult to analyse. However, the contradictions between these conventions serve both to foreground the tensions implicit within socially-constructed ideas of 'woman', or the female protagonist, and present interpretive problems for deciding which is the privileged discourse. This ideological juxtaposition can be observed as early as Act I, scene i, where three major questions are introduced: first, the political context of the play as a whole, specifically the first presentation of the Duchess as a reigning sovereign and public figure; second, the presentation of the brothers and their political and familial relationship to the Duchess; and third, the presentation of the Duchess as a private figure and the character's development of her unusual 'new world and custom' in her secret marriage to Antonio. The display of contesting ideologies characteristic of this scene may make the play difficult to analyse, but simplification of the work through unified readings deprives it of its ideological complexity.

In order to understand the ways in which the Duchess is figured as a political character, it is necessary to examine the political context in which this character is presented. Antonio's description of the ideal French court and its 'judicious king' does just this.[6] The description acts as a touchstone for the accepted Renaissance ideal of court life that is contrasted to Malfi and Rome, places the play within a political framework, and indicates that the entire first act is an examination of the political natures of the four 'princes' – three actual and one 'spiritual' – who appear in this play: the Duchess herself; Ferdinand, the 'perverse' Duke of Calabria; the corrupt Cardinal; and the 'spirit' of the King of France, the emblem of the 'judicious king'.

It is against this dual background of corruption and idealism that Webster places the political persona of the Duchess of Malfi. Her presentation as a sovereign in a courtly setting both reinforces Antonio's description of her as an ideal ruler who differs in some essential way from her brothers (I.i.187–205) and insists upon the necessity of her occupying a political space. The fact that his speech can, on one level, be seen as the idealised portrait of a 'woman', does not alter the fact that the opening line – 'the right noble duchess' (l. 187) – serves to indicate that the speech must be seen as relating to the idealised public figure that Antonio feels the Duchess, in contrast to her Machiavellian brothers, is.

That the major discussion between the Duchess and her brothers concerns their exercise of familial authority to forbid her to remarry makes this scene seem more private than public. Citing traditional early modern objections to a second marriage for widows – 'they are most luxurious / Will wed twice' (ll. 297–8) – the brothers appear to forbid her remarriage because she is their sister, not because of her political position as Duchess. Yet such overtly political references to the court as 'a rank pasture' (l. 306) whose deadly 'honey-dew' (l. 307) might tempt the Duchess to act against her brothers' interests reinforce the political sense of the scene. However, this is not to deny that the reference to the Duchess as a 'sister' seems to involve consideration of her natural rather than her political body. Thus, in less than 100 lines we appear to move from contemplation of the body politic of the Duchess – as exemplar of Antonio's ideal of courtly virtue – to a picture of her widow's body natural at the mercy of her brothers' fears of her remarriage and early modern notions of the hypersexuality of widows.

And yet this encounter can be seen as being as political as the description of the French court and involving exclusively the Duchess's body politic. Catherine Belsey and Susan Wells speak of the problems involved in trying to separate public from private space in the early modern period, especially as these spaces relate to the family. Belsey indicates that

> in the sixteenth and early seventeenth centuries these two meanings of the family – as dynasty and as private realm of warmth and virtue – are both in play and indeed in contrast. In 1527 and for many years to come it was the dynastic meaning which was dominant.[8]

But although the sense of 'family' as 'dynasty' was the paramount 'reading' of the concept, Belsey points out that an 'alternative' notion of the family as 'a little world of retreat' from the public space 'where the wife enters into partnership with the husband' was also beginning to emerge (p. 173). We are tempted, I feel, with our twentieth-century eyes to view things like early modern family relationships as though they were more like our own than less. Thus, the temptation throughout this play is to feel that Ferdinand and the Cardinal take an inordinate amount of interest in the potential marital (e.g., private) affairs of their sister. This is perhaps an appropriate twentieth-century reading, but not necessarily an appropriate early modern one. While I do not wish to minimise the 'private' complexity of the Aragon family's relationships, I do think it is important to acknowledge the 'political' or dynastic nature of the early modern aristocratic marriage.

The Duchess is a sovereign ruler, a fact her brothers never forget. Silvio announces the entrance of Ferdinand's family to him as 'your brother, the Lord Cardinal, and sister Duchess' (I.i.148) and the Cardinal recalls the 'high blood' (l. 297) – noble birth – that the Duchess possesses. The choral urgings of the two brothers to prevent the sister's marriage seem somewhat odd, especially when Ferdinand calls upon his 'father's poniard' (l. 331) to help with the argument, unless the objections of the brothers are viewed on dynastic grounds. Once we read the family as a Renaissance dynastic unit, it becomes easier to understand the brothers – and their father's spirit's – earnest arguments. It also becomes easier to understand Ferdinand's obsession with the Duchess's blood and her reference to 'all [her] royal kindred' (l. 341) who might lie in the path of her proposed marriage to a steward of lower rank, which would pollute this blood.[9] Thus, the argument over the marriage can be seen as a dynastic argument concerned with the Duchess's body politic. This highly political scene, then, initially focusing on the ideal court of the French king, also serves to present the Duchess as a political figure both in her own right and as a member of a political dynasty – whether of Malfi or Aragon. The focus on the Duchess, until her brothers' departure, is completely on her body politic.

However, viewing the early modern family as a dynastic unit does not fully account for the explicit sexual tension in this encounter of the Aragonian siblings. The brothers may be justified in taking an interest in their sister's marital affairs, but it is rather difficult to see how they can be justified in their inordinate interest in her sexual being as well. The nature of Renaissance dynastic marriage served almost totally to objectify the woman. She became an object of commerce who – passed from father to husband – sealed a bargain of greater or lesser economic significance.[10] As her body was seen as an object of trade to be owned by either father or husband, the products of her body – her children – were also seen as objects of commerce to be used to solidify further trade agreements between her (husband's) and other families. Thus, the woman's biological life – her ability or inability to produce viable offspring – becomes as much a possession of her male owners as her physical body itself. Thus, as Ferdinand and the Cardinal feel justified in controlling their sister's 'use' as a wife, they also feel justified in controlling the biological uses of her body – its ability to produce offspring. In this sense, their inquiry into the chastity of their sister's body is understandable, though grotesque, for her production of children the patriarchy considers illegitimate would decrease her value as a trade article for her family.

And yet the brothers – especially Ferdinand's – questions regarding her own use of her body go beyond questioning her chastity to expressing both fear of and desire for her sexual being. The very nature of woman's objectification within dynastic marriage leads to Ferdinand's obsessive sexual questioning. That a wife's body became, in essence, a vessel for reproducing her husband's or her father's bloodlines made it necessary for that vessel to remain unpolluted by sexual contact with unapproved males. This situation necessitated confining a woman and preserving her chastity at all costs. Yet the mere fact that the woman existed within the world and was a living being capable of disposing of her own body, of polluting her dynastic vessel through unauthorised sexual contact, led to extreme anxiety on the part of her male owners.

Ferdinand's obsessive desire to confine his sister and preserve her chastity – coupled with his equally obsessive fear that she will dispose of her body as she chooses – leads directly to his fearful imaginings of her as an excessively sexual creature. Thus she becomes, for him, one of those diseased women whose 'livers are more spotted / Than Laban's sheep' (ll. 298–9), or a whore, or witch who 'give[s] the devil suck' (l. 311). The reference to their father's poniard – in addition to recalling his patriarchal spirit – is, of course, phallic, as is the reference to the lamprey. While the references to whores and witches may be viewed as traditional early modern labels for a widow's sexual excesses,[11] Ferdinand's reference to the poniard (and his implicit threat to use it) and to the lamprey / tongue / (penis) imply the demand (and desire) for more intimate sexual knowledge. These references also serve to point out Ferdinand's technique of asserting his power over his sister by symbolically dismembering her body, a technique discussed by Nancy J. Vickers and Francis Barker.[12] Ferdinand's implication that all a woman can enjoy of a man is his tongue / penis suggests that all *she* is is a mouth / vagina, a container for these objects. Confusion results, however, in trying to discover whether the brothers try to control their sister's behaviour as 'private' widow or as 'public' Duchess. In fact, once they have left, it is difficult to say whether Webster is presenting the Duchess as either political or private woman, as embodiment of either body politic or body natural. The boundaries of the Duchess's two bodies are indistinct and perpetually slipping. In the speech denying her 'royal kindred' power to stop her marriage (I.i.341–9), she is represented as acting like a sovereign, willing to make her family into 'low footsteps' if they try to control her. But her assertion that she will choose a 'husband' – rather than a consort – seems to indicate that she is acting as a private woman. However, once Antonio appears, she again is represented in her political persona. Antonio is shown to respond to her as his Duchess, and she is shown to be in total control of both the scene and her secretary. It is as sovereign ruler that she shows Antonio what she 'make[s him] lord of' (l. 430) and it is as ruler that she laments 'the misery' of being born great, 'forc'd to woo, because none dare woo us' (l. 442). But later in the same speech, she is represented as shifting into a private mode:

I do here put off all vain ceremony,
And only do appear to you a young widow
That claims you for her husband, and like a widow,
I use but half a blush in't.

(I.i.456–9)

And she appears to continue in this mode for the remainder of the scene.

Even though the Duchess may not have acted precisely in her body politic at the end of the scene, she has acted in a political way. With the power of her body politic, the power of a sovereign prince, she has violated existing patriarchal conventions of marriage to create her own concept of the state. To do so, this character has drawn upon an ideology of marriage quite different from the dynastic union her brothers speak of. The Protestant notion of the 'companionate marriage' began, as John C. Bean indicates, as a rationalist humanist reaction to the emotionalism of courtly love and consisted, as John Halkett explains, of 'a relatively modern concept of marriage as a partnership of love and mutual helpfulness'.[13] Thus the Duchess chooses a man below her in estate to be, not her consort, but her husband: not a man to support her as a ruler, but a man to support her as a woman. She has eliminated the problems of the consort trying to wrest power from the woman ruler – who was thought to be subject to her male husband – by not naming Antonio as her consort.

The Duchess's marriage has occasioned much critical concern because it is to a person below her in degree and because she enters into it 'irregularly' or without her brothers' consent. Antonio is clearly represented as a worthy person whose 'nobility of character' validates the Duchess's free choice of him as a husband. Yet the nature of Antonio's character is a direct result of Webster's juxtaposition of contrasting discourses in the play. In direct contrast to the custom that placed women under the control of their male family members is a long humanist tradition that both recognised the great importance of nobility of character in a man and validated a woman's right to the free choice of a husband, a tradition reinforced in Henry Medwall's *Fulgens and Lucres* (c.1497).[14] In this play, a wealthy man from an ancient family and a poor man of personal integrity court Fulgens's daughter. Yet Fulgens refuses to choose Lucres's husband, stressing not only that the choice must be hers, but that she must also accept the obligation such freedom of choice entails.[15] This tradition of a woman's free choice even appears in Painter's story of the Duchess of Malfi, the source of Webster's play.[16] Fifteenth- and sixteenth-century women may have been coerced into propertied, political, or dynastic marriages, but they, theoretically, should have entered into them purely as a result of free choice. Thus, the Duchess's actively choosing Antonio can be seen as an action that recalls Lucres's acceptance of duty in choosing a husband.[17] Various men may be proposed to Lucres, but it is her moral duty to exercise her freedom of choice and choose the one who is best for her, whom she feels to be most honourable.

By having the Duchess choose a husband beneath her in rank, but virtuous, Webster calls on a tradition that is in direct contrast to the one he earlier presented as influencing the Aragonian brothers. The reflection of these two discourses within the play – one that validates male family members' rights over the bodies of their female 'property' and one that mandates a woman's free choice as a moral necessity – is an example of the ideologically contradictory nature of *The Duchess of Malfi*. The extreme difference of these two conflicting discourses as regards the position of women serves to foreground the character of the Duchess and her dilemma as woman and sovereign ruler. While the brothers are shown to support that tradition which validates the power of the patriarchal family over women, the Duchess can be seen as challenging that discourse either by creating a new one or by consciously harking back to a tradition which, at least philosophically, granted women a certain measure of autonomy. It is not surprising that the character should be aligned to this humanistic tradition since the power it grants a woman provides a space whereby the Duchess can use her political autonomy to create a marriage situation in which she, as rule, is not subsumed by the power the dynastic marriage paradigm would grant to any husband over any wife.

The Duchess is further represented as manifesting her political authority by engaging in an 'irregular' marriage – one that is not sanctified by any representative of the church. The Duchess's exchange of vows with Antonio constitutes a *sponsalia per verba de praesenti*. Such a marriage, as Margaret Loftus Ranald indicates, 'created the status of virtual matrimony at that moment, without future action on the part of the persons concerned. It could even be upheld in courts against a later, consummated contract'.[18] Thus, when the Duchess and Antonio exchange their *de praesenti* vows in Act I scene i, they are, in fact, legally marrying themselves, although in an unusual way. However, their promises are followed by a physical consummation which was not allowed partners in a *de praesenti* spousal. Such a union that resulted in physical consummation was still valid, though irregular, and the action was deplored. Ecclesiastical penalties were generally imposed which usually involved public penance and, in rare cases, excommunication. The latter sentence could be circumvented by payment of a fine. The couple were then required to ratify their marriage by recelebrating it in church.

It is clear, then, that although the Duchess's marriage to Antonio *itself* is legal, the *consummation* of it is irregular and would open the couple to ecclesiastical penalties. However, it also seems clear that the Duchess is aware of the Church's traditional role in a *sponsalia per verba de praesenti* for, after she and Antonio pledge their love, she questions:

> What can the church force more? ...
>   How can the church bind faster?
> We now are man and wife, and 'tis the church
> That must but echo this.
>   (I.i.488; 491–3)

Although the Duchess recognises the church's traditional role in legitimising a marriage contract, she is also depicted as scorning the church's ability to have power over her as a secular ruler. Her employing a marriage *per verba de praesenti* rather than a fully ecclesiastical wedding accomplishes more, it seems to me, than simply secrecy. In marrying Antonio the Duchess is shown to challenge her brothers first, by exercising her woman's 'freedom of choice' – as Lucres did – and second, by recognising and validating Antonio's personal worth over his social position. She is also shown to challenge them by exercising her power as a ruler both by denying the church its rights in the legitimising of her marriage as well as in courting a husband, rather than a consort.

In her marriage and its ramifications, the Duchess can be viewed as a subversive character. Marriage was the major means of controlling female sexuality and legitimising the means of inheritance between patriarchal families and governments. In challenging marriage in any way, therefore, the Duchess challenges the very essence of gender relations within patriarchal early modern society. I see the character's reaction to marriage as subversive on two levels: first, in her decision to keep her marriage 'private' and separate from her 'public' identity as ruler; second, in her unconventional concept of what a marriage between a man and a woman might be like. This marriage – both the choosing of a virtuous husband and the ceremony itself – represents the major conflict between the Duchess's natural and political bodies in the play. In actively choosing her own husband and in marrying him in a way that scorns accepted legal practices, the Duchess reinforces her sense of self as a political person. She is represented as demonstrating her own right to choose a husband and her right to determine how she – as ruler of Malfi – will legitimise her choice. However, despite her attempt to take political control over the marriage ceremony, the Duchess does not make the marriage part of her strategy for rule. That she is presented as opting to keep her marriage secret indicates that she has not determined an effective way to integrate marriage into her public life as ruler.

In Act I, scene i, the Duchess moves back and forth between acting as a prince and as a woman. Her political self exerts itself as she, being 'born great', proposes to Antonio despite her brothers' prohibitions against remarriage (l. 468). Yet her refusal to make Antonio her consort argues that her union is to be considered a 'private' marriage. Her political self also asserts its power to legitimise the marriage through a *sponsalia per verba de praesenti*. But it is the character's private self that urges her husband to lead her to their marriage bed. The confusion in this scene as to whether the woman or the prince prevails is part of the major problem of just how to read the Duchess throughout the play. We are invited to see her marriage to Antonio as a marriage for love between two attractive people, one of whom is a woman ruler. The problem with this view is that we are asked to accept the fact that this reigning woman – the living exemplar of a respected theory of rule – would make not only a non-political marriage, but a politically disastrous one as well. And yet this same woman has directed her talents to creating a new discourse of rule, one which does not simply replicate the patriarchal conventions determined by her society and its male rulers, but which attempts to fuse a traditional female role – wife and mother – with a non-traditional one – ruler. The ultimate effect of Act I, scene i, therefore, is to present us with a very political character. The Duchess may opt to keep her marriage 'private', but her doing so must be acknowledged a political decision. Keeping her natural and political bodies separate may not be the most effective political strategy. However, there is no doubt that this strategy must be recognised as a political one made by a sovereign who is conscious of the political implications of all activities she engages in.

Although the Duchess may have made an unfortunate political choice regarding separating her natural and political bodies, she makes a rather unique decision concerning the fundamental nature of her marriage with Antonio. Webster has represented the implications of such a marriage over time in Act III, scene ii, which depicts the first private view we have had of Antonio and the Duchess since Act I, scene i. This scene presents the Duchess as wife in the new 'private' family life she has created, and it reads as an inversion of the traditional Renaissance marriage where the husband has total control over the wife.[19] Yet it is also clear that while the Duchess may be shown to take the 'lead' in the bantering in the scene, Antonio is not exactly 'subject' to his wife in the same way that Renaissance women were expected to be subject to their husbands. His joking reference to his 'rule' being 'only in the night' (III.ii.8) indicates both that the marriage is sexually fulfilling and that Antonio is meant to accept the parameters of the marriage the Duchess has created and not to envy her position as ruler.

The Duchess is represented as being radically different from the traditional picture of the Renaissance wife in this scene. Not only is she a woman who is capable of commanding her husband specifically as regards his sexual desires (III.ii.4–6), and refusing him – 'you get no lodging here tonight, my lord' (l. 2). But she is also a woman who thoroughly enjoys her sexuality – 'Alas, what pleasure can two lovers find in sleep?' (l. 10) – and the products of it, her children (ll. 66–8). Antonio's behaviour is similarly radical for he is represented as not challenging his wife regarding his 'rights' to her body or bed, and chafes her with the observation that

> Labouring men
> Count the clock oft'nest ... [and]
> Are glad when their task's ended,
> (III.ii.18–20)

which forces her to 'stop' his mouth with a kiss (l. 20). The bantering continues with Antonio's begging another kiss and his sneaking off with Cariola so that the Duchess will be left speaking to herself. Antonio is depicted as teasing his wife in this way because he loves 'to see her angry' (l. 57).

Webster's extraordinary picture of marriage contrasts sharply with the prevailing early modern notion that women were marginalised or objectified creatures that required domination by men. Yet however much we may applaud this idealistic, egalitarian, and companionate marriage, we still must realise that it exists in almost direct conflict with the Duchess's position as sovereign ruler of Malfi. By keeping her body natural divorced from her body politic and secreting her husband, the Duchess opens herself to accusation as a whore and a witch – women who do not follow accepted patterns of behaviour. Her pregnancies convince her brothers and her subjects that she is sexually involved with a man – a situation that allows her to be viewed as an oversexed widow and play directly into Ferdinand's hands. That she has, in fact, married, but married in secret to a man some feel is inferior presents her as violating still more accepted patriarchal codes of female behaviour. By not actively challenging the Renaissance discourse of 'woman', the Duchess, effectually, allows herself to be read as 'whore'.

One way to contain women who acted in ways contrary to accepted patterns of female behaviour was to label them 'whores' or 'witches'. This technique of containment through stereotypic 'naming' has been used several times on the Duchess, as I have indicated above. Another way to contain women characters is to control representations of their bodies. As labelling marginalises women by giving them the 'names' of those who live on the margins of acceptable society – whores or witches – the focus on only certain parts of a woman's body 'dismembers' her by negatively contrasting her amputated / lacking condition to the completeness of the socially-acceptable male body. Ferdinand's depiction of his sister as a mouth / vagina (l.i) is just such an example of dismemberment. But the female body does not need to be 'dismembered' to be marginalised. Sometimes the mere focus on a woman's biology or her use of cosmetics serves negatively to contrast her body to the fixed image of maleness all men, by definition, possess. Bosola's discovery of the Duchess's pregnancy in Act II, scene i continues consideration of how the female body is represented in the play. Bosola is depicted, in this scene, as first condemning the Old Lady for her face-painting, or 'face-physic' (l. 23). In a series of particularly loathsome images, Bosola is shown to accuse the Old Lady – and, by association, all women – of engaging in thoroughly disgusting practices in order to present to the world a facial image that differs from reality. He tells of the French woman who flayed the skin off her face to make it more level (ll. 27–8), a process which made her resemble 'an abortive hedgehog' (l. 29). He then lists the cosmetic contents of a woman's closet and indicates that they are more suitable 'for a shop of witchcraft' (l. 35). The ultimate effect of this listing of disgusting objects and disagreeable practices is to stress Bosola's anti-feminism, which causes the character to aver that he 'would sooner eat a dead pigeon, taken from the soles of the feet of one sick of the plague, than kiss one of you [e.g., women] fasting' (ll.i.38–40). From this woman-hating stance, the character proceeds to describe the Duchess in her pregnancy:

> I observe our duchess
> Is sick o' days, she pukes, her stomach seethes,
> The fins of her eyelids look most teeming blue,
> She wanes i'th' cheek, and waxes fat i'th' flank;
> And (contrary to our Italian fashion)
> Wears a loose-body'd gown – there's somewhat in't!
>   (ll.i.63–8)

Although there is clearly as much revulsion in Bosola's description of the pregnant woman as in his earlier descriptions of cosmetics, revulsion regarding female nature is not the only thing these two descriptions have in common. Make-up and face-painting, no matter what the cosmetics contain, serve the purpose of 'disguising' a woman and hiding some part of her from the male gaze. The essential fear of men as regards cosmetics is that they will create a mask of beauty and gull a man into accepting a 'naturally' ugly woman as 'artificially' beautiful. In the same way, a loose-bodied gown – or 'bawd farthingales' (l. 148) – disguises a swelling body and 'the young springal cutting a caper in [the Duchess's] belly' (l. 151). Thus, from what we are shown to be the point of view of the intelligencer, women are adept as deceivers of men because they use cosmetics and costume to disguise/hide the defects of their bodies to present themselves as something they are not – beautiful or chaste.

But the image of the pregnant Duchess can be seen as something more than simply an emblem of disguise or trickery. The body of a pregnant woman is very different from the body of a non-pregnant woman, as Bosola's description of Act II, scene i, lines 63–8 attests. However, to go one step farther, a woman's body is radically different from a man's body because it *can* become pregnant. Thus, while for a man constancy of bodily image may be desirable, constancy of bodily image for a woman may not necessarily be desirable. Given the female body's ability to become pregnant, the necessity of that pregnancy for the production of heirs to the patriarchal line, and the lack of reliable birth control methods in the early modern period, the pregnant body must be seen as an alternative image of the female body with as much power as the traditional non-pregnant image. And since, despite the innate fallaciousness of the phrases, a woman may be 'slightly pregnant' or 'very pregnant', there cannot be *one* acceptable image of the 'pregnant' woman. Women in the sixteenth and seventeenth centuries – if they were not virgins – drifted into and out of pregnancy with alarming regularity. Thus, the female body – in direct contrast to the male body – is a body in a state of constant flux. And, as such, it is capable of producing a certain uneasiness. The nature of woman's biology necessitates a flexible image of her body which is in direct contrast to the fixed image of the male body. This fact accounts for both the Duchess's refusal to be concerned about the inevitability of the greying of her hair (III.ii.58–60), and Bosola's uneasiness at his inability to find the constant within the Duchess's vastly (and continuously) changing bodily shape. Women's bodies are threatening because they are ever-changing and cannot be confined to a single shape.[20] Bosola's wish to confine / define the Duchess's body by her clothes, to remove it from the loose-bodied gowns that hide it, is played out in Act II, scene ii when the Duchess is both literally and figuratively 'confined' during the birth of her child.

The Duchess's figurative confinement results from her failure to consider the implications her changing shape will have upon her subjects. In separating her body natural from her body politic, the Duchess has not provided a means for dealing with the fact that her married body natural is expected to become pregnant while her 'widowed' body politic is expected to remain 'unpregnant', constant of shape. When her pregnancy impinges upon her political body and its shape changes, she does nothing beyond wearing a loose gown to disguise it. Far from being successful at concealing her pregnancy, this strategem simply serves to call attention to both her stereotyped changing female shape and her stereotyped sexuality. In allowing these stereotypes room for consideration, the Duchess forces consideration of herself as *woman* rather than *ruler* and foregrounds her body natural at the expense of her body politic.

Bosola is not the only male character to espouse negative attitudes towards women. We can contrast this character's views on cosmetics, pregnancy, and old age with Ferdinand's views on the sexual nature of women's bodies, especially his sister's. I have already mentioned the lamprey/tongue/(penis) pun in Act I, scene i, lines 336–8 and the implication that the Duchess's interest in men is purely sexual, her body nothing more than a mouth/vagina to contain the tongue/penis of a man. In Act II, scene v, Ferdinand tells the Cardinal that the Duchess is 'loose i'th' hilts' (l. 3), another sexual reference, since the blade of a sword or dagger was inserted into its hilt. Finally, Ferdinand's anger and fury at his sister is represented as carrying him out of the realm of metaphor and into that of specific images where he 'sees' her

> in the shameful act of sin. ...
> Happily with some strong thigh'd bargeman;
> Or one o'th' wood-yard, that can quoit the sledge,
> Or toss the bar, or else some lovely squire
> That carries coals up to her privy lodgings.
>   (ll.v.41–5)

Thus his fury is directly the result of the Duchess's desire to keep her marriage secret. While Ferdinand does not learn of the marriage, he does learn of the children. The sexual activity necessary to engender them prompts his misogynistic outburst and is the direct result of the Duchess's failure to control the effects of her private life on her public one. Instead of defusing the threats to her political persona caused by her first pregnancy, she fuels them by having subsequent pregnancies. That this last image of his sister is less objectified than some of Ferdinand's earlier images does not discount the fact that it still represents the Duchess as an exclusively sexual creature who will couple with any man who is available.

Although in many respects Ferdinand's preoccupations with the Duchess's sexuality can be seen as simply obsessive or paranoid, on another level his fears are well-grounded, for Webster has represented the Duchess as being very different in regard to her sexuality from accepted images of early modern women. She is neither chaste virgin nor unregenerate whore (except, perhaps, in what Webster has depicted of Ferdinand's mind), yet she is something that normally does not appear in the early modern drama – a loving wife who is also a sexually mature and active woman. The Duchess is presented as marrying in order to fulfil her physical love for Antonio as well as her emotional attachment to him. Further, and as the play progresses, the Duchess and Antonio are shown to be loving parents to the children who are the products of their marriage. Thus, we can view the Duchess as a figure who values and takes control of her own sexuality by marrying against custom and her family. Further, by not making Antonio her consort, by not granting him a place in her political life, the Duchess is depicted as not granting her children by Antonio a place in her political life as well. Removed from the political realm, these children are never thought of as the heirs or commodities in a dynastic marriage, but as offspring who need a mother's care:

> I pray thee, look thou giv'st my little boy
> Some syrup for his cold, and let the girl
> Say her prayers, ere she sleep.
>   (IV.ii.202–4)

Since the Duchess's children are kept so secret, their existence so shadowy, they become completely invisible as regards the court of Malfi. But by removing the children from the public gaze, the Duchess is represented as controlling her biology through the products of it as completely as she is represented as controlling her sexuality.

Ultimately, the Duchess's marriage and sexual politics are represented as so revolutionary that she must be punished for her actions. After Ferdinand appears in her chamber in Act III, scene ii, the Duchess tries to avoid discovery by concocting a plot whereby Antonio and her children leave Malfi for a place of safety. Although the Duchess is represented as not having tried to integrate her private life into her public life, her decisive actions in her public persona are used to try to preserve her husband and allow the couple to live, eventually, as private individuals. But her plot does not work and she is punished, first by having her duchy taken from her and second by imprisonment in her own palace.

Since the Duchess has been stripped of her political power in Act III, scene iv, it is essentially as a private woman that she is punished in Act IV. As Bosola was shown to have chafed at the fact that it was impossible sufficiently to confine women or their bodies, in this act the Duchess is represented as finally being completely confined and the victim of various tortures. Her body is still depicted as being a subject both Ferdinand and Bosola focus on. And Ferdinand, perhaps for the first time, is depicted as viewing his sister's body as complete (IV.i.121–3), rather than as simply a vagina. This change of focus is interesting and perhaps refers to the fact that, for the first time, Ferdinand can be absolutely sure of his sister's chastity. Totally confined physically, the Duchess is denied the possibility of any and all sexual activity. She is now, finally, a vessel that may be trusted with the Aragon family's pure dynastic blood. Yet, despite this, Ferdinand is shown to see his sister as mad, for women who act in a way contrary to accepted social norms are often considered mad. Bosola's focus on the Duchess's body has also changed. Where earlier he was represented as seeing the Duchess's female body as swollen with pregnancy or concealed by clothing or disgusting cosmetics, he now describes it as being no more than 'a box of worm-seed' (l. 124) or a preserve of earth-worms. Although the images are not positive, they are not particularly sexist either. They are emblems of mortality, images common to both men and women, rather than socially-sanctioned images of anti-feminism.

Finally, the scenes of the Duchess's imprisonment give a mixed message regarding the Duchess herself. She is shown to indicate her position as victim both by the reference to her body as food – 'Go tell my brothers, when I am laid out, / They then may feed in quiet' (IV.ii.236–7) – and when she says 'I am chain'd to endure all your tyranny' (IV.ii.60). The character is also shown to be a martyr[21] and is represented as comparing herself to Portia 'the rare and almost dead example / Of a loving wife' (IV.i.73–4). In addition to these images of martyrs, Webster reminds us that the woman in prison had a political identity which she still claims: 'I am Duchess of Malfi still' (IV.ii.142). Yet despite her claims to a political self, the Duchess is totally powerless in prison and totally without her sovereign power. But in a very real way we are made to witness the punishment of the Duchess of Malfi as well as the wife of Antonio. The Duchess's line identifying herself as still Duchess of Malfi recalls her political identity and the nobility of her death reinforces it (IV.ii.230–4). There is a certain cosmic sense about the Duchess's death as though she both realises her position in the universe and accepts responsibility for both her life and her death. That she is shown not to cry out or beg for mercy places her at a moral advantage over Cariola, who is represented as begging for mercy, and Ferdinand, who is represented as denying the murder he is implicated in. Her death manages, for a moment, to cause Ferdinand to reconsider his part in it – 'I bade thee, when I was distracted of my wits, / Go kill my dearest friend, and thou hast done't' (IV.ii.279–80) – and Bosola to view her as a saint – 'Return, fair soul, from darkness, and lead mine / Out of this sensible hell' (IV.ii.342–3). In fact, Bosola's conviction that the Duchess has the power to lead his soul out of hell recalls Antonio's earlier boast to Delio that the Duchess's looks 'were able to raise one to a galliard / That lay in a dead palsy' (I.i.196–7). Yet there is something profoundly ironic in this scene.

This final representation of the Duchess as martyr, as woman idealised through suffering comes actually from a much more traditional discourse of womanhood than previous representations of the Duchess as ruler. This 'martyred' view of woman comes both from the patient Griselda stories, which validate the wife who is faithful, forgiving, silent, and patient, and the images of the Virgin Mary and Hecuba as mothers prostrate with grief.[22] In a society that limits women's options to those of wife or mother, creatures whose identities can easily be subsumed by their husbands or children, a talent for suffering nobly (and quietly) becomes the only means by which a woman can be viewed as 'heroic'. Thus the final representation of Webster's protagonist is not as ruler, but as idealised suffering wife / mother / woman. Her cry, 'I am Duchess of Malfi still', becomes ironic, for this seeming validation of her political self occurs within a context that more completely validates her private self as wife and mother.

The 'mixed messages' present in this scene are characteristic of the 'mixed messages' regarding the Duchess's character that are presented throughout the play and are what contribute to the play's ideologically contradictory nature. In Act IV, our final view of the Duchess is of a character punished primarily for her violation of social custom as a woman, yet also for her violation of political custom as a sovereign. Thus *The Duchess of Malfi* can be viewed as a subversive play because it challenges the basic concept of the early modern marriage, a marriage in which the woman was completely objectified, used only to serve the business or physical needs of her father, her husband, or their joint families. The Duchess is represented as reacting against this social construct of marriage by creating an entirely new concept of the estate, one in which men and women are companions, equal partners, friends, and lovers. She is shown to control her own sexuality, not simply by refusing her body to her husband, but by demanding a relationship with him in which her sexuality is acknowledged, validated, and fulfilled. Further, in spite of dynastic practices, she removes her children from consideration as heirs, seeing them as belonging to herself, rather than her family, thus allowing her effectively to control her biology as well as her sexuality. Even though her refusal to unite her body natural and her body politic – or to consider an alternative way to integrate her private married life into her life as a ruler – leads to her unsuccessful reign as a sovereign, the very nature of her marriage is so revolutionary and challenges social custom to such a degree that the Duchess must be punished for her audacity in creating it. Despite this attempt to contain the subversive nature of the Duchess, the overall impetus of Acts 1–IV remains subversive, especially since allowing the Duchess to die as a tragic figure in Act IV presents her as taking over even the powers of a male tragic protagonist, foregrounds her further, and invests her character and its subversive ideology with great power.

But if Act IV leaves us with a fairly strong picture of the Duchess as a character who would subvert her society's political and social ideologies by re-creating patriarchal discourses regarding marriage, what are we to make of Act V? This curious act appears to be an afterthought that abruptly changes the focus and mood of the play. By foregrounding the male characters, it attempts to contain all of the subversive aspects of the Duchess's rule and restore patriarchal order. And yet the containment is far from complete because the restored order is so dubious. Civil authority is represented by a lycanthropic Duke who robs graveyards and ecclesiastical authority by a Machiavellian Cardinal who murders his mistress. The naïvely innocent Antonio accepts the brothers at face value and is killed, accidentally, as Bosola murders them to avenge their sister. The Duchess's reign may have been threatening to accepted patriarchal notions of rule, but the final picture of Ferdinand, Antonio, Bosola, and the Cardinal hardly reassures an audience of any of the male characters' abilities to control the state or their moral right to do so. Even the honourable Delio's final entrance casts doubt upon this picture of restored patriarchal order. Antonio's friend appears with the child who will inherit 'in's mother's right' (V.v.113). To reinforce the patriarchal order this act ostensibly supports, this child should be the son of the Duchess's first marriage, the son of the dead Duke of Malfi. And he *should* inherit 'in his *father's* right'. But this son is curiously the child of the Duchess and Antonio, the son of the Duke of Malfi having somehow disappeared during the course of the play. Thus the inheritance pattern that should reflect primogeniture and support patriarchal order does neither. True it restores a male ruler to the duchy, but one who has no legal right to the title which he acquires through a matriarchal rather than a patriarchal inheritance pattern.

Act V, then, is a curious construct. In an attempt to erase or contain the power revealed by the Duchess in Acts I–IV, it focuses on 'traditionally' male questions of government and inheritance. Yet the rulers it presents – Ferdinand, the Cardinal, and the Duchess's son – are either totally reprehensible morally or come to the title illegally through the female line. Thus, while ostensibly attempting to reinforce the patriarchy and erase the subversive elements of Acts I–IV, Act V, in fact, questions the nature of the social constructs it reinforces and the men who represent them. While not actually arguing in favour of the marital / political paradigm the Duchess has created, this Act's insistence upon establishment of the son of the Duchess's irregular marriage in 'her' right does seem to reinforce her political power while simultaneously attempting to deny it. Finally, the discontinuous nature of Act V makes it as difficult to 'read' as earlier acts. While it must be acknowledged that an attempt is made to 'cover over' the subversive elements of Acts I–IV, the fabric of that covering certainly is dubious at best. It contains holes through which a newly-created, though contradictory, ruling practice can be viewed. Thus while presenting the 'official' patriarchal picture of rule, Act V allows simultaneous consideration of the Duchess's subversive attempts at rulership as a corrective to an existing system that is imaged as morally corrupt.

From *Studies in Philology*, 87 (1990), 221–45.

NOTES

[Body politics form the basis of Theodora Jankowski's essay, especially the problem of the female body – reproducing, ageing, cosmeticising, governing, and dying – in patriarchal culture. When the male body constitutes the cultural norm, the female body can only constitute tragic aberration. For reasons of space, some of the original notes to the essay have had to be cut. Ed.]

1. John Knox, *The First Blast of the Trumpet, Against the Monstrous Regiment of Women* (Geneva, 1558; rpt., Amsterdam, 1972) (STC No. 15070).

2. John Aylmer, *An Harborovve for Faithfull and Trevve Subjects, agaynst the late blowne Blaste, concerning the Gouernment of Vvemen* (Strasborowe, 1559; rpt., Amsterdam, 1972) (STC No. 1005).

3. Marie Axton (*The Queen's Two Bodies: Drama and the Elizabethan Succession* [London, 1977]) explains that by 1561 Queen Elizabeth I had been legally endowed with a body natural and a body politic.

4. Kathleen McLuskie, 'Drama and Sexual Politics: The Case of Webster's Duchess', in *Drama, Sex, and Politics*, ed. James Redmond (Cambridge, 1985), p. 88. [Reprinted in this volume – Ed.]

5. Joyce E. Peterson, *Curs'd Example: 'The Duchess of Malfi' and Commonweal Tragedy* (Columbia, MO, and London, 1978) p. 78.

6. John Webster, *The Duchess of Malfi*, ed. John Russell Brown (Manchester and Baltimore, MD, 1981), pp. 8–9 (I.i.5–22). All further references to the play will be to this edition.

7. Inga-Stina Ekeblad, 'The "Impure Art" of John Webster', in *Twentieth-Century Interpretations of The Duchess of Malfi*, ed. Normal Rabkin (Englewood Cliff, NJ, 1968), feels that there was a strong Renaissance attitude against the second marriage of widows. But there were, in fact, no legal or ecclesiastical prohibitions against such a remarriage. Paradoxically, though, the strong opinion against a widow's marrying was again under a man's control. As Lisa Jardine indicates, 'widows of wealthy men were married off again with quite undignified haste where those responsible for them considered it financially advantageous to the line to do so' (*Still Harping on Daughters: Women and Drama in the Age of Shakespeare* [Brighton and Totowa, NJ, 1983], p. 83).

8. Catherine Belsey, 'Disrupting Sexual Difference: Meaning and Gender in the Comedies', in *Alternative Shakespeares*, ed. John Drakakis (London and New York, 1985) p. 169. Susan Wells, *The Dialectic of Representation* (Baltimore, MD, and London, 1985), feels that during the Jacobean period, the family was not only beginning to have a history, but was establishing its own identity as an entity distinct from church and state (*Dialectic*, p. 69).

9. Leonard Tennenhouse (*Power on Display: The Politics of Shakespeare's Genres* [New York and London, 1986]) discusses the mutilation of the female body in Jacobean drama especially in terms of the 'metaphysics of blood' (chapter 3, esp. pp. 118–22).

10. Eve Kosofsky Sedgwick, *Between Men: English Literature and Male Homosocial Desire* (New York, 1985), p. 38.

11. The traditional sterotype of the oversexed widow is also discussed in Simon Shepherd, *Amazons and Warrior Women: Varieties of Feminism in Seventeenth-Century Drama* (New York, 1981); Katherine Usher Henderson and Barbara F. McManus, *Half Humankind: Contexts and Texts of the Controversy about Women in England, 1540–1640* (Urbana and Chicago, 1985); and Lisa Jardine, *Still Harping*.

12. Nancy J. Vickers ('Diana Described: Scattered Woman and Scattered Rhyme', *Critical Inquiry*, 8 [1981], 265–79) and Francis Barker ('Into the Vault', in Barker, *The Tremulous Private Body: Essays on Subjection* [London and New York, 1984]) discuss the prevailing Reniassance image of the female body as silent, dismembered, and therefore, powerless.

13. John C. Bean, 'Passion Versus Friendship in the Tudor Matrimonial Handbooks and Some Shakespearean Implications', *Wascana Review*, 9 (1974), 231–40 and John Halkett, *Milton and the Idea of Matrimony* (New Haven and London, 1970), p. 16. While the notion of marriage Webster's Duchess conceives of with Antonio is closer to the philosophical concept of the Protestant 'companionate marriage' than to the 'dynastic marriage' her brothers have in mind, it is important to remember that neither marriage concept granted the woman a right to choose her own husband.

14. Henry Medwall, *'Fulgens and Lucrece'*, in *Five Pre-Shakespearean Comedies*, ed. Frederick S. Boas (London, Oxford, New York, 1934; rpt., 1970), p. ix.

15. Catherine Belsey indicates that, while Lucres asks her father's advice, she clearly makes the unconstrained choice her freedom allows her in favour of virtue (*The Subject of Tragedy* [London and New York, 1985], pp. 194–200). 'The play thus affirms marriage as the location of liberal and affective values rather than as a guarantee of dynastic continuity' (p. 194). Belsey also indicates that *The Duchess of Malfi* 'claims for its heroine the right to choose a husband' (p. 200).

16. William Painter, 'The Palace of Pleasure, Vol. II, xxiii Novel' (1567) in *The Palace of Pleasure*, Vol. III, ed. Joseph Jacobs (1580; rpt., London, 1890), p. 13.

17. Richard Bodtke points out that the Duchess is 'true to earlier Renaissance humanistic values of true nobility' in seeing 'the man not his rank' (*Tragedy and the Jacobean Temper: The Major Plays of John Webster* [Salzburg, 1972]. p. 171). While Catherine Belsey indicates that in wooing Antonio the Duchess opts for personal virtue over nobility of birth (*Tragedy*, pp. 197–8), Frank Whigham ('Sexual and Social Mobility in *The Duchess of Malfi*', *PMLA*, 100 [1985], 167–186) argues that the Duchess violates her class rank by choosing a 'base lover' (p. 170) who could potentially contaminate the ruling elite (p. 168).

18. Margaret Loftus Ranald, '"As Marriage Binds, and Blood Breaks": English Marriage and Shakespeare', *Shakespeare Quarterly*, 30 (1979), 68–81.

19. Muriel C. Bradbrook sees the marriage as a reversal of order, and condemns the Duchess for acting contrary to accepted Renaissance pat-

terns of behaviour for women (*John Webster: Citizen and Dramatist* [New York, 1980], pp. 146, 150). But as critics like Kathleen McLuskie indicate, the point of the play is that it is *about* 'the possibility of so unconventional a marriage' (*Drama*, p. 86). In fact, by separating her private life from her public life, the Duchess is shown to adhere to a notion of family and marriage that is more similar to the 'private' notion of marriage outlined by Catherine Belsey than to the 'public' notion of dynastic marriage her brothers have been discussing.

20. Susan Wells contrasts the Duchess's ' static, remote, dedicated to matrimony' royal body – which she sees imaged in the alabaster tomb figure – to her 'eroticised, individual body'. She feels that the play most often places us in 'a world of fragile and fertile bodies' in which the social distinctions – class, status, etc. – that normally determine our experience of the body are subverted (*Dialectic*, p. 66). The fixed, alabaster royal body of the Duchess can also be seen as more like the fixed male body that Bosola finds easier to accept than the changeable pregnant body he is confronted with.

21. T. F. Wharton, '"Fame's Best Friend"': Survival in *The Duchess of Malfi*', in *Jacobean Miscellany I*, ed. James Hogg (Salzburg, 1980), p. 21.

22. Belsey, *Tragedy*, pp. 164–71. Lisa Jardine, *Still Harping*, pp. 181–95 and '*The Duchess of Malfi*: A Case Study of the Literary Representation of Women', in *Teaching the Text*, ed. Susanne Kappeler and Norman Bryson (London and Boston, 1983), pp. 207–8. Marilyn L. Williamson, *The Patriarchy of Shakespeare's Comedies* (Detroit, 1986), pp. 64–74.

5

Drama and Sexual Politics: the Case of Webster's Duchess

KATHLEEN McLUSKIE

To discuss sexual politics and theatre involves a fairly straightforward consideration of the material conditions of women and men in the theatrical profession – that paradoxical situation where women and to an extent gay men are excluded from the financial and executive power of the theatre world yet find in it a protected environment which offers certain possibilities for self realisation.[1] The question of drama and sexual politics is rather more problematic since criticism of dramatic texts, while occasionally recognising the critical importance of performance, has all too often dealt with texts as historically transcendent, with a life – and by implication a meaning – separate from changing conditions of performance. Yet plays from the past are continually recreated in different historical and political conditions of theatre. New meanings are constructed by an interaction between the play's original ideology and artistic form, the role of the play within high culture, and the prevailing ideology and cultural forms which make up the audience's expectations. This is particularly true of modern productions of Renaissance drama, whose radical potential is often submerged by modern theatrical expectations.[2]

Jacobean drama provides a dazzling range of roles for women. In *The Duchess of Malfi*, and for that matter in *The Roaring Girl*, the heroines have an autonomy, particularity and depth of presentation which is unparalleled in the English theatre until the translation of Ibsen. Yet the creation of these dramatic characters was a product of an articulation between ideology and form which must be unpacked in order to understand its historical specificity and to understand the way in which it is reproduced in the modern theatre. The roles of women in Renaissance drama were played by boys whose theatrical career was necessarily limited and who enjoyed only apprentice status in the theatre companies for which they worked. Moreover these heroines were created by men at a time when real women were, in Virginia Woolf's telling if tendentious phrase, 'locked up and beaten and flung about the room'.[3] Recent work by social historians has revealed patterns of sexual relations in the Renaissance which were no less complicated than those of today and yet the sets of ideas from which seventeenth-century dramatists constructed their women reflect the simple polarities which lay behind the earliest versions of the *querelle des femmes*. Discussion of the nature of women had from earliest times rested on the simple oppositions of a debate. Misogynists from the Church fathers onwards insisted on woman's direct descent from Eve which gave her the attributes of lust and duplicity, while those who defended women – and there were many in the reign of a virgin queen – concentrated on the long line of women worthies from the Nine Muses to Queen Elizabeth herself. Those who defamed women used arguments from history combined with *a priori* attacks on woman's very essence; those who defended them simply reversed the arguments. At no point did the defenders of women question the moral and intellectual basis for the argument; indeed even the few women who joined in accepted the division of women into opposing categories of 'familiar doxies', 'religious matrons' and 'prostitute strumpets'.[4] For the debate constantly isolated women, saw them as aberrant and focused entirely on them as sexualised, 'other', seen *vis-à-vis* men.

The theatrical representations of women in the sixteenth and seventeenth centuries tend to follow ideologically similar lines. By and large the women can be divided into the witty wives of city comedy and the doomed victims of tragedy. Yet this distinction was as much a feature of different theatrical styles as of difference of ideology. At the turn of the seventeenth century writers had available to them a range of styles from the formal show and spectacle associated with older open-air theatres to a more intimate and realistic mode of theatrical form. These theatrical forms were partly a matter of theatre history but they could carry the greatest ideological importance.

In *The Duchess of Malfi* the action dramatises the extremes of oppression as the heroine is tortured and murdered by her brothers, who object to her assertion of her right to marry the man of her choice. Webster's source for the play clearly presented the Duchess's end as just punishment for her lust in choosing her own husband and her disobedience to her brothers, and the play has been similarly interpreted by modern critics. Yet the form and structure of the play question this ideology of oppression and not only by making the brothers into villains but by dramatising the story in ways which foreground the relationship between static ideas and dynamic action. It is critical commonplace to note that Webster used the full range of theatrical forms available to him.[5] What has not been fully recognised is that the clash of theatrical forms, the contrast between statement and action which it sets up, creates a continual shift of focus in the play. Descriptions of character and moral judgements pronounced in set speeches are tested by realistic action which exposes their internal contradiction.

Webster's particular technique is to juxtapose stage image with verbal image so that one comments on the other, opening out the range of meaning which the significant moments of the play will allow. In an early scene, Webster has Antonio describe the 'three fair medals / Cast in one figure', the Duchess and her brothers. In a series of set speeches he describes the Cardinal's blatant intrigues in pursuit of the papacy and Ferdinand's sinister behaviour as a magistrate, defining the brothers by their relations with the outside world, their positions of power and their ability to manipulate others. In the Duchess, on the other hand, he notes more personal qualities; the idealised virtues of a pious, continent, sweet-countenanced woman. While Antonio is speaking, the figures he describes are on stage, a silent tableau which neither confirms nor denies his judgement. However, when we next see the Duchess with her brothers the emblem comes to life; Webster has given voices to the three fair medals and we have immediately to modify our impression of their relationship. The way in which each brother completes the lines of the other's speeches (I.ii.189–225) shows Webster using his verse to suggest their attempted manipulation of the Duchess, which confirms Antonio's report. The Duchess's reply, however, is made the more dramatically startling in its wit and independence: 'Diamonds are of most value / They say, that have passed through most jewellers' hands' (ll. 196–7). The still and silent figure of Antonio's imagination, who 'stains the time past, lights the time to come' (I.ii.126) wakens into life and reveals a figure from comedy, rather than an emblem from a legend of good women.

The imagery, both visual and verbal, with which Webster presents Antonio himself and his liaison with the Duchess is similarly double edged. Antonio opens the play by discussing the state of the French court in terms which show his concern for political stability and his understanding of such affairs. We next hear that he has 'taken the ring' in the courtly horsemanship contest and he himself shows the significance of this action by asserting that 'out of brave horsemanship arise the first sparks of growing resolution, that raise the mind to noble action' (I.ii.62–3). These indications of his courtly qualities are given a final seal in the Duchess's assurance that

> If you will know where breathes a complete man,
> I speak it without flattery, turn your eyes
> And progress through yourself.
> (I.ii.332–4)

The idea of royalty suggested by 'progress' (a king's journey to survey his realm) and the neoplatonic union of action, passion and contemplation in the notion of a 'complete' man places the Duchess's attraction to him on a far higher plane than the ticklish instigations of her wanton flesh suggested by Painter, one of Webster's sources, as the reason for her love. Just as Antonio idealises the Duchess as an emblem of female virtue, so she finds in him the harmonious combination of the ideal Renaissance man. The ambiguity of Webster's images, however, prevents this idealised Antonio from being a bloodless prig. His courtly skill in horsemanship involves catching a ring off a lance, surely a sexual metaphor, and the extended range of implication which Webster can pack into metaphor and action is further demonstrated in the moment when the Duchess places her ring on Antonio's finger. The action which creates this stage image symbolises their forthcoming sexual union but it also provides a physical point of reference for the succeeding poetic image of the harmonious circle of the spheres imitated by their love (I.ii.376–8). The full dramatic message of the sequence combines a bawdy joke about rings and fingers with more rarified neoplatonic images of perfect harmony to create an effect which transcends both sentimentality about pure love and moralising condemnation of a widow's lust.

Placing the ring on Antonio's finger is a symbolic action in the range of meaning it can embody but this must not obscure the fact that it is an exciting moment in the development of the scene. It is a turning point which commits the lovers to a course of action from which no retreat is possible. As such it is part of the sequence of revealing dramatic moments which provide a structure for the play. Webster has been accused of indulging in cheap *coups de théâtre* in order to affect his audience with the maximum horror and surprise; but the dead man's hand and the dance of madmen which Ferdinand inflicts on his sister, macabre and grotesque as they are, must take their place in a complete visual pattern which equally includes the image of the Duchess kneeling by her coffin or the Cardinal taking on the habit of a soldier.

These significant visual moments often take the form of tableaux through which we can chart both the narrative and conceptual movement of the play. In Act I, scene ii we see the Duchess with her brothers and later in the same scene the plot advances as she places her ring on Antonio's finger. In Act III, scene ii the exciting moment comes when she is combing her hair, oblivious of Ferdinand, his dagger unsheathed, standing behind her. It is a moment of theatrical suspense; but by providing a visual echo of a similar moment in Act I, scene ii (ll. 228–9) when Ferdinand presented her with a dagger, it also reminds the audience of the context in which her love and marriage have existed from the very start.

After Act III, scene ii this context changes and we see the Duchess opposed not only by Ferdinand's overt and sinister violence but also by political and military power. In the scenes which follow Act III, scene ii we are shown the extent of this power which, though less psychologically horrible than Ferdinand's twisted imagination or his midnight visit, has a much more destructive effect on the Duchess. She could bravely oppose Ferdinand's disapproval with

> Why might not I marry?
> I have not gone about, in this, to create
> Any new world, or custom
> (III.ii.115–17)

but she has no resources against the Cardinal's might. Webster underlines her impotence and the almost casual process of tyranny by presenting these plot developments in tableaux commented on by more or less neutral observers. When the brothers receive their spy Bosola's intelligence about the identity of the Duchess's husband they are at a military camp and their reactions are seen on stage but at the same time described by two noblemen looking on. This gives a curiously dislocated effect, emphasising not simply the brothers' anger and disapproval but the fact that neutral observers realise the error of what is taking place but do nothing to oppose the evil in this politic power. In Act III, scene iii we hear how the Cardinal's 'worth' has found favour with the Emperor, Charles V, and this is followed in Act III, scene iv by his solemn 'instalment in the habit of a soldier' after which he banishes the Duchess along with Antonio and the children '*by a form of banishment in dumb-show expressed towards them by the Cardinal and the state of Ancona*' (III.iv.8 SD). The effect of the silent tableaux is that the Cardinal's military and political power are presented as sheer unopposed dramatic fact, emphasised in the visual contrast between the powerful Cardinal in military dress with his train of 'divers Churchmen', and the vulnerable family group. However much the pilgrims might ask 'What power hath this state / of Ancona to determine of a free prince?' (III.iv.30–1) the Duchess has now become and remains a victim. Her will to act independently could prevail against psychological restrictions, but unsupported by military strength, can have no lasting effect as she is delivered over to Ferdinand and Bosola.

Interspersed with these visual set pieces which suggest one kind of interpretation for the play are the verbal set pieces, the long speeches, the meditations and sententiae which present another perspective on the action. In the pattern of Webster's dramaturgy they often provide the generalising explanation with which characters attempt to make sense of events. Taken out of context, they are often 'impressive', if conventional, expressions of received wisdom; but just as the visual set pieces can only present the bare dramatic event, so these speeches must be seen in relation to the dramatic structure of a particular scene. A long speech allows a character to dominate a scene or a situation and we find Webster using set speech to suggest a character's attempts to do this. For example, in Act III, scene ii the commonplace sermonising of Ferdinand's speech on Reputation, Love and Death brings that hectic sequence to a more controlled close. His earlier monologue (ll. 94–115) had verged on hysteria as he shouted curses at the absent Antonio; the Duchess cuts into this ranting with 'Why might not I marry' (l. 115), but instead of answering this question, he retreats into moralising platitudes about Reputation. The abstractions which he uses have no reality in the world of the play as we see from his description of Love:

> Love gives them counsel
> To inquire for him 'mongst unambitious shepherds,
> Where dowries were not talked of, and sometimes
> 'Mongst quiet kindred that had nothing left
> By their dead parents.
>
> (III.iii.133–7)

This description sounds like an emblem picture of unmercenary love and is in no way supported by the real experience of the play. Earlier in this scene we have been shown the humour and passion of true married love in the exchanges between Antonio, Cariola and the Duchess; a scene whose harmony was destroyed by Ferdinand's prurient violence. Moreover, when faced with a real love 'where dowries are not talked of', Ferdinand's reaction is one of snobbish contempt for

> A slave, that only smelled of ink and counters
> And ne'er in his life looked like a gentleman,
> But in the audit-time.
>
> (III.iii.75–7)

There is a great discrepancy between the moral position of parable and stereotype, and Ferdinand's reaction to the realities of experience. Webster's dramatic method, with its constant comparison between what is said and what is shown, exposes the empty conventionality which informs Ferdinand's oppressive violence.

It is significant, as a result, that the Duchess almost never resorts to sententiae to explain or excuse her conduct. On the one occasion when she is given a formal set speech – the tale of the salmon and the dog-fish at the end of Act III, scene v – the dramatic function of the episode is as significant as the moral point of her little homily. She uses the speech to reassert her control over the hopeless situation; overcome by the physical strength of Bosola and his troop of armed soldiers, she asserts her psychological superiority by reminding both Bosola and the audience of her rank. Her clear insult to Bosola in implying that he is a mere dog-fish with temporary power over the more naturally aristocratic salmon – herself and Antonio – is her last wry joke before the darkness of Act IV. It is also the beginning of that 'strange disdain' (IV.i.13) with which she 'fortifies her melancholy' in Act IV and which so enrages Ferdinand.

This ability to convey the shifts of psychological dominance in a scene and to suggest a variety of points of view on the action gives Webster's dramaturgy its particular force and makes the formal devices of dumb show and set speech effective. The visual and verbal set pieces provide a firm structure for individual scenes and the play as a whole, carrying the plot and its ethical context. Around them Webster uses more flexible broken verse lines and passages of prose to suggest the dramatic tension which exists between different characters. The verbal sparring between Antonio and Bosola during their midnight encounter in Act II, scene iii (ll. 11–49) is echoed most effectively in the uncompleted half lines. Webster gains a similar effect in the attempted seduction of Julia, the Cardinal's mistress in Act II, scene iv, while the opposite effect of complicity between two characters can be seen in the way the brothers complete one another's sentences (I.ii.202–25) or in the verse of the 'loving palms' dialogue between Antonio and the Duchess (I.ii.376–81).

These dramatic moments as much as their grand conclusions about the relations of man to the universe, make Webster's characters 'live' on the stage, make their relationships and their passions believable. But the life of Webster's play is in more than its characters and more than its poetry; the complex effects of his drama create a varied experience for the audience which is compelling at the level of the story but which also foregrounds without resolving a number of political questions.

'OF GREATNESS OR OF WOMAN'

One of the issues which Webster most tantalisingly refuses to resolve in the play is the question of the rights and wrongs of the Duchess's remarriage. Contemporary attitudes to the remarriage of widows have attracted a good deal of critical attention[6] and it is clear, as Clifford Leech points out, that 'there was indeed a strong prejudice against remarriage which could be presented as a joke at the widow's expense ... or could be sententiously enunciated'.[7] However, the flexibility of Webster's dramatic method in presenting these prejudices from a variety of angles has the effect of extending the problem beyond the narrow legal and ethical issue of remarriage to a wider consideration of women's actions and possible attitudes to them.

Webster's treatment of the women in his play involves a whole range of responses taken from both comedy and tragedy. The Duchess first impresses us as a figure whose wit and vitality are more appropriate to a comic setting and yet by the end of the play she has undoubted tragic stature. Many commentators have had difficulty in reconciling the forthright and determined woman who woos and wins her lover in Act I with the stoical Christian heroine of Act IV. However, by combining a figure from comedy with a tragic action of tyranny and oppression Webster gives us a greater insight into the process which imposes this change in the Duchess's action.

At the beginning of the wooing scene the Duchess states that defying her brothers is taking her

> into a wilderness
> Where I shall find not path, nor friendly clue
> To be my guide.
> (I.ii.226–8)

The conventional moral values seen in the empty banter of the opening court scene or imposed by the veiled threats of Ferdinand and the Cardinal are inadequate guides for a woman who feels able to emulate 'men in some great battle' who 'by apprehending danger, have achieved / Almost impossible actions' (I.ii.241–3). Her tentativeness in wooing Antonio shows that she recognises the moral norms imposed by her society and she complains that her sex and her status force her

> to express our violent passions
> In riddles and in dreams, and leave the path
> Of simple virtue ...
> (I.ii.342–4)

At the end of this ambiguous scene, when the Duchess and Antonio have retired to consummate the love which they prayed would bring the harmony of the spheres, Cariola comments

> Whether the spirit of greatness or of woman
> Reign most in her, I know not, but it shows
> A fearful madness. I owe her much of pity.
> (I.ii.398–400)

Cariola's opposition between 'greatness' and 'woman' reveals a great deal about the values of the world in which the Duchess has to act. As a woman she is expected to exhibit certain qualities and Antonio's early eulogy of her (I.ii.113–31) suggests that she does indeed portray traditional feminine virtues. However, her 'greatness' also consists of an independent spirit and an awareness of her own sexuality.

Webster very clearly places the Duchess's independent action in a frame which dramatises the attitudes of the men who surround her. The comedy of the wooing scene is enclosed by Ferdinand's and Bosola's views of women, each presenting a powerful image of the horrid fantasies which dominate their understanding of female sexuality. Just before Antonio's entrance, Ferdinand approaches the Duchess with his dagger unsheathed:

> This was my father's poniard: do you see?
> I'd be loth to see't look rusty, 'cause 'twas his.
> I would have you to give o'er these chargeable revels;
> A visor and a masque are whispering rooms
> That were ne'er built for goodness. Fare ye well –
> And women like that part which, like the lamprey,
> Hath never a bone in it.
>
> (I.ii.228–34)

The reference to his father suggests that Ferdinand is invoking some notion of family honour, but the remainder of the speech, together with the physical image of Ferdinand holding the dagger, dramatises the sexual aggression of his remarks. His earlier opposition to remarriage had focused only on its lustfulness (I.ii.194–5) and this speech equally shows him denying the possibility of beauty and joy in any encounter between men and women. The 'chargeable revels' which he sees as only an excuse for misconduct could be an expression of the princely virtue of magnificence and hospitality and we have seen how they gave Antonio, at least, an opportunity to display the courtly skills which 'raise the mind to noble action' (I.ii.63–4). Ferdinand's dirty-minded joke about the 'part which, like the lamprey, / hath never a bone in it' suggests an obsessive hatred of sexuality which sees all courtship as deception.

More problematic, because more conventionally acceptable, is the judgement on women presented by Bosola at the beginning of Act II. He seizes on the unfortunate Old Lady who crosses the stage and, taking upon himself the role of satirist and preacher, describes in hideous sensual detail the supposed contents of her private dressing room:

> One would suspect it for a shop of witchcraft, to find in it the fat of serpents, spawn of snakes, Jews' spittle, and their young children's ordures, and all these for the face.
>
> (II.ii.34–6)

Carried away by his own rhetoric, he urges her, and all women, to feel for themselves the same loathing he feels, in his generalised 'meditation' on the decay of the flesh and the folly of any human pride:

> What thing is this outward form of man
> To be beloved? We account it ominous
> If nature do produce a colt, or lamb,
> A fawn or goat, in any limb resembling
> A man; and fly from't as a prodigy ...
> And though continually we bear about us
> A rotten and dead body, we delight
> To hide it in rich tissue: all our fear
> Nay, all our terror, is lest our physician
> Should put us in the ground, to be made sweet.
>
> (II.i.43–59)

These lines have the impact of conventional wisdom, but Webster does not given them enough dramatic support to allow them the general application which Bosola wishes to claim. Castruchio is presented as something of a fool, and his name implies that he is physically inadequate, but neither he nor the Old Lady need demonstrate the kind of physical decay which Bosola excoriates. He is mouthing the clichés of mediaeval complaint but these are shown to have no particular application to the events or the characters of the play.

It is worth noting that by 1613–14 when the play was first performed, the figure of the self-appointed malcontent satirist had come under attack[8] and Bosola's railing presented only one view in a debate. As early as Act I, Bosola has been described as a 'court gall' (I.i.23) one who 'rails at those things which he wants' (I.i.25); his pessimistic and disgusting reminder of the frailties of human flesh is only further undermined when he refers to the Duchess herself in similar terms:

>   I observe our Duchess
> Is sick a-days; she pukes, her stomach seethes ...
> She wanes i'th' cheek, and waxes fat i'th' flank ...
>   (II.ii.62–5)

When the Duchess herself appears, she refers to her physical condition quite openly and uses it to demonstrate her affection for Antonio in public with 'Your arm, Antonio; do I not grow fat?' Her body has changed from its first youthful beauty but it has done so for the sake of the procreation which undermines the pessimism of Bosola's vision of human frailty. Thus Ferdinand's and Bosola's attitudes to the Duchess's sexual potential need not be endorsed by the performance. They have no special status in the dramatic dialectic even though they are closer to the clichés of conventional morality. They are, however, the judgements of those who wield power and who therefore can destroy the Duchess's more independent stance. For we must not underestimate the originality of the Duchess's 'dangerous venture'. Cariola comments (I.ii.400) that 'it shows a fearful madness', and the attitudes of the other characters demonstrate how difficult it is to understand the possibility of so unconventional a marriage. When Bosola meets Antonio at night during the Duchess's labour (II.iii) even he, the arch intelligencer, does not draw the correct conclusion on finding him with the child's horoscope. Antonio seems to Bosola such an unlikely candidate for the Duchess's lover that he can only conclude 'this precise fellow / Is the Duchess' bawd' (II.iii.71–2). Ferdinand's reception of the news that his sister has had a child is to rage and then descend into prurient fantasy, imagining her engaged in 'the shameful act of sin' with a variety of partners chosen for their sexual prowess (II.v.45–9). The marriage is judged as secret fornication by the spy, acrobatic sexual indulgence by the obsessive Ferdinand and a deviation from family honour by the politic Cardinal.

After the wooing, the Duchess is given only one more private scene in which her relationship with Antonio can be represented. In Act III, scene ii we see once again a scene from comedy; contrasting with the world of the court and the intrigues of powerful men, we are presented with a scene of domestic intimacy in which humorous banter about love making and the Duchess's frank admission that she is going grey provide a point of view to set against Ferdinand's obsession with sex and Bosola's denunciation of the inevitable decay of the flesh. We are shown that the opposite of lust is not absolute chastity and that the inevitability of decay is not only to be countered by ascetic other-worldliness; a more creative alternative exists in the reassertion of human love and its consummation in fruitful marriage. Where Ferdinand and the Cardinal see marriage as a means of increasing family prestige, something to be arranged by the men (see III.i.43–4 and V.ii.127–9), the scenes between the Duchess and Antonio show an alternative view of marriage in an assertion of individual fulfilment.

By setting the case of the Duchess against that of Julia, the Cardinal's mistress, Webster extends his audience's awareness of the circumscribed choices open to women in the world of the play. Julia's role in the play need not merely expose the Cardinal's immorality, nor simply contrast a virtuous Duchess with a vicious whore. It illuminates the different paths to greatness which each woman takes. Julia, like the Duchess, has abandoned 'the path of simple virtue' but the alternative route which she has taken is one more recognised and accepted by the men in the play. Her sexuality is accepted, as we see from the way the men joke with her in Act I (I.ii.23–33) because as the loose wife of an old man she fits into a conventional category. In becoming the Cardinal's mistress she achieves status and power (see V.i.26–50) but in doing so is exposed to the oppression of his sexual egotism. Peter Thomson[9] records a student's interesting suggestion that the first scene between Julia and the Cardinal (II.iv) should show them coming from making love, and the idea of post-coital bad temper would certainly explain the Cardinal's unkindness. Even without this direction, it is clear that the Cardinal's description of the affair (II.iv.27–36) expresses only satisfaction at his sexual prowess. He compares Julia to a falcon, a creature whose flight is completely controlled by the falconer who is, of course, the Cardinal himself:

> I have taken you off your melancholy perch
> Bore you upon my fist, and showed you game,
> And let you fly at it.
>
> (II.iv.28–30)

The repeated 'still you are to thank me' with which the Cardinal punctuates this speech indicates a pose of complete self-satisfaction; he regards Julia as completely his creature with no independent contribution to make to the affair.

In the dialogue between Julia and Delio which ends this scene, there is an interesting twist which exposes the limitations of stereotyped judgements of women. Delio tries to seduce Julia and, to his astonishment, is rejected. As one of the virtuous characters of the play his comment is especially revealing. He asks 'Is this her wit, or honesty that speaks thus?' (II.iv.85) and his comment, like Cariola's about greatness, shows how the women of the play are circumscribed by conventional norms. Julia is categorised as a whore so why should she not be his whore? Wit in women is associated with deviousness and so cannot coexist with honesty or chastity; greatness is incompatible with womanliness. Both Julia and the Duchess assert their independence in the only way open to them, by sexual choice, and Webster's drama places these choices against the commonplace and limiting values of the men in the play.

In terms of the stated ideologies of Webster's own day, *The Duchess of Malfi* seems a remarkable play. There was little in the contemporary discussion of women which could have prefigured Webster's sympathetic portrayal of the Duchess's strong-willed sexuality and it is doubtful that he would have recognised the terms of the interpretation which I have suggested. Nonetheless he may have shared with his more radical contemporaries (most notably John Marston) a recognition of the ideology of dramatic form, a dissatisfaction with convention and stereotype and a search for a more realistic mode of theatrical presentation. However, the forms of realism which were radical in the seventeenth century later became the received norms of both drama and the novel, and the variety of theatrical devices which Webster used has important consequences for the reception of the play today. How is a modern audience to respond to the spectacle of a woman totally oppressed or the expression of such complete mysogyny as shown by Ferdinand or Bosola? One response to these elements in the play is to deny their political import by relating them only to the particular case of the story on stage and this is made possible in Webster's case by the power of his characterisation. Since his characterisation of the Duchess transcends a single theatrical tradition her character gains an impression of realism: since he constantly frees her from the oppression of either side of the debate over women she gains an apparent autonomy from ideology. The combination of wit, domesticity and heroism suggests a certain idiosyncrasy of character which, together with her defiant assertion of individuality – 'I am Duchess of Malfi still' – fits very easily into a bourgeois liberal notion of the autonomous integrated subject asserting individual rights against antiquated and oppressive systems and appears to focus on 'real', i.e. individual, sexual relations between men and women. It is thus allowed to enter the sacred canon of texts which are not for an age but for all time.

However, attempts completely to assimilate the play to the demands of realism militate against a full discussion of the play's sexual politics. Realism demands that individuals be presented in terms of personal feelings and coherent psychology, as the critical history of the play has clearly shown. In the study men have argued whether the Duchess deserved her fate and about the motivation of her brothers. The first question reflects a critical unease with a woman character who so impertinently pursues self-determination and shows how little sexist thinking in the nineteenth and twentieth centuries escaped the polarities of the Renaissance debate over women. The question of the brothers' motivation was nonetheless seen in terms of a separate concern with individual personalities and was most ingeniously solved by the suggestion that Ferdinand is motivated by incestuous passion for his sister.[10] Such interpretation pays full attention to the realism of Ferdinand's hysterical obsession with the Duchess's sexuality but can make nothing of his formal account of the parting of Reputation, Love and Death with which he lectures her in Act III. The play's formal elements have, in general, met with dissatisfaction among modern critics for they do indeed disrupt the pleasure afforded by becoming involved in the tragic story of an individual defiant woman oppressed and destroyed by an individual sadist and an individual psychopath.

The 1981 production of the play at the Manchester Royal Exchange, for example, completely cut the dumb show at the centre of the play in which the Cardinal takes on his military persona before banishing the Duchess and her family. It is easy to see why the cut was made: the scene is slow, long-winded, and adds nothing to the narrative line. It is one of the 'flaws' in the play's otherwise powerful realist coherence. The production was totally committed to bringing out the realist power of the play. Bob Hoskins's snarling Cockney all but removed the knotted paradoxes of Bosola's language; Mike Gwilym's sinister Duke was a cold study in psychological verisimilitude with a *tour de force* in his barking, frothing lycanthrope of the final act. The design worked magnificently to bring out the play's emotional tones, contrasting the rich colours of the scenes in the Duchess's court with the pale monochrome of the scenes where she is tortured and killed. Yet the very pleasure afforded by its realist truth militated against the effectiveness of the play's sexual politics. By creating a powerful sense of emotional realism the production invited the audience to feel for the Duchess's plight but in no sense to understand the combination of military power and sexist ideology which made it inevitable. The production presented the world of the court, the political dimension of the play, as a cliché of glittering corruption – a decadent background to the personal drama of the Duchess, Bosola, Ferdinand and to a lesser extent the Cardinal. In this context and with this style of acting it was impossible to place, or distance, the political and ideological implications of the play's set pieces and the design of the play completely endorsed the malcontent view of the world of Malfi and the nature of women. This was particularly the case in the casting of the Duchess. The sexual politics of twentieth-century theatre make it inevitable that a starring actress will also be a beautiful woman and in this production Helen Mirren's dress and style emphasised her sexuality above all. The sexual sub-text of Ferdinand's feeling for her was allowed full rein, positioning the audience as voyeurs in a sexual drama. As Laura Mulvey[11] has shown, this is the most common positioning of an audience in realist spectacle and the one which affords the greatest pleasure, but it is a pleasure which needs to be examined. There was of course explicit sympathy created for the Duchess and exposure of her brothers' corruption and sadism. However, the direct power of that simple moral line only served to soothe away the sexual anxieties involved in the pleasure at the sadistic spectacle of the torture and humiliation of a beautiful woman. It is, after all, hardly radical to suggest that sexual torture leading to the murder of women is wrong – and by placing the action in a costume-drama world of the past the production blots out the more complex sexism involved in the casting of the play and the relations this creates with the audience. The mere evocation of sympathy for oppressed individuals short circuits the true recognition of oppression. The realist nature of the production co-opts the liberal views of its audience, their approval of a self-determining individual, while at the same time preventing their reflection on those views by setting them in the closed off historical world of the past.

The programme notes for the play further reinforced this process. They quoted only the reactionary and misogynist statements of the *querelle des femmes*, disguising their controversial status with Lawrence's Stone's much criticised[12] and partial account of the sixteenth-century ideology of marriage. They provided a context in which the play's performance can console the atavistic sexism of some of its audience and reassure the remainder that things were worse in the past. The potential radicalism of Webster's theatrical strategies, in his calling into question of the clichés of sexism, was suppressed in favour of that mixture of sympathy and consolation called tragedy.

From *Drama, Sex and Politics*: *Themes in Drama*, Vol. 7, ed. James Redmond (Cambridge, 1985), pp. 77–91.

NOTES

[Kathleen McLuskie's essay is most concerned with the play as a perform-ance text, asking how issues of gender and power literally get played out in the theatre. Woman is physically (at least in modern productions) and sym-bolically centre stage and the tragic limitations of her capacity to act define as well as refine traditional conceptions of tragedy. References to *The Duchess of Malfi* are to the text edited by John Russell Brown (London, 1964). Ed.]

1. See Michelene Wandor, *Understudies* (London, 1981), p. 20.

2. Notable exceptions have been Michael Bogdanov's 1978 production of *The Taming of the Shrew* and Peter Brook's 1979 production of *Antony and Cleopatra*.

3. Virginia Woolf, *A Room of One's Own* (Harmondsworth, 1977), p. 42.

4. Constantia Munda, *The worming of a mad dogge: or a sop for Cerberus Taylor of Hell* (1617), CIV–C2. Constantia Munda's pamphlet was a reply to Swetnam, *Arraignment of Lewde, idle, froward and inconstant women: or the vanitie of them, choose you whether* (1615).

5. See T. S. Eliot, 'John Webster' in 'Four Elizabethan Dramatists', *Selected Essays* (London, 1924), pp. 109–17.

6. See Clifford Leech, *John Webster, A Critical Study* (London, 1951) and F. W. Wadsworth, 'Webster's *Duchess of Malfi* in the Light of Some Contemporary Ideas on Marriage and Remarriage', *Philological Quarterly*, 35 (1956), 394–409.

7. Clifford Leech, 'Three Times Ho and a Brace of Widows: Some Plays for the Private Theatre', *The Elizabethan Theatre*, vol. III, ed. David Galloway (Toronto, 1973), p. 31.

8. See Alvin Kernan, *The Cankered Muse: Satire of the English Renaissance* (New Haven, CT, 1959).

9. Peter Thomson, 'Webster and the Actor', *Mermaid Critical Commentaries*, ed. Brian Morris (London, 1970), p. 32.

10. See F. L. Lucas, *The Complete Works of John Webster*, vol. 2 (Chatto and Windus, 1927); the idea has been restated a number of times since.

11. Laura Mulvey, 'Visual Pleasure and Narrative Cinema', *Screen*, xvi: 3 (1975), 6–18.

12. For a critique of Stone's view of the affective life of the early modern family see Keith Wrightson, *English Society 1580–1680* (London, 1982), ch. 4.

6

The Heroics of Marriage in Renaissance Tragedy

MARY BETH ROSE

I

No Shakespearean tragedy focuses exclusively on a strong, central female figure. That in *Othello* Shakespeare should diffuse female heroism between two figures, distinguishing the sexual styles of waiting woman and lady, has significant implications for determining his interests, as well as for assessing the tragic representation of sexuality. Before turning to these crucial issues, however, I would like to introduce a comparison with *The Duchess of Malfi* (c.1613–14), written approximately ten years after *Othello*. Here it suffices to note that it is, of course, Othello's heroism that assumes central importance in the earlier play. Although Shakespeare clearly recognises and explores the potential for female heroism in the qualities inscribed in the Protestant idealisation of marriage, he remains primarily concerned to examine the decline of the heroism of action by dramatising its inadequacy when faced with the challenges of private life. In his next tragedy of love, *Antony and Cleopatra* (1607), rather than elaborating his insights into the contradictions inherent in marriage itself, he chooses instead to focus on the conflict between eros and public service, continuing his intense scrutiny of the tragic obsolescence of the epic-chivalric heroic style.

In *The Duchess of Malfi* the process of decline characterising the representation of the heroism of action in Jacobean tragedy is already complete, its logic manifest. As in *Othello*, the distinction between public and private domains demands scrutiny and redefinition. Conflicts centred on these issues are initiated by an aristocratic woman's decision to disobey her male relatives and to marry a man not her social equal, thus defying traditional social and sexual hierarchies and opening the way for their dissolution. But what is striking in comparing *Othello* and *The Duchess of Malfi* is less the similarity of the elements constituting each play than the differences with which they are emphasised and arranged. For example, in *Othello* the state is both rational and just; the hero's harmonious relationship with the state involves rewarded merit and dignified gratitude. In need of Othello's services and respecting his abilities, the political hierarchy of Venice easily accepts his unusual marriage. The complex psychological and sociocultural factors that combine to undo Othello do not stem from political absolutism, then, but are more subtle and diffuse.

The Duchess of Malfi also begins with a picture of the state as traditionally conceived by humanist idealism: governed by a rational prince with the aid of learned and truthful counsellors, setting an example of judiciousness for the people, and inspiring the nobility to virtuous action (I.i.5–23).[1] But this idealised state is dislocated to France. It quickly becomes apparent that Italy, where the play takes place, has a decadent and corrupt court, dominated by a vicious, melancholy, and hypocritical Cardinal ('the spring in his face is nothing but the engendering of toads' [I.i.167–8]) and his pathological brother, Ferdinand ('a most perverse and turbulent nature; / What appears in him mirth is merely outside. / ... He speaks with others' tongues, and hears men's suits / With others' ears: will seem to sleep o' th' bench / Only to entrap offenders in their answers; / Dooms men to death by information. / Rewards by hearsay' [I.i.179–85]). In a further perversion of the humanist political ideal, each brother surrounds himself with sycophants and 'never pays debts, unless they be shrewd turns' (I.i.191). The profitable counsel to be exchanged between prince and advisers has degenerated into rigid, mindless, absolutism. 'Methinks you that are courtiers should be my touchwood, take fire when I give fire; that is, laugh when I laugh, were the subject never so witty,' advises Ferdinand, in one of his eeriest speeches (I.i.127–30). Given the diseased nature of the state, how can its defence be valued? Military heroism is evoked only in brief allusions and associated with the Cardinal, Ferdinand, and their savage, discontented henchman.

Bosola (e.g., I.i.76, 89–126; III.iii; III.iv). The steward Antonio's victories at games become nostalgic exercises, staged by servant courtiers for the amusement of their betters. 'When shall we leave this sportive action, and fall to action indeed?' asks Ferdinand, disingenuously (I.i.92–3).

Webster is dramatising an anachronistic neofeudal regime in the process of decline: in short, to use Lawrence Stone's terms, a crisis of the aristocracy. Though scholars have noted this fact, until a short time ago analyses have subordinated the political and socio-cultural issues that generate conflict in the play to moral assessments of guilt and innocence: shall we blame the Duchess or praise her for courageously compromising the demands of her position in order to marry her steward for love? How shall we assess the guilt and latter-day conversion of the dangerous, tortured, victimised Bosola? – itself a question that leads to assessments of the relevance of the play's fifth act, from which the Duchess has disappeared.[2] In a recent essay, however, Frank Whigham has forcefully redirected analysis, demonstrating that moral judgements of the characters are at best peripheral to an understanding of the play and locating the action precisely within Jacobean social processes.[3]

Whigham partially couches his arguments in the terms set down by Raymond Williams's conception of culture as a perpetually dynamic network of processes of change. In relation to a hegemonic dominant culture, Williams isolates several formative modes that 'are significant both in themselves and in what they reveal of the characteristics of the "dominant"'. His notions of 'residual' and 'emergent' processes are most illuminating in terms of *The Duchess*. Williams defines the 'residual' as a process by which a culture relates to the elements of its own past: 'thus certain experiences, meanings, and values which cannot be expressed or substantially verified in terms of the dominant culture, are nevertheless lived and practised on the basis of the residue ... of some previous social and cultural institution or formation.' Although this aspect of the resid-ual can have an oppositional relation to the dominant culture, it is distinct from 'that active manifestation of the residual ... which has been wholly or largely incorporated into the dominant culture'. Where the residual describes a culture's relation to its past, Williams's notion of 'emergent' formations delineates a process by which a dominant culture confronts the present and future. 'By emergent', he argues, 'I mean ... that new meanings and values, new practices, new relationships and kinds of relationship are continually being created.'[4]

These concepts enable Whigham to explain mechanisms of cultural change that generate irreconcilable conflicts in *The Duchess of Malfi*. For example, he argues that Ferdinand is an embattled aristocrat, resisting an onslaught of upward mobility. Ferdinand's pathology is rooted in a residual exclusivity that now appears deranged, an obsessive pride in purity of blood that becomes the basis of an incestuous attachment to his sister. Antonio, on the other hand, participates in the (to Ferdinand) threatening emergent cultural forces. Whether Antonio's motives for marrying the Duchess are ambitious is arguable, but it is clear that his valuable skills are administrative rather than military; and that his managerial abilities match those that became increasingly important to upwardly mobile men in sixteenth-century England, men who sought and attained advancement at court through education and achievement, rather than assuming elite status as a birthright. The isolated, perplexed Bosola perceives the evil of the neofeudal regime of the Aragonian brothers but cannot imagine a place for himself within another political formation. A veteran soldier without an occupation in times of peace, the neglected henchman embodies the socioeconomic transition from a collectivist ethic of service to an ascribed aristocracy to a mobile bourgeois economy of wages, employment, and individualistic achievement. As Whigham explains, Bosola, losing his belief in rank, finds himself caught between residual and emergent cultural modes:

> As the human origin of rank was gradually revealed, it became clear that the power to confer it was freely available to those who could pull the strings of influence or purse. When ascriptive status emerged as a commodity, the king's sacred role as fount of identity began to decay, and with this shift came a change in the nature of identity itself. It became visible as something achieved, a human product contingent on wealth, connection, and labour. Later, when Marx described it theoretically, the notion could seem a conceptual liberation. ... But in the Renaissance, when this insight began to be visible, it seemed a loss rather than a liberation. The obligation to found identity on one's actions seemed to sever the transindividual bonds that bound the polity together; it left one on one's own.[5]

Although he is describing Bosola, Whigham provides in this passage a cogent analysis of the historical conditions that make female heroism possible in Renaissance tragedy. Bosola, himself of 'base descent', remains enmeshed in an unholy and dependent alliance with the corrupt and anachronistic past embodied in Ferdinand; for him the glimpse of a possible future, though poignant, is belated and brief. Yet it is not Bosola but the Duchess herself who is the hero of the play, precisely because it is she who most fully embodies the 'coincidence of loss and possibility' located in the shifts of cultural identity taking place in the Renaissance.[6] Proud of her royal birth and stature, the widowed Duchess is also in love with her steward and determined to disobey her brothers, woo Antonio, and marry him. Thus she is caught between classes, between sexes, between tenses: as a young widow, she has a past and seeks a future; as an aristocrat who is also royal, she is independent, politically central, a ruler; but as a woman she is marginal, subordinate, and dependent – a status that her brothers' tyranny makes abundantly clear. With her conjoined, paradoxical attachments to present, future, and past, to status granted at birth as well as status gained by achievement, to female independence and female subordination, the Duchess is in a position as fluid and anomalous as the social conditions of Jacobean England. Viewed in this context, it becomes clear why Webster chooses an aristocratic woman as the figure that could represent most fully the irreconcilable conflicts of tragedy.

Understanding the play's class and sexual conflicts in terms of emergent and residual cultural modes allows us to connect the two dominant types of Renaissance sexual discourse examined in this book more firmly with historical process, with the shifting relations among present, past, and future, than is possible to do when exploring *Othello*. Specifically, the polarising mentality that idealises or degrades women and eros is associated in the play with the decadent, tyrannical Ferdinand and the alienated, paralysed Bosola. As Whigham shows, Ferdinand's obsessive attachment to his sister constitutes not a desire for sexual union, but a deranged purity, in which her absolute chastity becomes the equivalent of his exclusivist, aristocratic territoriality.[7] In his narcissistic identification with the Duchess as his twin, he insists that she remain unmarried, her life sexless. 'And women like that part, which, like the lamprey, / Hath never a bone in't', he warns obscenely (I.i.343–4).[8] Ferdinand's association of sex with pollution is echoed by Bosola's misogyny, which is second only to Truewit's in its nauseated specificity and is distinct in intensity from that of the comic wit only by being completely gratuitous. 'I would sooner eat a dead pigeon, taken from the soles of the feet of one sick of the plague, than kiss one of you fasting', Bosola tells an old lady, who at first appears to enter the play for the sole purpose of being abused by him (II.i.44–6).[9] The other character who associates the Duchess with absolute purity is Antonio, who, in his role as obedient steward at the beginning of the play, construes her as divine, an unattainable ideal, associated with rebirth, an exception to her sex:

> Whilst she speaks,
> She throws upon a man so sweet a look
> That it were able to raise one to a galliard
> That lay in a dead palsy; and to dote
> On that sweet countenance: but in that look
> There speaketh so divine a continence
> As cut of all lascivious and vain hope.
> Her days are practiced in such noble virtue
> That, sure her nights, nay more, her very sleeps,
> Are more in heaven than other ladies' shrifts.
>   (I.i.205–13)

The Duchess recognises her brother's grotesque misogyny and Antonio's rapturous idealisation as equally life-denying; indeed, she resists the dualising sexual sensibility that would relegate her to aestheticised inactivity and permanent widowhood in terms and imagery that recall the destinies of Zenocrate and Desdemona. 'Why should only I, / Of all the other princes of the world / Be cased up, like a holy relic? I have youth, / And a little beauty', she protests to Ferdinand (III.ii.137–40). And she exhorts Antonio to marry her by resisting in a similar vein immobilisation as an icon, associating the widow's enforced chastity with stasis and death: 'This is flesh, and blood, sir, / 'Tis not the figure cut in alabaster / Kneels at my husband's tomb' (I.i.459–61).[10]

Much of the scholarly debate about the Duchess's actions has centred on her sexuality. She has been blamed for being irresponsible, overly passionate, too bold, in analyses that often focus on the demands of her social position and/or on the conservative body of Renaissance thought that regarded a widow's remarriage as lustful and disloyal. Or she is praised for being both courageous and nurturing, in analyses that often pit the individual against society and, in post-romantic terms, privilege the former while regarding the latter as oppressive.[11] In order to escape these terms, Whigham rejects entirely an analytic focus on the erotic, which he regards as moralistic and trivial: 'the Duchess's actions should be seen not as erotic (a common male reduction of women's issues) but as political', he insists.[12]

Yet to view eros as a comparatively trivial, non-political issue is also to miss the point. The Duchess repeatedly emphasises her sexuality, indicating in precise and definite terms its centrality to her identity ('This is flesh, and blood, sir ...'). Throughout the play Webster not only stresses the strength of her desire for Antonio, but also focuses on her pregnancies, her erotic playfulness, and her tender, nurturing motherhood. 'I pray thee look thou givest my little boy / Some syrup for his cold, and let the girl / Say her prayers ere she sleep', she instructs her waiting-woman at the moment of her death (IV.ii.203–5).[13] The Duchess's erotic identity, then, is omnipresent in the play and central to it. The point is not that erotic issues are separate from, and/or less important than, political ones; to adopt this position is to accept the sexual stance of Bacon, Donne, Tamburlaine, Othello, and – what is decidedly less appealing – of Ferdinand. As we have seen, this point of view does not adequately account for the number of great Jacobean tragedies that centre on private experience. Rather than representing public and private life as a hierarchy that subordinates the latter to the former, *The Duchess of Malfi* attempts to draw the two domains together and to confer upon them equal distinction. The point is a crucial one, because in this play, unlike *Othello*, the effort constitutes a central, rather than a subordinate action, and its failure provides the primary tragic material of the play.

The effort to unite public and private life and to confer upon them equal prestige is formulated in the Protestant idealisation of marriage. This is the discourse in which the Duchess is inscribed. As we have seen, in the Protestant conception of marriage as a heroic endeavour, a military idiom is absorbed and transformed from the heroism of action, and this idiom, though sometimes applied exclusively to males, frequently ignores gender or explicitly includes women as subjects. It is precisely this military vocabulary of conquest and defeat that the Duchess uses to define her marriage to her steward. In response to her brothers' demand that she remain widowed, for example, she reflects:

> Shall this move me? If all my royal kindred
> Lay in my way unto this marriage,

I'd make them my low foot-steps. And even now,
Even in this hate, as men in some great battles
By apprehending danger, have achieved
Almost impossible actions: I have heard soldiers say so –
So, I through frights and threatenings, will assay
This dangerous venture. Let old wives report
I winked, and chose a husband.

(I.i.348–56)

'My laurel is all withered', she says, characterising her eventual defeat; and she adds, 'I am armed 'gainst misery' (III.v.90, 141). Finally, the Duchess's conception of her marriage as a dangerous but necessary venture also takes on the lonely, absolutist commitment shared by the tragic hero and the hero of marriage ('I am going into a wilderness, / Where I shall find nor path, nor friendly clue / To be my guide' [I.i.367–8]), leading her inevitably to ponder her own condition in universal terms, as Desdemona never could, and to her prolonged encounter with death. It has been argued correctly that the Duchess's confrontation with 'ultimate universal hostilities' distinguishes her as 'the first fully tragic woman in Renaissance drama'.[14] I would add to this crucial point that it is the full recognition of the importance of private life, here claiming equal status with public concerns, that makes her tragic stature possible; in turn, the Duchess's heroism helps to define and clarify the heroics of marriage.

It has also been argued that the Duchess's metaphysical confrontation with the foundations of human identity contains 'the kind of speculation familiar from Shakespearean tragedy, where the elevated are crushed as they inaugurate new conceptual options'.[15] Despite her disclaimers to Ferdinand ('Why might not I marry? / I have not gone about, in this, to create / Any new world, or custom' [III.ii.110–27]), this argument continues, the Duchess is in fact thoroughly committed to constructing a revolutionary future, viewing herself, like Tamburlaine, as a pioneer who will ignore traditional class barriers and chart a course through the wilderness to discover and colonise a new world, disdainful of the past and independent of it.[16] 'All her particular worth grows to this sum: / She stains the time past; lights the time to come', says Antonio; and keeping social history in mind, we can recall that this observation reflects the hopes of a steward who, whether he achieves greatness or has it thrust upon him, unquestionably becomes a protagonist of upward mobility in the play (I.i.218–19).

How revolutionary is the Duchess? Her assertiveness in wooing Antonio has been characterised as androgynous, an attempt to conjoin male and female modes.[17] This idea can lead us to compare the behaviour of the Duchess and that of the disguised female comic hero, whose androgyny gives her the freedom actively to pursue her mate. As discussed earlier in this study, the female comic hero's androgynous disguise exists in a holiday world over which she reigns, but the holiday world functions solely to renew and perpetuate the orderly world of every day. At the end of a romantic comedy, therefore, the festive world is left behind; the female hero, who has been free from sexual constraint throughout the play, surrenders her disguise along with her control, in a gesture of commitment to her future as an obedient, subordinate wife. In romantic comedy the contradictions between the woman's present freedom and her future constraint are contained in the final, harmonious, comic focus on the present.

In *The Duchess of Malfi* the Duchess's widowhood, with its temporary and limited freedoms, can be viewed in aesthetic terms as the symbolic equivalent of an androgynous disguise. Unlike a married woman, a widow in Renaissance England had a distinct legal capacity that she was progressively consolidating in the late sixteenth century, and unlike a single woman, she had an acknowledged right to choose her own mate. Just as the female comic hero does, the widowed Duchess identifies her future mate and follows eros into an alternative world. But as scholars have demonstrated, the widow's freedom constituted an anomaly that was difficult for Jacobean culture to absorb. On the one hand, an independent woman running her own household presented a contradiction to English patriarchal ideology; on the other, a widow who did remarry was criticised as lustful and disloyal, particularly in the threat her remarriage posed to a family's retention of property.

Like Moll Frith's male clothes, then, the Duchess's widowhood calls attention to the irreconcilable contradictions in Jacobean sexual values. But while, unlike the female hero of romantic comedy, Moll refuses to surrender her clothes, she also removes herself from participating in marriage. Thus her androgyny does not constitute a radical threat to the existing social structure. In contrast, the Duchess both marries and attempts to remain independent from the dominant culture, conceptualising her marriage as autonomous: 'All discord, without this circumference / Is only to be pitied and not feared' (I.i.472–3). There is, of course, no place within the absolutist state of the Aragonian brothers to absorb and contain the Duchess's unusual marriage. The vision of the future cannot be amalgamated, put off, or distanced, as it can in a comic structure. In tragedy the future has arrived, and it is unquestionably violent, revolutionary.

Webster, then, clearly recognises the radical potential of female heroism in the process of cultural change. From this perspective, distinct conceptual alliances and antitheses begin to take shape in our consideration of the play. The dualising mentality that either idealises or degrades women and eros becomes associated with an embattled and declining aristocracy, tyrannical political absolutism, and obsolete heroism of action, a receding past. In contrast, the heroics of marriage is associated with the bourgeois recognition of merit in determining status, rather than the aristocratic reliance on birth; with administrative rather than military skill; with upward social mobility and female independence; an impending future.

Yet the Duchess's identity and greatness – her heroism – are grounded in the past as well as projected into the future. Though on one level the dichotomy between a corrupt and decadent past and a more promising future is confidently formulated and supported in the play, on another the relation between past and future emerges in contrast as one of conflicting loyalties between two worthwhile modes of thought and being. This second, more subtle, syndrome, which assigns not only corrupt power but sympathy and value to the past, can be perceived by locating the Duchess precisely within the heroics of marriage, the discourse that she creates and adheres to and that defines her.

Like Desdemona, the Duchess is forced to defy male relatives (i.e., authorities) in order to marry the man she wants. Again like Desdemona, she becomes embroiled in the contradictory injunctions of the idealisation of marriage that both do and do not encourage woman to have a say in selecting her spouse and do and do not demand familial consent to a match. Yet while Shakespeare dramatises this issue as a subtle and significant but subordinate theme, Webster brings it to the very centre of the action, embodying its consequences in the career of a female hero whose private life subverts the established order. Although Desdemona's marriage matters to the established political order, its primary public importance rests in the state's need for her husband's services; her elopement with Othello precedes the action and takes place offstage. In contrast, the Duchess is a ruler; it is *her* marriage that has crucial importance to the state and shakes its foundations, a fact that, conjoined with her brothers' tyranny, makes the radicalism of her action at once more apparent and more urgent than that of Desdemona. Because the marriage between the Duchess and Antonio is fully dramatised on stage, the ambivalences conjoining family consent and female independence, which are reduced in *Othello* to the receding residue of Brabantio's displeasure, constitute the major, irresolvable, tragic conflicts in the later play. The Duchess and Antonio's marriage contract *per verba de presaenti* itself has an ambiguous status. As historians have demonstrated, clandestine marriage, or vows made between consenting adults with a witness present, constituted a perfectly legal union in England until marriage laws were clarified in the eighteenth century. But the social status of such a marriage, contracted without banns, solemnised outside the church, and associated with both poverty and illicit sexual activity, was at best marginal.[18] All throughout her wedding ceremony, the Duchess both abjures and affirms the need for legitimating institutions and traditions, thus unwittingly emphasising the problematic vulnerability of her marriage. Citing the legality of the ceremony, she demands, 'What can the Church force more?' adding insistently, 'How can the Church build faster? / We now are man and wife, and 'tis the Church / That must but echo this' (I.i.489, 493–5). Later, when Ferdinand calls her children bastards, the Duchess counters angrily, 'You violate a sacrament o' th' Church / Shall make you howl in hell for 't' (III.v.39–40).

But the most powerful contradictions that work to undermine the Duchess's marriage are those centred on status and rank. Though the inequalities that separate Othello and Desdemona (the Moor's age and blackness) are profound, they are nevertheless sufficiently intangible to be easily absorbed by the state: the marriage challenges prejudice, rather than established, class-based social and political hierarchy.[19] In contrast, the discrepancies in rank between the Duchess and Antonio comprise officially institutionalised boundaries, not to be crossed: 'Of love, or marriage, between her and me, / They never dream of', Antonio realises (III.i.36–7), referring not only to the ruling elite, but to the rest of the populace as well. By locating the foundation of identity in merit rather than birth, then, the Duchess drives a radical, irreconcilable wedge between the natural and social orders, previously regarded as identical. 'If you will know where breathes a complete man, / I speak it without flattery', she tells Antonio, 'turn your eyes, / And progress through yourself' (I.i.440–2).

Yet the Duchess does not adhere entirely to this commitment to achieved rather than ascribed status. Although the greatest obstacles to her marriage take the form of the brothers' tyranny, an external impediment, it is important to note the extent to which the Duchess herself continues to rely on her royal birth. It is not simply that she takes the lead in the wedding scene ('The misery of us, that are born great, / We are forced to woo because none dare woo us' [I.i.445–6]); she also delivers a very mixed message on the question of rank. Thus she defines Antonio as a 'complete man' and claims to 'put off all vain ceremony', begging to be regarded not as a royal Duchess, but merely as 'a young widow / That claims you for her husband' (I.i.460–2). At the same time, however, she reminds him 'what a wealthy mine / I make you lord of' and adds, in what is probably the clearest example of the double bind created by her superior power. 'Being now my steward, here upon your lips / I sign your *Quietus est*. This you should have begged now' (I.i.434–5, 467–8). As is often observed, the Duchess continues to take the lead throughout the play, whereas Antonio repeatedly demonstrates his helpless inability either to confront the dreaded brothers or to outwit their villainy: 'I am lost in amazement: I know not what to think on 't,' he says at one point, in what could stand as a summary statement of his position (II.i.182).[20]

Based in a problematic awareness of a wife's possible social superiority to her husband, the perception of a potentially severed relation between hierarchies of gender and power is also a central issue in the heroics of marriage. 'But yet when it hapeneth, that a man marrieth a woman of so high a birth, he ought (not forgetting that hee is her husband) more to honour and esteeme of her, than of his equall, or of one of meaner parentage, and not onely to account her his companion in loue, and in his life, but (in diuers actions of publike apparance) to hold her his superior,' advise Dod and Cleaver. Yet they contradict themselves by adding, 'She ought to consider, that no distinction or difference of birth and nobility can be so great, *but that the league which both Gods ordinance and nature hath ordained betwixt men and women, farre exceedeth it: for by nature women was made man's subject.*'[21] What bond is more 'natural', birth or marriage? Dod and Cleaver lean toward the radical position of granting greater importance to marriage, but continue perplexed. Their perception of the problem, which comes from the thwarted attempt to unite not only gender and power, but public and private domains, is itself subversive, but it remains unresolved and, as such, sheds light on *The Duchess of Malfi*. 'You are a lord of mis-rule', the Duchess teases Antonio, who counters playfully, 'My rule is only in the night' (III.i.6–8). The fact that their marriage must remain exclusively private – within 'this circumference' – does indeed become the sign of its doom.

The contradictions about rank, status, gender, and power that characterise the heroics of marriage perpetuate rather than resolve the conflicts between past and future. At the moment of the Duchess's death, the irreconcilable loyalties that are the source of tragic conflict become most clearly visible. On the one hand, the Duchess's rank plays a central role in the construction of her tragic heroism. 'For know, whether I am doomed to live, or die, / I can do both like a prince', she tells Ferdinand (III.ii.70–1). Later, when Bosola confronts her with chaos and destruction, she asserts her identity in the play's most famous line, 'I am Duchess of Malfi still' (IV.ii.142). The Duchess's courage and dignity in facing death are indissolubly conjoined with her royal stature. On the other hand, the sociopolitical conditions that make heroism possible in the play unquestionably reside in the decay of and need to defy the order from which her stature derives. Antonio correctly defines the heroic response to the resulting untenable position as one of active, chosen suffering: 'Though in our miseries fortunes have a part / Yet in our noble sufferings she hath none: / Contempt of pain, that we may call our own' (V.iii.55–7).

As I have tried to show, with its background in stoicism, religious martyrdom, and medieval treatises on the art of dying, the heroism of endurance that Antonio defines is connected in Protestant moral treatises with the idealisation of marriage and the elevation of the private life, a combination of elements particularly amenable to the construction of female heroism. Much recent scholarship has demonstrated that unstable social conditions often generate female heroism and creativity, which in turn play a major role both in demolishing an old order and in constructing a future.[22] In this context, an interesting example of Shakespeare's relative conservatism in representing women emerges from contrasting the Duchess's death with Desdemona's. The two scenes offer a remarkable instance of a reverse parallel. Both women are unjustly strangled for misconceived sexual crimes; both die martyr's deaths, accompanied by loyal and loving waiting women. As we have seen,

Desdemona's understanding of her own situation, along with her responsibility for it, recedes throughout *Othello*. At the moment of her murder, she begs for her life, an action that, however sensible it may appear in isolation, is definitely not characteristic of a tragic hero. Desdemona's final act is one of self-cancellation; courageous self-assertion is instead assigned to the waiting woman, Emilia, who is given the noble lines: 'Thou hast not half the power to do me harm / As I have to be hurt' (V.ii.163–4). By distributing the components of female heroism between the two women, Shakespeare confers independent selfhood on the subordinate character, while merging Desdemona's identity entirely with Othello's. Thus the stage is cleared for Othello's final, climactic consideration of his own, more active heroism, and the focus centres entirely on the lost past. The emphases in the Duchess's death scene are, of course, different. The most prolonged moment in the play, the Duchess's death is made to carry the full burden of tragic significance, as her debates with Bosola on the meaning of life and the effects of her death on the other characters make clear. Summoning all her princely dignity, the Duchess also dies thinking of her children's welfare, thus dissolving the distinction between 'woman' and 'greatness' that her waiting woman, Cariola, makes after her marriage (I.i.505). The Duchess's dual role as agent and sacrifice is never simplified to an emphasis on her victimisation. Instead, her courage in facing death is emphasised ('Pull, and pull strongly, for your able strength / Must pull down heaven upon me,' [IV.ii.230–1]), along with her acceptance of responsibility for her own actions. 'Doth not death fright you?', asks Bosola. 'Who would be afraid on 't?' she replies, 'Knowing to meet such excellent company / In th' other world' (IV.ii.211–14). A final contrast occurs when Cariola provides a foil to the Duchess's heroism by begging for her life, the exact reverse of the situation in *Othello* (IV.ii.231–55).

Despite the Duchess's greater prominence, however, she is assigned precisely the same fate as Desdemona and, for that matter, Zenocrate: she is removed from the active resolution of the conflicts of the play and granted instead the indirect role of inspiration. In one critic's useful terms, she ceases to be the maker, and becomes instead the bearer, of meaning.[23] A varied range of crucial activities occupies the stage for an entire act after the Duchess's murder, when, like Desdemona, she returns from the dead as a disembodied voice, an echo and 'thing of sorrow' meant to protect her husband (V.iii.24). In order to clarify her permanent status as an unattainable ideal, Webster specifically constructs her death as a work of art, relegating her value to the state of bodiless, aestheticised inactivity that she had heroically resisted in life: 'This is flesh, and blood, sir, / 'Tis not the figure cut in alabaster / Kneels at my husband's tomb' (I.i.459–61). 'Who do I look like now?' she asks Cariola in preparation for her death. 'Like to your picture in the gallery, / A deal of life in show, but none in practice; / Or rather like some reverend monument / Whose ruins are even pitied.' 'Very proper', replies the Duchess, ready now for death (IV.ii.30–5).

As the hero of the play the Duchess embodies its major conflicts; thus in order to remove her from their active resolution, Webster has had, as it were, to rewrite her part. The Duchess is inscribed in the heroics of marriage, a discourse that inevitably breaks down from a combination of external opposition and its own internal contradictions, which emerge as an irresolvable conflict of loyalties between future and past. At the end of the play, Webster resolves the conflict by discarding the future and reinscribing the Duchess in the dualistic discourse that idealises (or degrades) women, thus placing her above and beyond the action, in a position that she, pursuing the future, had specifically resisted and that is unambiguously associated in the play with death and the disappearing past. As Bosola seeks to avenge her murder and the Cardinal and Ferdinand die, leaving 'no more fame behind 'em than should one / Fall in a frost, and leave his print in snow' (V.v.114–15), the associations of the past with pathology and corruption also recede, while the dead Duchess's elegiac role assumes greater prominence. Viewed in the context of the polarising sexual discourse that defines her final position, the construction of the Duchess's death can be seen as reactionary: she is removed from the potentially radical conflicts of the heroics of marriage that have fully defined her, and the sympathy and value assigned to her life are unambiguously allied instead with a compelling tribute to the lost past.

II

Webster's removal of the hero from the last act of the play is so striking and bold a move that it raises important questions about the nature of English Renaissance tragedy. Indeed, given its pointed critique of political absolutism (the form of government favoured, if not enacted, by James I), its recognition of the centrality of the private life, and its profound exploration of female heroism, *The Duchess of Malfi* becomes an excellent text from which to assess the nature and extent of radicalism in Jacobean tragedy. By embodying major tragic stature exclusively in a woman, Webster acknowledges the female hero's pivotal role in the process of historical change, exploring the workings of the contradictory components of female identity in Renaissance sexual ideology as Shakespeare never does.[24] Recalling the comparison between Tamburlaine's revolutionary career and the Duchess's role as a social pioneer who courageously disregards traditional class and rank barriers, one can perceive the impossibility of finding either figure in Shakespeare's plays, where shepherds who gain power turn out to be princes in disguise; and powerful, central women preside exclusively over the comic world, not the more elevated and prestigious tragic one. The figures of Malvolio and Antonio provide a similarly telling contrast. A Renaissance playwright creating an upwardly mobile steward clearly had options in his representation of that figure. Should he be a pompous ass, a vain, deluded buffoon, easily outwitted and finally expelled by the aristocracy? Or should he be able, competent, appealing and, if perhaps also mediocre, nevertheless aware of his own limitations and capable of winning a Duchess's love?

My purpose in making these comparisons is not to find fault with Shakespeare, but to point out that, given the variety of conceptual options available in Jacobean culture, he often chooses the conservative ones, a pattern that becomes obvious when we view him not on his own, but in relation to his fellow playwrights. Because Shakespeare is indisputably the greatest writer of English tragedy, his conservatism relative to his contemporaries should have a great deal to tell us about the nature and purposes of that form of drama. Despite Webster's considerably greater interest in, and sympathy for the future, for example, he nevertheless ends *The Duchess of Malfi* by diminishing the future and paying a powerful tribute to the past. Recent scholarship concerned with the relation of tragedy to history has emphasised the foundations of tragedy in the failures of the past.[25] With its relentless, subversive scrutiny of obsolete modes of heroism, tyrannical forms of government, unjust social systems, and inadequate sexual ideologies, tragedy is seen to play a radical role of negation, to clear the way for a new order by participating in the dissolution of archaic cultural formations. Not only has this scholarship rescued Renaissance drama from being assessed in terms of a non-reflective identification with the construct of unified hierarchy known as the 'Elizabethan world picture'; it has also been invaluable in calling attention to tragic discourse as an historical process that plays a crucial role in the course of cultural change. But in correctly emphasising the function of tragedy as a social critique, these analyses have tended to assume that the tragic exposé of social injustice is more real than the focus on loss and death, thus underestimating tragedy's considerable allegiance to the past. As Webster's elegiac conception of the Duchess's death makes clear, no matter how pronounced the criticism of the past and sympathy for the future may be in a play, the separation between past and future that is the defining purpose of radicalism never occurs within Jacobean tragedy. Instead, attention is focused on the radical act as one of sacrifice and extinction, and the future is diminished in deference to the past: 'We that are young / Shall never see so much, nor live so long.'[26] In this context Jacobean tragedy can be viewed not as radical, but as conservative and nostalgic: a lament for a long lost past from the point of view of the aristocracy. Seventeenth-century English tragedy tended increasingly to become a predominantly aristocratic form.

How can we reconcile the evident radicalism of Jacobean tragedy with its equally compelling nostalgia? As is well known, great tragedy, unlike comedy, has erupted in Western history in infrequent, irregular bursts, particularly in fifth-century Athens and sixteenth- and seventeenth-century Europe. Attempting to account for tragedy's simultaneous alliance with the past and future, Timothy J. Reiss has joined other scholars in pointing out that in each of its major appearances, tragedy has accompanied the rupture of a familiar order, in which 'the essential relationships between physical, social, and religious life are now losing their reference to any "experience of totality"'. At the same time, however, in both ancient Greece and Renaissance Europe, the major developments in tragedy coincide with the rise of science, the struggle to realise an emergent rationality for which analytic, referential knowledge, rather than mystery and mythical thinking, becomes 'the true expression of reality'. Reiss argues that during this process of change, 'a sense of injustice appears, compounded of ignorance, fear, unfulfilled desire, and suffering, the mark of an "absence" which of necessity escapes organisation' – that is, meaninglessness. The function of tragedy is not simply to represent irreconcilable ambiguity, suffering, and injustice, but also to contain these ruptures precisely by defining them, giving them meaning and form. Tragedy's unique role in this process is to underline the moment at which the previously meaningless becomes legible and articulate, what Reiss describes as '*the moment of accession to referentiality*'. Whereas other discourses (e.g., history) 'take for granted the possibility of a discursive ordering of chaos, of the as-yet unknown ... tragedy *performs* the overcoming of that "absence"', the enclosure of meaninglessness that 'disappears as the very consequence of its naming'. Reiss also emphasises a dislocation between the protagonist and spectator of a tragedy. The protagonist is active but blind or, in the terms of this book, trapped in the past, the spectator, on the other hand, becomes conscious of a capacity to organise and to know, to create a future: 'the discourse of tragedy may be ambiguous internally, but that is just the point: it is an ordered and enclosed ambiguity... . It presupposes a knowledge.' By clearly defining and finally immobilising the destructive ambiguities of suffering and injustice, then, tragedy provides an affirmation that a future imposition of order is possible.[27]

As Reiss makes clear, once tragedy has performed its function in the processes of cultural change, tragic plays may continue to be written, but no further development takes place within the genre. As he recognises, these conceptions take different forms when embedded concretely in distinctive cultural situations. Reiss's formulations thus become particularly helpful for understanding the changing representation of love and sexuality in English Renaissance tragedy. As we have seen by examining *Tamburlaine*, in Elizabethan tragedy, created during a period of relative patriotism and optimism, the private life plays a marginal role in the representation of a heroism of action, to which it is at best subordinate, at worst destructive. In this context love and sexuality are constructed from a dualising perspective that either idealises or degrades women and eros, removing them from the significant centre of action. Such a perspective of course lingers as a conceptual option in our culture, and as John Donne's marriage sermons, written between about 1620 and 1630, make clear, it remains prominent in Jacobean and Caroline England. Although this dualistic sensibility is never superseded, during the late sixteenth and early seventeenth centuries it gradually recedes before the Protestant idealisation of marriage, a more multifaceted sexual discourse that elevates the private life and grants greater centrality to women as necessary protagonists in its enactment. Conjoined with a complex of sociocultural factors, including both the absolutism and pacifism of the king and the attempt to halt and consolidate the social mobility of the sixteenth century, the heroics of marriage becomes the primary subject of Jacobean tragedy. While *Othello* dramatises the beginnings of this process by scrutinising the decline of the heroism of action, *The Duchess of Malfi* manifests its logic completely by granting full attention and distinction to the private life and making visible the pivotal role of the female hero in the process of cultural change. During the development of Jacobean tragedy, the dualising sexual discourse becomes associated with the disappearing past, the heroics of marriage with the promise of the future. But, as we have seen, the heroics of marriage breaks down, both from external (and reactionary) opposition and from its own unresolved contradictions. As these ambiguities assume greater centrality in tragic representation, they are immobilised within a final, elegiac tribute to the lost past, a process of containment clarified in the deaths of Desdemona and the Duchess of Malfi. In this way tragedy serves its complex function of articulating the need for a future by destroying the past and then mourning its disappearance. Once again this point becomes clear from examining the tragic representation of sexuality, in which no further development takes place. Either the scrutiny of the private life becomes increasingly involuted, focusing on corruption and extremes, as in the depictions of female villainy and incest in *The Changeling* (1622) and *'Tis Pity She's a Whore* (1629); or the portrayal of endurance and suffering becomes increasingly static, as in *The Broken Heart* (1629). Fresh impulses in the development of the English drama are no longer articulated in tragedy, but in a less demanding and idealistic form, tragicomedy.

From Mary Beth Rose, *'The Expense of Spirit': Love and Sexuality in English Renaissance Drama* (Ithaca and London, 1988), pp. 155–77.

NOTES

[Mary Beth Rose addresses the great adventure of Protestant marriage as the primary subject of early modern tragedy. Marriage was a perilous journey, which required not only courage and fortitude, but also – crucially – the agency of women. Ed.]

1. All references to *The Duchess of Malfi*, identified in the text by act, scene, and line numbers, are to *Drama of the English Renaissance*, ed.

Russell A. Fraser and Norman Rabkin, vol. 2, *The Stuart Period* (New York, 1976), pp. 476–515.

2. These questions indicate the principal directives of almost all of the scholarship on *The Duchess of Malfi*. Representative examples of different ways in which these issues are addressed include James L. Calderwood, 'The Duchess of Malfi: Styles of Ceremony', *Essays in Criticism*, 12 (1962), 133–47; and Susan C. Baker, 'The Static Protagonist in *The Duchess of Malfi*', *Texas Studies in Literature and Language*, 22:3 (Fall 1980), 343–57.

3. Whigham, 'Sexual and Social Mobility in *The Duchess of Malfi*', *PMLA*, 100 (1985), 167–86 [Reprinted in this volume – Ed.] Whigham's essay includes a good bibliography of criticism of the play. See also Margaret L. Mikesell, 'Matrimony and Change in Webster's *The Duchess of Malfi*', *Journal of the Rocky Mountain Medieval and Renaissance Association*, 2 (January 1981), 97–111.

4. Raymond Williams, *Marxism and Literature* (Oxford, 1977), pp. 122–3.

5. Whigham, 'Sexual and Social Mobility', p. 177.

6. Ibid.

7. Whigham, 'Sexual and Social Mobility', pp. 169–71.

8. For a discussion of erotic imagery in the play, see Dale Randall, 'The Rank and Earthy Background of Certain Physical Symbols in *The Duchess of Malfi*', *Renaissance Drama*, 18 (1987).

9. Actually, like the character Julia, the Cardinal's mistress, the old lady seems to be in the play as a comment on and warning about the Duchess's marriage. Her odd appearances (see also II.ii.1–27) can be linked with the complex of witch imagery that pervades the play (see, e.g., III.i.78, III.ii.140–1, III.iv.57–8, and III.v.54–5) and the misogynistic connections of the Duchess with the lady-of-pleasure tradition, traced by Randall.

10. Cf. *Othello*, V.ii.3–5: 'Yet I'll not shed her blood, / Nor scar that whiter skin of hers than snow, / And smooth, as monumental alabaster.'

11. See, e.g., Calderwood, 'Styles of Ceremony'; and Baker, 'The Static Protagonist'.

12. Whigham, 'Sexual and Social Mobility', p. 184.

13. See Alan Dessen, 'Modern Productions and the Elizabethan Scholar', *Renaissance Drama*, 18 (1987); Dessen points out the ways in which excluding these lines from a production of the play, as was done in the recent National Theatre production (1985–6), tend to alter the audience's view of the Duchess and to reduce the complexity of her character.

14. Whigham. 'Sexual and Social Mobility', p. 174.

15. Ibid.

16. Cf. Paula S. Berggren, 'Womanish Mankind: Four Jacobean Heroines', *International Journal of Women's Studies*, 1 (1978), 349–62; 353; and Whigham, 'Sexual and Social Mobility', p. 172.

17. See, e.g., Lois E. Bueler, 'Webster's Excellent Hyena', *Philological Quarterly*, 59 (1980), 107–11. Bueler provides a fascinating account of the associations of sexual ambiguity with the hyena, alluding to Ferdinand's pathological fantasies of his sister's sexual relations: 'Methinks I see her laughing – / Excellent hyena! – talk to me somewhat, quickly, / Or my imagination will carry me / To see her, in the shameful act of sin' (II.iv.36–41). Also see III.ii.222 for an intriguing reference to Antonio as a hermaphrodite.

18. See Lawrence Stone, *The Family, Sex and Marriage in England, 1500–1800* (London, 1977), pp. 35, 317, 629.

19. Interestingly, Othello justifies his marriage to Desdemona by alluding to his royal birth as well as his personal merit: 'I fetch my life and being / From men of royal siege, and my demerits / May speak unbonneted to as proud a fortune / As this that I have reach'd' (I.ii.21–4).

20. Cf. Whigham, 'Sexual and Social Mobility', p. 176. Whigham remarks of Antonio that 'he agreed to his wife's coercive marriage proposal with the deference of the subordinate he feels himself to be'. Whigham notes several instances of Antonio's inability to keep up with the aristocratic world he has furtively and reluctantly embraced, including his remaining in hiding when Ferdinand approaches his wife with a dagger (III.ii) and, finally, his futile journey in Act V, when he attempts a reconciliation with the Aragonian brothers: 'Antonio's final action, the desperately naïve journey to the Cardinal for reconciliation, freezes him for us, as one whose unsought elevation never brought much sense of how to navigate the webs of alliance and enmity'.

21. John Dod and Robert Cleaver, *A Godlie forme of householde Government* (London, 1598; rpt. 1630), signs. K and K2.

22. See Mary Beth Rose, 'Gender, Genre, and History' in Rose (ed.), *Women in the Middle Ages and the Renaissance: Literary and Historical Perspectives* (Syracuse, 1985), Mary Ellen Lamb, 'The Courtesy of Pembroke and the Art of Dying', in Rose (ed.), *Women*, pp. 20–8, and Jane Tibbetts Schulenburg, 'The Heroics of Virginity', in Rose (ed.), pp. 29–72. See also Penny Schine Gold, *The Lady and the Virgin: Image, Attitude, and Experience in Twelfth-Century France* (Chicago, 1985). For a very interesting treatment of female heroism in Restoration and eighteenth-century tragedy, see Laura Brown, 'The Defenseless Woman and the Development of English Tragedy', *Studies in English Literature*, 22 (1982), 429–43.

23. Laura Mulvey, quoted in Nancy J. Vickers, 'Diana Described: Scattered Woman and Scattered Rhyme', in *Writing and Sexual Difference*, ed. Elizabeth Abel (Chicago, 1980), p. 109.

24. I do not regard Shakespeare's Cleopatra as an exception to this observation. Arguably, *Antony and Cleopatra* moves beyond tragedy and into romance. Certainly Cleopatra's 'infinite variety' is unique, not characteristic; rather than embodying the contradictions of Renaissance sexual ideology, which becomes the central focus of the play, she provides an alternative ethos that is opposed to the public/political world: i.e., the conflict is between love and duty. Finally, Cleopatra is not the sole hero of her play, as Lear, Hamlet, Macbeth, Othello, Coriolanus, and the Duchess of Malfi are of theirs.

25. See especially Jonathan Dollimore, *Radical Tragedy: Religion, Ideology, and Power in the Drama of Shakespeare and his Contemporaries* (Chicago, 1984); Franco Moretti, '"A Huge Eclipse": Tragic Form and the Deconsecration of Sovereignty', in *The Power of Forms in the English Renaissance*, ed. Stephen Greenblatt (Norman, OK, 1982), pp. 7–40; Whigham, 'Social and Sexual Mobility'; Walter Cohen, *Drama of a Nation* (Ithaca, NY, 1985); Ihargot Heinemann, *Puritanism and Theatre* (Cambridge, 1980). For other scholars who have addressed the issue of subversion and authority in Tudor–Stuart drama, see Stephen Greenblatt, *Renaissance Self-Fashioning: From More to Shakespeare* (Chicago, 1980), esp. pp. 193–254, and 'Invisible Bullets: Renaissance Authority and its Subversion', in *Political Shakespeare: New Essays in Cultural Materialism*, ed. Jonathan Dollimore and Alan Sinfield (Manchester, 1985), pp. 18–47; and Louis Montrose, '"Shaping Fantasies": Figurations of Gender and Power in Elizabethan Culture', *Representations*, 2 (1983), 61–94.

26. I owe this point to Northrop Frye, who, quoting these lines, which are the last two lines of *King Lear*, comments (p. 6) that in Shakespeare the social contract that forms at the end of a tragedy is always a diminishment of the present and future: 'the heroic and infinite have been; the human and finite are' (*Fools of Time* [Toronto, 1967]).

27. Timothy J. Reiss, *Tragedy and Truth: Studies in the Development of a Renaissance and Neoclassical Discourse* (New Haven, CT, 1980), pp. 19, 36, 20, 21 (italics his), 24, 35 (see, in general, pp. 1–39). On p. 36 he remarks that 'the reaction to tragedy ... would be at once the fear of a lack of all order and the pleasure at seeing such lack overcome.'

7

Dominance of the Typical and *The Duchess of Malfi*

SUSAN WELLS

THE TWO REGISTERS AND REPRESENTATIONAL STRATEGIES

In the first chapter [of *The Dialectics of Representation*], I referred to a 'dominant' register. *Dominant* means that one register sets the problems that occupy the text, or that it generates reading strategies under which a full interpretation can be subsumed. Dominance of one register does not imply, however, that it contains the key to the text, or that any text can be understood without coming to terms with its full working as a representation. Nor does dominance of a single register mean that interpretive work must begin with that register. Since a dialectical method tries to see in each part the operation of the whole, our interpretation can begin anywhere in the text.

The relations between the two registers, however, are not exhausted by two bare possibilities – dominance of the typical and dominance of the indeterminate. Within a text, the registers may be at odds, may contest for domination. Within a genre, a strategy may evolve that balances the two registers to set or resolve some representational problem. Such a strategy, internalised by readers, creates a frame of expectations that later writers may satisfy or violate.

In analysing representational strategies, I will use a method like the one Marx proposed in *The Grundrisse* – working from an abstraction through mediating concepts to more determinate ideas. I will move from the initial abstract discussion of representation, through the mediating concept of the dominant register in this chapter, to the determinate instances of historically situated genres in subsequent chapters. By following this path, we will, perhaps, be able finally to arrive at representation again, 'as a rich totality of many determinations and relations'.[1]

To discuss the dominant registers, I will use a traditional form, explication of texts, looking at John Webster's *The Duchess of Malfi* (1613), in which the typical register dominates, and Henry James's *The Turn of the Screw* (1898), a text dominated by the in-determinate. In both these texts, the protagonist is an isolated woman, and both of them recount stories of unequal love, super-natural visitations, secrets and mysterious deaths. And in both texts, the dialectic of representation is quite complex.

DOMINANCE OF THE TYPICAL AND *THE DUCHESS OF MALFI*

The Duchess of Malfi is marked by the uneasy dominance of its typical register. The problem this play takes up resembles those posed in Shakespeare's history plays – relations of sovereigns and subjects, of public life and private intimacy. Like Shakespeare's his-tories, *The Duchess of Malfi* investigates these problems as ques-tions of representation, questions of the relations of parts to wholes, of individuals to groups, of the hidden to the manifest. And, like *Richard II, The Duchess of Malfi* phrases this investiga-tion in the language of the typical register. But while the indeterm-inate elements in *Richard II* are consistently subordinated, in *The Duchess of Malfi* they make a bid for autonomy, if not domination. Interpreting this play, then, will broaden our understanding of the representational possibilities of the typical register and will sharpen our analysis of the dialectic between the typical and the indeterm-inate registers.

Since *The Duchess of Malfi* is not so familiar as *Richard II* or *A Midsummer Night's Dream*, perhaps a summary of the play's action would be useful. The widowed Duchess of Malfi, against the wishes of her brothers, secretly marries her steward, Antonio. Bosola, who has been paid to spy on her household by the brothers, discovers and betrays the marriage. The Duchess's brother

Ferdinand imprisons, torments, and finally murders her. In the last act, Bosola helps Antonio to revenge the Duchess, while the brothers deteriorate rapidly – Ferdinand hallucinates that he is a wolf, and the Cardinal sees ghosts. Antonio and Bosola are both killed in the final carnage.

This grisly, but by no means unusually tangled plot weaves together two strands of discourse that Jacobean drama normally separated. The matter of domestic tragedy – questions of fidelity, family ties, and the good order of the household – is joined with the matter of historical tragedy – questions of honour, legitimacy, and the good order in the state. The typical register of the play phrases both the public state questions and the private family questions in terms of part-whole relations and concentrates them through the character of the Duchess and the indexing image of her body. *The Duchess of Malfi* is thus a quite different play from *Richard II*, in which the public sphere is a sphere of isolation, developed as a reflex to the contradictions of public life. Here, public and private are both contradictory, and together they form a system of problematic part-whole relations. The play's typical register is organised by the contradictory relations of its private sphere.

The Duchess of Malfi begins by invoking a conventional view of the relations between sovereign and subject, between public and private life. Antonio says that the French court is admirable because, 'in seeking to reduce both state and people to a fixed order', their king has begun 'at home' (I.i.6–7, 8). Home, for the king, is the court, the foundation of honour, the source of all public and private virtue. To reform the king's home, then, is to replace politic flatterers with good counsellors. The opening of the play provides us with a series of ideological equations: the king, as an individual, represents the kingdom; the king's public life represents the private lives of his subjects; the king's private life is represented by his public activity. These equations prescribe a double replacement: the king substitutes for his subjects, and the king's public life substitutes for his private life – a twofold substitution that favours both public life and sovereignty. *The Duchess of Malfi* does not, however, take this ideological figure at face value, but challenges its representational logic by disturbing the play's initial equations. In *Richard II*, as we have seen, the private sphere was ordered by either the claims of private 'right' or the interior world of private subjectivity. In *A Midsummer Night's Dream*, the family mediates public and private, satisfying both the claims of individual passion and the sanctions of social norms. In *The Duchess of Malfi*, however, the family becomes identified with privacy and interiority, a domain of peculiarly intersubjective meaning. The state and public life, on the other hand, are emptied of representational power, and become the arena for a combat of wills and appetites. We can read the play as an experiment in moving the typical register from the sphere of the public to the sphere of the private, radically altering the structure of each sphere and their relation to each other. In the play, the Duchess performs this transformation for us.

> Cariola Whether the spirit of greatness, or of woman
> Raigne most in her, I know not, but it shewes
> A fearefull madnes.
>
> (I.iii.576–8)[2]

As the Duchess's maid perceives, there is a contradiction for her between the 'spirit of greatness', that magnanimity held to be the crowning virtue of princes, and a 'spirit of woman', a spirit that chooses out Antonio, woos him with 'only half a blush', and marries him in a private, unconventional ceremony. These two 'spirits' both try to 'reign' over her. The figure of the Duchess is a scandal because she cannot be assimilated to the normal system of public-private relations or of part-whole relations. She has established a virtuous court, but that court has not exhausted her subjectivity. She has established a family, but within that family she does not maintain her proper subordinate role. She has enforced a split between private life and public life, establishing Antonio as ruler of the night and lord of misrule, while she rules the public world of day. Finally, in setting herself against her brothers and establishing a secret family, she has also divided herself, making herself incapable of the public display of an untouched self, of the instrumental deployment of subjectivity, that the exercise of Renaissance sovereignty required. To reject the state and public relations of representation in favour of domesticity and the family may seem unproblematic. What could be less controversial, for conventional ideology, than for a woman to renounce public life for the sake of domestic intimacy? This reaction, however, assumes a nineteenth-century valuation of family life rather than an understanding of the relationship of public and private that was contemporary with the play. As Adorno said: 'To antiquity this intimacy was wholly alien; according to Plato's *Phaido*, Socrates, who generally speaks just in favour of inwardness, sends his closest relatives away just before his death, in order to be able to converse undisturbed with his friends. Only in modern times did the family transpose the demands of society to the interior of those entrusted to the family, make them into the family's own affair, and thereby "internalise" the human beings.'[3] Such a change in the valuation of domestic life, which probably did not reflect a radical shift in family size or structure,[4] reached its most intense expression in Reformation spirituality, that crucial vehicle for the creation of an autonomous sphere of the private. It was within the family that the inward spirituality and Christian liberty that characterised Reformation doctrine were to be expressed.[5] For English reformers, this implied spontaneous family prayer, searching counsel and admonition, and mutual corroboration of religious experience – a whole machinery, in fact, for generating a private life, a vocabulary for discussing it, and a set of norms controlling it. When the Duchess laments, 'in the eternall Church, Sir, I doe hope we shall not part thus' (III.v.84–5), she echoes the Reformation commonplace that every household should be a 'little church'.

To interpret this text, then, requires us to bracket some of our normal assumptions, to see family relations in an unfamiliar light. We cannot construct a reading of the play that mirrors its reception by Webster's contemporary audience. In fact, to attempt such a recreation would be the last refuge of reflectionism: if the play does not contain a mirror image of the world, we might try to find in it a blueprint for a vanished consciousness, the consciousness of its original audience. But if we cannot resurrect that audience's consciousness, we can do justice to the intersubjective force of the play's typical representation. By confronting us with an image of domesticity as it was being invented, *The Duchess of Malfi* invokes everything that is for us still difficult, promising, and subjectively dangerous about the family. The Duchess says, as she prepares to woo Antonio:

> I am going into a wildernesse,
> Where I shall find nor path, nor friendly clewe
> To be my guide.
>
> (I.i.404–68)

And the text places us in a wilderness, too – not the same wilderness as the Duchess's, but one that has a common border with it.

Thus, when we speak of the typical register locating *The Duchess of Malfi* in history, we face a certain paradox. History simultaneously links us to the play and separates us from it. We live in a world for which the equation between domesticity and intimacy has been taken for granted, sentimentalised, and exposed as a means of domination. But our world is also fundamentally the same as Webster's, in that both are structured by a division between public and private life. The private emerges in this play as a new sphere, uncompromised and radiant with possibilities – a vision of domesticity it is not easy for us to share. But the structure of this private world, the relation between it and public life, and the utopian hopes that formed it: these are not alien categories, but arcs in a horizon of consciousness that encloses both us and the original audience of the play, although we scan that horizon from different positions.

As a sort of index or 'friendly clewe' to these structures and relations, the play provides us with the image of the Duchess's body. In our analysis of *Richard II*, we have already referred to the convention of the king's two bodies, an interpretive topic traditionally associated with that play. In *The Duchess of Malfi*, we encounter a different sort of royal body, invoked most memorably by the Duchess in her courtship of Antonio:

> This is flesh, and blood (Sir),
> 'Tis not the figure cut in Allblaster
> Kneeles at my husbands tombe.
> (I.i.519–21)

While for received ideology the king's royal body is an image of the whole nation and is invested with typical force, in this play the Duchess's royal body, the alabaster figure, is static, remote, dedicated to mourning. Typical force resides in her eroticised, individual body. We encounter that body whenever we enter the Duchess's domestic world. She is the 'sprawling'st bedfellow' (III.ii.16); she vomits; she eats apricots greedily; she calls out in childbirth; her hair turns grey. We are continually placed by this image in a world of fragile and fertile bodies: the symbolic distinctions that normally shape our experiences of the body – experiences of division, status, and class – are subverted. The body emerges as an expression of common experience, to provide an index for the play's pattern of typicality. We are continually reminded that we share some common bonds with the Duchess, bonds the Renaissance would have characterised as those of 'kinde', and that Marx analysed as these of 'species being'.[6]

These relations of representation are grounded, for the Duchess and Antonio, in intersubjectivity, specifically in intersubjective dialogue. As Habermas puts it:

> The intersubjectivity of the world ... is not a generality under which individuals are subsumed in the same way as elements under a class. It is, rather, the case that relations between I, You (other I) and We (I and other Is) are established through an analytically paradoxical achievement. The speakers identify themselves with two mutually incompatible dialogic roles and thereby secure the identity of the I as well as that of the group. The one (I) affirms his absolute non-identity *vis-à-vis* the other (You); but at the same time both recognise their own identity by accepting one another as irreplaceable individuals.[7]

This formulation suggests a homology between intersubjective dialogue and typical representation: both are relations of inclusion that do not require the subordination of individual moments or speakers. In *The Duchess of Malfi*, the dialogue between the Duchess and Antonio simultaneously transfers value and significance from the public world to the world of the family, creating the play's typical register, and establishes an intersubjective relationship between the Duchess and Antonio as non-identical speakers:

> **Antonio:** These words would be mine,
>   And all the parts you have spoke, if some part of it
>   Would not have savour'd flattery.
> **Duchess:** ('You speake in me this, for now' we are one.)
>   (I.i.541–3, 569)

Each finds in the other's speech an expression of subjective intimacy, but each one's speech remains the discourse of an other.

Since it must be created by discourse, intersubjectivity is not simply given to us as a virtual image in this play; something must happen before we can see it. The first act of the play permits us to do that work, establishing the play's typical register as we move from the received ideology to a new sphere of the private, a sphere of domestic intimacy. In the course of this act, the ideological equation of the sovereign's public life with the subject's private virtue becomes associated with the Duchess's two wicked brothers, and is therefore dramatically compromised. The brothers, to anticipate our analysis of the play's indeterminate register, see the public significance of the sovereign's private life as a vehicle for self-aggrandisement, thus abstracting and negating received ideology. When the brothers warn the Duchess that her private life will inevitably have public consequences, for example, they enforce this warning by hiring Bosola to spy on her. And Ferdinand blatantly imposes his subjectivity on his subordinates: he forbids them to laugh before he does. In the brothers, the representational power of the sovereign has become a vehicle for domination and deceit.

The Duchess, on the other hand, opens a new terrain for the private by creating a language of domestic intimacy, a language that she teaches to both Antonio and the audience. She renounces all equivocating public language – 'a tyrant doubles with his words' – and insists that degree and domination will not affect the world of her marriage. And the guarantee of that world is her own body, 'flesh, and blood (Sir)', the body that embraces, desires, and ultimately joins Antonio.

The Duchess invokes a world of domestic intersubjectivity, but we see that world only intermittently in this play: the marriage is hidden, emerging only when it is in danger, its secrecy enacting its intimate and interior quality. What we see when the marriage is dramatised, however, is not a realm exempt from the relations of domination, but one in which they have become objects of play, pretexts for joking. In the play's domestic world, normal systems of subordination have not been abolished; the Duchess's utopian invocation of the 'birds, that live i' th' field / on the wilde benefit of Nature', who 'may choose their Mates / and carroll their sweet pleasures to the Spring' (III.v.25–6, 27–8), is not realised in her own life. In the play's domestic world two systems of subordination are at odds: Antonio is the Duchess's inferior in political rank, but her superior in gender. This dissonance, rather than generating tragic discord, allows Antonio and the Duchess to establish themselves simultaneously as identical and non-identical, to use Habermas's cumbersome term. They are not equals – the notion of equality, in fact, was profoundly alien to the Jacobeans – but they are able to play the relations of subordination off against each other, so that neither character is subsumed by the other. And, since neither character is exhausted by conventional systems of representation, both characters appear at once as individuals, exempt from stereotyped constraints, and also as representations of the basic relations of domestic life rather than its conjunctual details.

The intersubjective world of the Duchess and Antonio, then, joins the rhetoric of the play to its logic. Our assent to these two characters re-enacts the intersubjective dialogue they have initiated. We find, first, in the image of the Duchess's body, an answering voice, a response to our interrogation of the play. That body, the dramatisation of which must have been a scandalous breach of decorum to the Jacobeans, is for us a reassuring sign of commonality. The Duchess's individual physical being is a recognition of our own. Our interpretive dialogue with the play, then, can begin with a recognition of the 'identity' of the play as speaker. We begin to interpret its typical register by seeing the Duchess and Antonio as people like ourselves, by affiliating with the group (family members, lovers) for which they are such compelling representations.

But this affiliation is too simple. That which, in this play, seems most exempt from history is also that which is most deeply determined by history: family sentiment, tenderness of the body, desire for homely intimacy. All of these categories, which seem natural and obvious to us, the play struggles to establish as bases of significance. We are led, then, to recognise the play as a 'non-identical' speaker, since its assertion of domestic life as sphere of meaning is distorted by the terms of our initial access to it. This assertion, for Webster's audience, was not a truism to be consumed, but a difficult mediation to be performed. We can trace the path of their performance, even though we cannot re-create its subjective quality: to see the private in this way meant to put at risk the normal relations of subordination, setting them at odds with one another. It also meant leaving the public sphere without adequate representation: if the prince's power to invoke a commonality is transferred to private life, then how can the public be invested with significance? How can it even become intelligible?

Paradoxically, when we approach the play as a mediated, historically determined representation, as an expression of a subjectivity quite different from our own, we open a final horizon of consciousness that includes both us and the play's original audience, and find a link between its representational strategy and our interpretive strategy. Both for the Jacobeans and for us, private matters were entering the domain of history, pressing, by different routes, into the world of public discourse. For the Jacobeans, the family was entering history, coming to have a history, establishing itself as a reflex to the newly defined sphere of the public, differentiating itself from the other corporate entities associated with church and state. For us, the family is entering history on a conceptual level; new feminist scholarship and social history have enabled us to understand the family as a historical rather than a 'naural' or 'given', form, and we see domesticity as an institution situated in time rather than as an eternal refuge from the cares of public life. In both cases, the sphere of the subjective, of privacy, requires re-presentation. We share with the Jacobeans the need to rethink the relation of the public and the private, although our reflections are cast in different terms.

To fully understand the play's typical register, however, we must move beyond those aspects of the play that invite our identification, that announce their resemblance to social life. We must also confront what is resistant to interpretation if we are to see the play as a representation, a performance linked to social life but also alienated from the norms of received experience. Let us turn, then, from the play's typical register to its indeterminate register.

INDETERMINANCY AND CONTESTED REPRESENTATION IN *THE DUCHESS OF MALFI*

If the typical register of the play subverts received ideology and establishes a realm of domestic intimacy, the indeterminate register receives that subverted ideology and presents its own distorted version of the Duchess's domestic world. This indeterminate world is structured by a reduced, abstracted, negated version of intersubjectivity.

Let us examine first the indeterminate negation of received ideology. Traditional ideology provided the brothers with a rationale for domination and the naked exercise of power; their own private lives are so distorted by this use of power that they recognise no non-identical subjects, to use Habermas's term. For example, when the brothers first confront the Duchess, warning her against remarriage, they rehearse bits of conventional wisdom, drawing from the truisms of sexual lore:

> So most Widowes say:
> But commonly that motion lasts no longer
> Than the turning of an houreglasse.
> (I.i.335–7)

of politics:

> You live in a ranke pasture here, i'th Court.
> (I.i.340)

of morality:

> Those lustful pleasures, are like heavy sleepes
> Which doe fore-run mans mischiefe.
>   (I.i.363–5)

It is, as the Duches says, 'terrible good councell' from characters who have already been established as amoral villains. Indeed, this series of platitudes is followed by the Duke's joke about the 'part without a bone' and his gift of his father's dagger to the Duchess. Thus, the catalogue of received ideas, a catalogue, that devalues the private and the bodily, is followed by a threat, an invocation of the penis, a reminder of patriarchal power.

The indeterminate register of the play discredits received ideology by associating it with the disturbed and disordered subjectivity of the brothers: it joins skewed common sense with psychosis. The Duchess enters a wilderness so that she can create a world of domestic intimacy: the brothers wander in a wilderness of their own, a wilderness in which ideological forms and subjective experience are both self-referential. Received ideology rationalises their self will; subjective experience is for them self-enclosed and resistant to interpretation.

If the Duchess lives in a world of other subjects, however compromised that world may be, the brothers negate intersubjectivity. For them, all social forms are reflections of themselves; all other individuals present simple commensurable variables, to be taken into account instrumentally, but ruthlessly suppressed if they become inconvenient. For the brothers, other subjectivities are so abstract that they can be represented by the bare figure of exchange: any subordinate can be bought. Neither the Cardinal nor the Duke recognises any independent private sphere; neither of them hesitates to use his office for private purposes. The Cardinal banishes his sister by ecclesiastical authority; the Duke uses the law for his own ends. In place of a private intersubjective world, the Duke and the Cardinal have constructed a world of secrecy and concealment, a world built on subordinates whose services are purchased for cash – a network of informers, a mistress kept by gold and fear – a world controlled by the habit of plotting and bribing.

In this world, the ties of family are not dialogic. As a private relation, the family does not rise to the brothers' consciousness; only as a dangerous extension of the boundaries of the self does the family become a problem for them both. For Ferdinand especially, family is incomprehensible and incommunicable, a material and irrational tie of blood:

> Damne her, that body of hers,
> While that my blood ran pure in't, was more worth
> Than that which thou wouldst comfort, (call'd a soule).
>   (IV.i.146–8)

If the public body is more valuable than the private body, it is infinitely more valuable than private subjectivity, 'call'd a soule'. If the Duchess's body was for use as a clue to the typical register of the play, it is to Ferdinand a galling reminder of his own body. Ferdinand is trapped by the equation he had himself constructed: if his private will is the sole legitimate source of public power, then all other wills are simple reflections of his own. They have been absorbed into his subjectivity, and he then becomes vulnerable to their aberrations. Ferdinand's desire for domination, like the search for pleasure that Hegel described, confronts him with the recalcitrant, irreducible other he had sought to evade, and confirms the power of others over him. When the Duchess marries in secret, she reverses the relations of power and representation. Ferdinand rightly feels that the very integrity of his body has been lost. He is suddenly vulnerable; his individuality has been dissolved into a public sphere that is now unaccountably out of control. He longs to apply 'desperate physike' – to the Duchess, to himself, to the realm. The boundaries between the world of others, the members of his family, and himself, never very securely conceptualised, collapse:

>   I could kill her now,
>   In you, or in my selfe.
>   (II.v.82–3)

This mad vision is an abstraction and a negation of the Duchess's project. In place of her concealed world of domestic intersubjectivity, the Duke creates a concealed world in which his subjectivity absorbs all others, in which the family is a self-referential web of appetite, eroticism, and the desire to dominate. If the Duchess's is a world of domestic intimacy, we can describe the world of the brothers as its negation, or borrowing Freud's term, as an uncanny world.[8] And in fact, Freud's word for uncanny, *unheimliche*, is derived from *heimliche*, which means, among other things, home-like, cosy, domestic. The uncanny shapes the indeterminate register of this play; this is a theme to which I will return.

I have said that the indeterminate register is an abstraction and negation of the Duchess's domestic world. For the brothers, subjectivity is an abstraction. While the Duchess raises and enriches her servant Antonio, the brothers degrade and waste their dependants. They are surrounded by interchangeable monads, any one of whom – they think – can substitute for any other. All offices – except the naked, original use of force – can be deputised; there is no other who cannot be manipulated, suborned, or eliminated. For the brothers, reason and discourse, like the hoariest ideological clichés, are simple pretexts, embodiments of desire with no density of their own. Thus, Ferdinand expresses his hatred of his sister in whatever grammar of desire comes to mind at the moment – sexual appetite, pride, greed for 'an infinite mass of treasure', zeal for the family honour – all are, abstractly, interconvertible, since there is never anyone, least of all the Duchess, to whom they must be communicated.

The dialogue between the Duchess and Antonio has created an intersubjective world; they find themselves performing the 'analytically paradoxical achievement' of recognising the non-identity of one another. But neither brother attempts such discourse. They cannot use speech for any other reason than to convey orders and threats or to elicit information. It is not surprising, then, that the brothers cannot speak to each other or to the Duchess. For them, speech is an act of will, a way of imposing on subordinates, so that in their scenes with each other, the Duke and the Cardinal often carry on simultaneous monologues. And neither of them can speak to the Duchess, especially after her remarriage. The Cardinal confronts her only in the ceremony of banishment, a transformation of the 'noble ceremony' of pilgrimage. The sacramental vows, sacrifices, and gifts of rings that should structure that ceremony are placed at the service of a purely private passion. And so transformed, they require commentary and interpretation. They become indeterminate.

> **1st Pilgrim** What was it, with such violence he took
>   Off from her finger?
> **2nd Pilgrim** 'Twas her wedding ring,
>   Which he vow'd shortly he would sacrifice
>   To his revenge.
> (III.iv.39–42)

The Duke also communicates with his sister by means of shows: the presentation of a dagger, an appearance by night, the unveiling of corpses, a masque of madmen. Like the Cardinal's, Ferdinand's spectacles are essentially demonstrations of force. He is all too ready to supply an interpretation for them, and that interpretation almost always is an assertion of his power over his sister's subjectivity:

> *(SD)   Here is discover'd (behind a Travers;) the artificiall figures of Antonio and his children: appearing as if they were dead.*

Bosola   He doth present you this sad spectacle,
That now you know directly they are dead,
Hereafter you may (wisely) cease to grieve
For that which cannot be recovered.
                              (IV.i.64–6, 68–71)

These spectacles summarise and concentrate the indeterminate register of the play: they abstract and negate the relations presented concretely and positively in the typical register. The Duchess hides her family; the Duke reveals them to her, no longer hidden, no longer her family. The Duchess creates an intersubjective sphere based on her participation in the commonality of domestic life: the Duke tries to control that domestic life without being subjected to it. The Duchess establishes relationships based on dialogue: the Duke creates a sphere of meanings divorced from public discourse, but inaccessible to intersubjectivity. Both brothers' spectacles are displays of power, attempts to reduce both the audience and the performers to abstract counters that the brothers can deploy at will. The Duchess's maid, Cariola, describes the effect of these shows; she says that the Duchess has become:

> Like to your picture in the gallery,
> A deal of life in shew, but none in practise:
> Or rather like some reverend monument
> Whose ruines are even pittied.
>   (IV.ii.33–6)

The Duke's spectacles undo what the Duchess and Antonio had done, by reducing her to a public, monumental image and making her an abstracted representation of herself.

And these spectacles are deeply indeterminate. They announce their obscurity by being performed in the dark; the Duke always provides an explanation for them, but his explanation is not always convincing. Just as the Duke will use any language that comes to hand to explain his hatred of the Duchess, he multiplies reasons for his torment of her. But all these reasons negate the Duchess's privacy, assert that he is in control of her subjectivity:

Bosola   Why doe you doe this?
Ferdinand   To bring her to despaire.
                                (IV.i.139–40)

Servant   I am come to tell you,
          Your brother hath entended you some sport:
          A great Physitian, when the Pope was sicke
          Of a deepe mellancholly, presented him
          With severall sorts of mad-men, which wilde object
          (Being full of change, and sport,) forc'd him to laugh,
          And so th' impost-hume broke: the selfe same cure,
          The Duke intends on you.
                                (IV.ii.40–7)

Duchess   Even now thou said'st,
          Thou wast a tombe-maker?

Bosola   'Twas to bring you
          By degrees to mortification.
                                (IV.ii.175–9)

Further, the density of the Duke's last spectacles – the masque of madmen and Bosola's series of disguises as tomb-maker, bellman, and executioner – seems to transcend the limits of the Duke's self-referential vision. They achieve this density of terror because their indeterminacy allows them to become independent of the characters who present them. What the Duchess faces in those final spectacles is no personal opposition; rather she confronts the dangerous, unknowable aspect of the world she has constructed. Domestic intimacy, here, presents its indeterminate face; it becomes *unheimliche*.

Freud defines the *unheimliche* as 'that class of the terrifying which leads back to something long known to us, once very familiar'.[9] And he gives a catalogue of uncanny objects and events, a virtual prop list and précis of the *The Duchess of Malfi*: wax figures, reflections in mirrors, doubles and twins, a severed head ('Second Antonio to me; I want his head in a business', III.v.35), a hand cut off at the wrist, spirits and ghosts. Freud sees all the items on this gory list as expressions of an anxiety about the self, death, and castration. Fearing a loss of self, an uncanny consciousness creates a world of protective doubles, a world made of material more friendly than the alienated world outside. But these doubles

become invested with the anxiety that created them; they are re-
minders of vulnerability and mortality, an anxiety expressed as castration fear.

In the fourth act, when the brothers have full control of the
Duchess, the indeterminate and typical registers contest for domination of the play. The act presents us, first, with an indeterminate
world, one in which identities shift, in which Bosola will appear
four times in four different roles. It is a world in which the boundaries between public and private vanish: the madmen are consumed
by their old occupations; the Duchess's noble rank is used to mock
her. It is a world in which the body is not an intersubjective bond,
but a source of vulnerability, 'a little cruded milke, phantasticall
puffe-paste' (IV.ii.24–5). There, familiar things become threatening.
The site of the Duchess's torment is her own palace. All this terror
threatens some loss of self: Bosola presents death to the Duchess as
the erasure of her noble status, the annihilation of her public self:

> Much you had of Land and rent
> Your length in clay's now competent.
> (IV.ii.185–6)

her reduction to an inert body:

> Duchess Thou art not mad sure, do'st know me?
> Bosola Yes.
> Duchess Who am I?
> Bosola Thou art a box of worme-seede, at beste, but a salvatory of
> greene mummey.
> (IV.ii.121–4)

It is a world in which the abstract state of subordination exhaus-
tively defines social being, in which Cariola and the children are
killed for the mere fact of their relation to the Duchess. And it is a
world in which Ferdinand feels anxiety only when he faces, in the
Duchess, an alienated image of himself:

> She, and I were Twinnes:
> And should I die this instant, I had liv'd
> Her Time to a Mynute.
> (IV.ii.285–7)

This uncanny world is a self-referential and unhappy version of
the intersubjective, intimate domesticity of the Duchess; the two
worlds are in contradiction. In this contradiction is the source of

the play's representational power. Webster will reassert the dominance of the typical register, but had he not contested that dominance by allowing the indeterminate register to take over certain portions of the play, *The Duchess of Malfi* could not have become a full representation. It is the brothers' opposition that enforces the secrecy of the Duchess's marriage; their indeterminate bond with her requires her to construct an overt representation of the inwardness and retirement that mark her domesticity. The secret marriage, then, grounds the Duchess's project in the deepest relations of public and private. Without the brothers, the Duchess would face no experience of negativity, absence, or abstraction. The family would have been a vehicle for easy transcendence. Because of the brothers, she must confront those aspects of domesticity not easily expressed in intersubjective discourse: unconscious eroticism, the desire for domination. Without the brothers, the sphere of private intimacy would be only a refuge from public life; because of their opposition, it must be constructed in the face of a public attempt to dominate the private. Without the brothers and the indeterminate world they so vividly constitute, the Duchess's story would be a simple exemplary tale, the presentation of a polished image, an alabaster body to be consumed without being understood. We should therefore take very seriously the Duchess's assertion that:

> Even in this hate (as men in some great battailes
> By apprehending danger, have atchiev'd
> Almost impossible actions: I have heard Souldiers say so),
> So I, through frights, and threatning, will assay
> This dangerous venture.
>
> (I.i.385–9)

Given the crucial role of indeterminacy in *The Duchess of Malfi*, why have I said that the typical register dominates this play? There are a number of reasons. First, while the play's representation is contested between its typical and its indeterminate register, the typical register absorbs and transforms the indeterminate at the climax of the play, the long scene of the Duchess's murder. Second, Bosola, who acts as an agent of exchange between the two spheres, is at the end of the play absorbed within the typical register, and establishes its dominance.

Let us see how these dynamics work in the final actions of the play. The Duchess, as I said earlier, is not immune to the Duke's oppression. At one point, she is reduced to a mere image of herself.

She loses even her sense of her own body:

> I am full of daggers:
> Puffe: let me blow these vipers from me.
>   (IV.i.107–8)

And faced with a deranged attempt to reorder her private life, she feels herself completely absorbed by a debased form of the public:

> I account this world a tedious Theater,
> For I doe play a part in't 'gainst my will.
>   (IV.i.98–9)

But faced with Bosola's final disguises, the Duchess recovers herself and her vision of intersubjective commonality. She locates the sphere of domestic intimacy in the 'other world', borrowing the religious trope of a heavenly union, but her dramatic presence establishes that sphere, those norms of representation, in the subjective present. She regains her sense of the body as an index of commonality:

> What would it pleasure me, to have my throate cut
> With diamonds? or to be smothered
> With Cassia?
>
>   (IV.ii.221–3)

During the Duchess's long dialogue with Bosola, the play's indeterminate register is subordinated to typical intersubjectivity.

Let me unfold that statement a little. Bosola, of course, has been the brothers' creature throughout the play, but he has done their errands with an increasingly uneasy conscience, has been more and more ready to question Ferdinand. Ferdinand delegated Bosola as his final emissary to the Duchess, but Bosola chooses, finally, to appear only in disguise. He takes his place as a kind of second – or third – author of the final spectacles of the play, speaking always under the brothers' authority, inhabiting their uncanny world quite comfortably, but busy about his own affairs.

We cannot know, of course, what those affairs are: as a 'melancholy', Bosola is a deliberately enigmatic character. We know that he is drawn to the Duchess and that he is deeply nihilistic. His shaping presence in Act IV deepens its indeterminacy, since the final spectacles cannot be read as expressions of any one subjectivity, and the subjective intention of Bosola, one of the chief performers, is simply irretrievable.

But Bosola's actions are shaped by some subjective intention. Even though this intention is not accessible to us, it is clear that in him the Duchess meets someone who recognises her as a speaker, a partner in intersubjective dialogue. Bosola shifts and equivocates, but he also questions and answers, pacing the shifts in his perform- ance to match the Duchess's mood and tone. Bosola is not the Duchess's equal; there is no affection or friendship or recognised dependency between them, and so in this last dialogue the Duchess has left the terrain of normal relationships entirely. But still, between them there is a dialogic bond, and that, for the Duchess, is enough. She re-creates with Bosola a grisly version of the world of domestic intimacy she had constructed in wooing Antonio. Both scenes are marketed by images of concealment, rings, cords, circles, oaths, and kneeling. In both of them, received ideas are subverted: with Antonio, the valuation of the public; with Bosola, the terror of death. In the last scene, the Duchess is able to assert with equal seri- ousness the claims of domesticity, privacy, and daily life, to recon- cile her subjective identity with her noble status in the public sphere:

> I pray-thee, looke thou giv'st my little boy
> Some sirrop, for his cold, and let the girle
> Say her prayers, ere she sleepe.
> (IV.ii.207–9)

> I am the *Duchess of Malfy* still.
> (IV.ii.141)

The Duchess reinterprets each of the indeterminate spectacles she confronts, recasting it into typical terms: each becomes a way of as- serting her subjectivity, an occasion for establishing her member- ship in the 'excellent company' to be met in the other world. There the Duchess hopes for a full realisation of her intersubjective project; the barriers of rank and public occupation dissolve as she welcomes death on her knees. Her final request reasserts in the sim- plest terms her concern for that body that we have seen, in so many guises, as the indexing image of the play's typical register;

> Dispose my breath, how please you, but my body
> Bestow upon my women, will you?
> (IV.iii.235–6)

With the Duchess gone, the burden of the typical register is carried by the unlikely figure of Bosola. He has demonstrated the infinitely malleable quality of his subjectivity, appearing in one role after another, casting off each costume without regret or rationalisation. Bosola now finds himself implicated in the Duchess's subjective project: he worries about her state of mind and guards her corpse from dishonour. That body, index of the typical sphere, reveals to him his subjection to the abstract norms of exchange. Bosola describes his awakening in terms that shift from his familiar language of exchange to the language of subjective vision: he begins by speaking of a register, here meaning a ledger, and then refers to a perspective, a painting that formed a coherent image only when the viewer looked at it from the correct angle:[10]

> a guilty conscience
> Is a blacke Register, wherein is writ
> All our good deedes; and bad, Perspective
> That shows us hell.
>
> (IV.ii.384–7)

Bosola's vision is temporary and fragmented; it cannot save him, but it does condemn the brothers. He dedicates himself to the discovery of secrets, to the resolution of indeterminacy – the protocols of revenge in this play.

And so the play ends with Bosola's spectacle, a reversal of the self-referential and uncanny shows of the brothers. If he blunders into killing Antonio, he murders the brothers according to his own script: he designs their deaths. The brothers have refused any dialogic relations. Their retainers are primed to ignore their final cries for help. Ferdinand has made public forms into a vehicle for private desires; he is deluded into seeing his final scuffle in an obscure room as a glorious battle. The brothers have used their subordinates as direct extensions of themselves; they will be held accountable for all their intended and unintended crimes:

> **Roderigo** How comes this?
> **Bosola** Revenge, for the Duchesse of *Malfy*, murdered
>   By th'*Aragonian* brethren: for *Antonio*,
>   Slaine by this hand: for lustful *Julia*,
>   Poyson'd by this man: and lastly, for my selfe.
>
> (V.v.102–5)

If these lines of Bosola's are a final assertion of the problems of subordination and exchange, the final lines of the play summarise its treatment of subjectivity:

> Integrity of life, is fames best friend,
> Which noblely (beyond Death) shall crowne the end.
>   (V.v. 146–7)

Spoken by Delio, the reliable confidant, these sententious lines pose the problem of forming a complete subjectivity, one that has overcome divisions to become *integer* – whole, untouched. Such wholeness, we are told, can be reconciled with that extended public being that the Jacobeans valued as 'good fame', although such a reconciliation is ruefully projected to the impossible territory beyond death. The play's last words affirm, however, tentatively, the relevance of the Duchess's vision and the dominance of the play's typical register. Neither register of the play, however, can be understood or expressed except through the agency of the other. Without the brothers, there is no concealment of the Duchess's marriage, no representation of the essential inwardness of her subjective life. Without the Duchess's marriage, the brothers' attempts to abolish the boundaries between public and private would have remained the conventional activity of tyrants and villains, rather than becoming an uncanny doubling of selves.

In analysing a representation dominated by the typical register, then, we find that we cannot evade the indeterminate. The indeterminate register enables us to read this text seriously; it is a precondition of our hermeneutic interrogation of the play.

From Susan Wells, *The Dialectics of Representation* (1985) (Baltimore and London), pp. 61–80.

NOTES

[Susan Wells's essay takes up the theoretical profundities of deconstruction to ask about how power worked for and against women in early modern England. In Webster, woman is both object and subject, and her structural position within the conceptual topography of Renaissance society leads, inevitably, to her tragedy. Ed.]

1. Karl Marx, *Grundrisse*, trans. Martin Nicholaus (New York, 1973), pp. 100–1.

2. John Webster, *The Duchess of Malfi* (Cambridge, MA, 1964), p. 34. Subsequent references are given parenthetically in the text. A full review of the literature on *The Duchess of Malfi* can be found in Joyce E. Peterson's *Curs'd Example: The Duchess of Malfi and Commonweal Tragedy* (Columbia, MO, 1978), pp. 1–13. To the works cited by Peterson should be added William Empson's essay 'Mine Eyes Dazzle', *Essays in Criticism*, 14 (1964), 80–6, and several recent works: R. B. Graves, 'The Duchess of Malfi at the Globe and Blackfriars', *Renaissance Drama*, 9 (1978), 193–209; Leslie Duer, 'The Landscape of Imagination in *The Duchess of Malfi*', *Modern Language Studies*, 10:1 (1979–80), 3–9; M. C. Bradbrook, *John Webster* (New York, 1980); Jacqueline Pearson, *Tragedy and Tragicomedy in the Plays of John Webster* (New York, 1980); and Lee Bliss, *The World's Perspective* (New Brunswick, NJ, 1983).

3. Theodor Adorno, *Aspects of Sociology*, trans. John Viertel (Boston, MA, 1972), p. 135. See also Lawrence Stone, *The Family, Sex, and Marriage in England: 1500–1800* (New York, 1971). Stone holds that family relations in the sixteenth and early seventeenth centuries were so impoverished that many people 'found it difficult to establish close emotional ties with any other person' (p. 99).

4. New historical research seems to indicate that English families during the period of the play were relatively small, averaging about four persons per household, and usually consisted of a married couple, children, servants, and perhaps an additional inmate or two. These barren empirical statements could be made with equal accuracy about English families at any point from the early Renaissance through the nineteenth century, but they do not exclude the possibility of an ideological redefinition of the family that was not reflected in demographics. For research on the family, see Philippe Ariès, *Centuries of Childhood: A Social History of Family Life*, trans. Robert Balick (New York, 1962); Peter Laslett, 'Mean Household Size in England since the Sixteenth Century', in *Household and Family in Past Time*, ed. Peter Laslett and Richard Wall (Cambridge, 1972), pp. 125–9; and Stone, *The Family, Sex, and Marriage*.

5. I cite again the work by Michael Walzer, *The Revolution of the Saints: A Study in the Origins of Radical Politics* (New York, 1970), as well as an earlier essay by Christopher Hill, 'The Spiritualisation of the Household', in his *Society and Puritanism in Pre-Revolutionary England* (New York, 1964), pp. 443–82. The work by Hill analyses the theme of the family as a 'little church' (p. 455).

6. See also Marie Axton, *The Queen's Two Bodies: Drama and the Elizabethan Succession* (London, 1977).

7. Jürgen Habermas, 'Critical Hermeneutics', in *Contemporary Hermeneutics: Hermeneutics as Method, Philosophy, and Critique*, by Josef Bleicher (London, 1980), p. 196.

8. Freud's essay 'The "Uncanny"' can be found in vol. 4 of his *Collected Papers*, ed. Ernest Jones (London, 1925), pp. 368–407.

9. Ibid., pp. 369–70. I am using Freud in the spirit suggested by Fredric Jameson's observation in *The Political Unconscious* (Ithaca, NY, 1981): 'So great has been the suggestiveness of the Freudian model that terms and secondary mechanisms drawn from it are to be found strewn at a great distance from their original source, pressed into the service of quite unrelated systems.'

10. See Inga-Stina Ekeblad, 'Webster's Realism or "A Cunning Piece Wrought Perspective"', in *John Webster*, ed. Brian Morris (London, 1970).

8

Sexual and Social Mobility in *The Duchess of Malfi*

FRANK WHIGHAM

> The real subject is not primarily sexual lewdness at all, but 'social lewdness' mythically expressed in sexual terms.
> (Kenneth Burke on *Venus and Adonis*)

Most readings of *The Duchess of Malfi* apply two categories of analysis: psychological inquiry (what are Ferdinand's motives? how should we understand Bosola?) and moral evaluation (what is the status of the Duchess's marriage to Antonio? how does he measure up to it?). But prior questions can be asked. *Why* does Webster give us a wandering Duchess? an incestuous brother? an eager yet remorseful henchman? And why are these figures in the play together? How are their features and actions linked? Correlations between incest and promiscuity, ascribed and achieved status, community and alienation can help us chart this sprawling yet impacted play by situating it more firmly in Jacobean culture. Such analysis would align the play with many other efforts, from those of James I to those of Hobbes, to articulate and construe the friction between the dominant social order and the emergent pressures toward social change.

I treat first the noble brother and sister in the light of class strata and anthropological notions of incest and then the experience of their mobile servants Antonio and Bosola as employees and self-conceived social inferiors. In each instance I seek to read Webster's interrogation of the highly charged boundary phenomena of a stratified but changing society.

I SEXUAL MOBILITY

During the last fifty years anthropologists have developed an extensive body of theory about incest. Debate continues on many issues: origin versus structure and function, incest and exogamy (sexual versus marriage regulation), and animal versus human social behaviour.[1] Still, a basic outline is now visible. A narrowly psychological – that is to say, universal – explanation of incest (via, for instance, 'instinctive repulsion') is stymied by the diverse data available from non-Western cultures. Jack Goody has found considerable variation in the object of the defining 'horror' that incest supposedly 'inevitably arouses'. Sometimes intercourse with blood relatives arouses the repulsion; on other occasions only relatives by marriage are forbidden.[2] Moreover, as Kenneth Burke notes, 'psychoanalysis too often conceals ... the nature of exclusive social relations behind inclusive [i.e., universal terms for sexual relations'.[3] A vocabulary of 'human nature' obscures crucial variations specific to different social formations. To deal with such variations, we need to reconceive such 'givens' of human psychology as social products.

Anthropologists propose two general sets of social explanation for the incest taboo: arguments from factors internal to the nuclear family (such as competition among males for females) and from factors external to it. The latter argument, from the larger social situation, fits neatly with Webster's play. It specifies, in Talcott Parsons's words, that

> it is not so much the prohibition of incest in its negative aspect which is important as the positive obligation to perform functions for the subunit and the larger society by marrying out. Incest is a withdrawal from this obligation to contribute to the formulation and maintenance of supra-familial bonds on which major economic, political and religious functions of the society are dependent.[4]

This notion of public determination of private social structure is quite flexible, as Raymond Firth noted long ago:

> I am prepared to see it shown that the incest situation varies according to the social structure of each community, that it has little to do with the prevention of sex relations as such, but that its real correlation is to be found in the maintenance of institutional forms in the society as a whole, and of the specific interest of groups in particular.[5]

This powerful account also explains exceptions to the rule, such as those of ancient Egypt or Hawaii (and, as we will see, exceptions of individual inclination such as Ferdinand's). 'Where interest of rank or property steps in', says Firth, 'the incest prohibition is likely to melt away.'[6] Both the taboo and its infringements are thus seen as social products, similarly determined by the pressures and limits of particular social formations.

The model thus far presented is derived from traditional societies, where intermarriage is the most important device for ordering 'the interpenetration of memberships among the different elements in the structural network.'[7] Jacobean England, though much more differentiated in many ways, exhibits many of the structural relations of such a traditional society. Lawrence Stone judges that 'in the sixteenth century, kin groupings remained powerful in politics, [and] much of the political in-fighting of the century revolved around certain kinship rivalries. ... In local affairs, kin ties undoubtedly continue to be important well into the eighteenth century.'[8] Aberle and his colleagues generalise the notion:

> For the bulk of pre-industrial complex societies, the functions of the incest taboo in its extended form remain important at the community level. There, the regulation of affairs is not impersonal and legal. ... The nexus of social life and cooperation continues to be based on kinship to a significant degree, until societies with well-developed market-economies appear.[9]

The politics of kinship thus continued in importance among the hereditary aristocracy throughout the Jacobean period.

With the development of a differentiated class structure there arises a new sort of pressure that, contrary to the pressure in traditional societies toward intermarriage, tends to limit exogamy. In moving from traditional toward differentiated structure, Jacobean England was marked by this new constraint. Among other ideological pressures, Stone says,

> the custom of the dowry, according to which brides from all ranks of the propertied classes were expected to contribute a cash sum, together with the great sensitivity to status and rank, meant that there was a very high degree of social and economic endogamy [i.e., required marriage within the group, here defined in terms of class]. Since marriage involved an exchange of cash by the father of the bride for the settlement of property by the father of the groom for the maintenance of the couple and a pension for the widow, it was inevitable that the great majority of marriages should take place between spouses from families with similar economic resources. ... The fact that most [elite] families aspired to maintain status and

enlarge connections through marriage meant that in most cases like would marry like.[10]

These limits to intermarriage were further stressed in aristocratic consciousness by a gradual contamination of the ruling elite by invasion from below – a process that Stone has described in *The Crisis of the Aristocracy*. Although the elite responded with hegemonic contempt to most of these penetrations, widespread public fascination testifies to the issue's continuing potency. Castiglione's *Book of the Courtier* was functionally a prolonged sneer at what Thomas Hoby translates as those 'many untowardly Asseheades, that through malapartnesse thinke to purchase them the name of a good Courtier.'[11] And Shakespeare explores the problem repeatedly, from Bottom to Bassanio and Edmund and Othello. This problem of ontological mobility, or mobility of identity, is palpably at the centre of the cultural consciousness, certainly in London, nowhere more than in the theatre, where I believe it shaped depictions of sexual and marital patterns. In *The Duchess of Malfi* in particular, the class-endogamy pressure assigns to licit marriage an outer frontier, which the Duchess trespasses, just as the incest taboo marks the inner wilderness, where Ferdinand longs to dwell. But to grasp the significance of these symmetrical vectors of social force, we must mark the details of the play.

First, though, a glance at the history of critical opinion about Ferdinand's incestuous desires. F. L. Lucas first addressed the possibility, though he thought it dubious.[12] Clifford Leech presented the view fully, in *John Webster*.[13] Leech's argument occasioned resistance, from, for instance, J. R. Mulryne, as implying too readily 'the desire to consummate the passion'.[14] In response Leech itemised his evidence in *Webster*:

> The grossness of his language to her in Act I, the continued violence of his response to the situation, his holding back from identifying her husband and, when that identity is established, from killing him until the Duchess is dead, his momentary identification of himself with her first husband, his necrophily in Act V – all these things ... seem to point in one direction.[15]

These items have been widely accepted as suggesting incestuous desires, but they do not address Mulryne's doubts, nor do they clearly relate the incest theme to other elements in the play. The anthropological view of incest, which emphasises not sex relations but the maintenance of institutional forms, allows us to add to Leech's evidence, make a virtue of Mulryne's objection, and integrate Ferdinand's behaviour with the otherwise all-embracing issue of social mobility.

The core of this hypothesis can be briefly stated. I conceive Ferdinand as a threatened aristocrat, frightened by the contamination of his ascriptive social rank and obsessively preoccupied with its defence. This view, when coupled with Leech's evidence, suggests that Ferdinand's incestuous inclination towards his sister is a *social posture*, of hysterical compensation – a desperate expression of the desire to evade degrading association with inferiors. Declining Muriel Bradbrook's substitutive position that the notion of Ferdinand's incest 'can satisfactorily compensate for inaccessible Jacobean theological or social moods',[16] I propose to retrieve the social mood and read the two explanations as one, through an understanding of the ideological function of the incest taboo. The taboo enjoins trans-familial bonding: when Ferdinand flouts the taboo, he violently refuses such relations. His categorical pride drives him to a defiant extreme: he narrows his kind from class to family and affirms it as absolutely superior, ideally alienated from the infections of interactive social life. The Duchess then becomes a symbol, flooded with affect, of his own radical purity. In reaching for her he aspires to the old heroic tag *par sibi*, to be like only himself, excelling, transcendent, other.[17]

This obsession is made clear by, and accounts for, many small touches early in the play. Webster initially presents Ferdinand expressly addressing his alienation from those below. When Castruchio, making small talk, avers that the prince should not go to war in person but rather 'do it by a deputy', Ferdinand replies: 'Why should he not as well sleep, or eat, by a deputy? This might take idle, offensive, and base office from him, whereas the other deprives him of honour' (I.i.99–102). While this hallowed pursuit of distinction warrants personal participation, Ferdinand otherwise enacts his alienation precisely by eschewing participation and employing prosthetic agents: 'He speaks with others' tongues, and hears men's suits / With others' ears … dooms men to death by information, / Rewards by hearsay' (I.i.173–4, 176–7). His courtiers are to be his creatures, will-less, without spontaneity: 'Methinks you that are courtiers should be my touch-wood, take fire, when I give fire; that is, laugh when I laugh' (I.i.122–4). (It is common to describe this behaviour as usual for flatterers and ambitious men;

for the prince to require it publicly involves a different emphasis altogether.) Ferdinand especially enjoys the distancing trick of surprise: 'He will seem to sleep o' th' bench / Only to entrap offenders in their answers' (I.i.174–5). Nicholas Brooke emphasises how Ferdinand's courtly appearance constitutes an 'absolute spectacle' ('laugh when I laugh', 'the Lord Ferdinand / Is going to bed' [III.i.37–8], 'The Lord Ferdinand laughs' [III.iii.54]).[18] Bosola's criticism suggests that this may be an intentional effect: 'You / Are your own chronicle too much; and grossly / Flatter yourself' (III.i.87–9). This pattern of distancing objectifies those below Ferdinand as mere reflective witnesses to his absolute surpassing. His embattled sense of excellence insists on ontological separation from those below, but his frenetic iteration of the motif suggests a strategic failure. For there is an inherent contradiction in this device, as in Hegel's master–slave relationship:

> The master was actually dependent on the slave for his status as master; both in the general society and in the eyes of the slave, the master was recognised as such only because he controlled slaves. What is worse, the master could not achieve the recognition he originally fought for in this relationship because he was recognised only by a slave, by someone he regards as sub-human. ... He needed an autonomous person to recognise his desire as human, but instead of free recognition, he received only the servile, dependent recognition of the slave.[19]

Self-defeated, Ferdinand also fails his subjects: instead of acting as the traditional fount of identity to them, he generates the loss of their identity, striving to become more himself by reducing others. His strategy of domination reduces them to tools, to things.

Ferdinand's fascination with his sister is equally strategic. His leering assurances to her that all her most private thoughts and actions will come to light mark the invasive urge to control of the authoritarian voyeur. The news of the Duchess's liaison brings the social element firmly into view, for Ferdinand's fantasy leaps to the assumption of class disparity. He imagines 'some strong thigh'd bargeman: / Or one o'th'wood-yard, that can quoit the sledge, / Or toss the bar, or else some lovely squire / That carries coals up to her privy lodgings' (II.v.42–5). (When he actually discovers Antonio's identity, he describes him as 'A slave, that only smell'd of ink and counters, / And ne'er in's life look'd like a gentleman, / But in the audit-time' [III.iii.72–4].) This anger specifies cross-class rivalry, and the debasement by occupation marks the intensity of the aversion. For him invaders are mere labourers, well-equipped with poles and bars, false, and potent; by coupling with the Duchess they couple with him and contaminate him, taking his place. He desires exclusiveness, which he pursues not by intercourse but by blockage. Mulryne is right, I think, to doubt the urge to physical consummation: for Ferdinand the passion's fruit is in denial, closed and whole in his pe-emptive possession. To use Firth's terms, the point of Ferdinand's incestuous rage is not the achievement of sexual relations but the denial of institutional slippage through contaminating relation. Just as the taboo takes the form of a denial but functions as a positive pressure outward, so Ferdinand's infringing attitude looks like a desire but functions as a hostile withdrawal inward. As James Nohrnberg has suggested in another context, 'incest has some claim to being a kind of intentional chastity'.[20]

This formulation deciphers another recalcitrant fact. Firth notes that 'in general the harmony of group interests is maintained' by the taboo; 'the "horror of incest" then falls into place as one of those supernatural sanctions, the aura of which gives weight to so many useful social attitudes.' But sometimes the reverse is true: 'Where [group interests] demand it for the preservation of their privileges, the union permitted between kin may be the closest possible.'[21] If Ferdinand's incestuous impulse is determined by class paranoia, then he might well feel a cognate but reversed horror for the outmarriage that contravenes what he needs to believe about social absolutes. Firth frames just this affective reversal in terms of racial rather than class outmarriage:

> The attitude toward incest has something in common with a popular, uninformed view about union of the sexes in the 'colour problem'. Here one meets with a comparable repugnance to the idea, the same tendency to put the objection on a 'natural' or 'instinctive' foundation. Close family sentiment is even invoked as the clinching argument in favour of the impossibility of the admission of such unions – in the well-known formula, 'Would you like to see your sister marry. ... ' ... Here, as in the case of the prohibition of the union of very close kin, is an irrational emotional attitude, developing from a set of powerful complex social institutions.[22]

Hamlet is horrified that his own mother would 'post with such dexterity to incestuous sheets'. Ferdinand's horror is equally aroused by posting and dexterity, but instead of incest the referent is the Duchess's horrifying outmarriage.[23]

Her action is also threatening to Ferdinand because it suggests that the supposedly ontological class categories are brittle and imperilled by the powers of flexible self-determination exhibited by the Duchess and her base lover. Such rewriting of the rules threatens to reveal the human origin, and thus the mutability, of the ultimate elevation on which he rests himself. He cannot tolerate the suggestion, and its source makes it even more frightening – one of his own kind become heretic, apostate. His cruel execution of the Duchess may thus have several overlapping motives. To destroy her is to destroy the necessarily potent source of doubt, and the process of destruction reconstitutes them both: she is now the felon, the outlaw; he the transcendent judge. His imprisonment of her reisolates her, puts her in her place, and so restores her status as untouchable, in a private realm that only he can enter. And if her murder counts as a kind of rape, a consummate possessing, he typically employs an agent, a debased and dehumanised prosthesis used teasingly, like the dead man's hand. So he maintains the style of alienation we have seen on the bench (or, for that matter in the voyeuristic boudoir scene). Such devices allow this forbidden conduct while punishing hers, and then allow him to deny his implication in them. This final evasion is couched in revealing terms, for he returns to the issue of disparity in rank when interrogating Bosola for what has now become an unauthorised murder: 'Let me but examine well the cause: / What was the meanness of her match in me?' (IV.ii.281–2). Her marriage was for him an adulteration that his fantasy of possession was designed to occlude. He now averts his eyes from his aversion and so alienates himself from himself.

This usurping investment in denial can only be maintained by increasingly radical devotion to the task, a surgical practice degenerating toward ultimate alienation: the solipsism of insanity.[24] Ferdinand had already long contracted his ground of being to the two of them; when he sees that he has accomplished his revenge for her divisive betrayal, he reveals (at IV.ii.267) the striking fact that they are (were) twins, restoring a lost unity between them even as her death makes him singular. The enormous condensation at work here may be partially untwisted with the aid of Pausanias's alternative version of the Narcissus fable (the Ovidian version having been pertinent all along). Narcissus in fact had a beloved twin sister.

> Upon her death, he is said to have come to a fountain alone, and suffering from desire, gazed upon his own image there. But although

that seemed somewhat of a solace, he at length perished with great desire, or, as is more pleasing to others, threw himself into the fountain and perished.[25]

When Ferdinand looks down into his dead sister's dazzling eyes, he sees himself, faces his own death too. The circle shrinks again, becoming more and more rapidly only his own. When asked why he is so solitary, he replies that the noble eagle flies alone: 'they are crows, daws, and starlings that flock together' (V.ii.30–1). Next he tries to divest himself of his shadow, attacking even this inherent multiplicity (V.ii.31–41). His lycanthropia, unitary wolf at last, brings him to his logical end in total isolation. Walled in alone, not in a secret garden but in an inward hair shirt,[26] he is finally sui generis, a peerless class of one – an entropic apotheosis of the superb Renaissance hero.

Webster presents the Duchess in terms precisely symmetrical to her brother's hypertrophy of will. Ferdinand, as we have seen, is pathologically endogamous, investing his energies much farther inward toward the nuclear core than is normatively fitting. His paranoia digs an ontological moat around itself. In contrast, the Duchess is excessively exogamous: fettered in Ferdinand's enclosure, she seizes self-definition by reaching out not only past the interdicted purity of her family but beyond the frontiers of her class, to marry her admirable steward. What Ferdinand would hoard, she circulates. He fastens on the absolutes of ascriptive identity; the Duchess, on the earnables of achieved character. And where Ferdinand's denials issue in unpolluted sterility, the Duchess's self-assertion is fecund, both biologically and ideologically.[27]

These opposed actions rest on the same base of will: each sibling has the compulsive focus of Marlowe's protagonists. If Ferdinand is an ingrown Tamburlaine (who, Puttenham tells us,[28] was punished with childlessness for his presumption to absolute status), the Duchess is a family pioneer who ruthlessly carves out for herself the privatised domestic realm of the future, based on personal rather than familial or class imperatives – a heterosexual Edward II. This fetish of will allows a reading via negative stereotypes for wilful women: those, for instance, that lie behind Cleopatra, Lady Macbeth, Benedick's Beatrice – temptress-whore, monster, shrew. But Webster obviates these constructions by emphasising the biologically and divinely sanctioned maternal motive and the antagonistic stimulant of Ferdinand. In the face of such pressures the

Duchess seeks to evade a reductive code by creatively adapting strategies of self-determination hitherto restricted to the masculine world of social action. Sadly, they are the very strategies of mobility that have activated Ferdinand's psychotic defences. That is to say, the Duchess's enterprise is not primarily private and romantic: it is, rather, a socially adaptive action that extends to the zone of gender conflict a manoeuvre actively in play in the arena of class conflict. Like Ferdinand's incestuous bent, it is irredeemably social.[29]

The Duchess begins the play as a widow. Upon her husband's death she entered a new realm of freedom from male domination, the only such realm open to Jacobean women, and it is this transformation that directly enables her outlaw marriage. Much has been written of late about the liberated status of Renaissance widows: I will here point out only that the Duchess privately assumes the unmistakably male tone of the Renaissance hero.

> Shall this move me? If all my royal kindred
> Lay in my way unto this marriage
> I'd make them my low footsteps: and even now,
> Even in this hate, as men in some great battles
> By apprehending danger, have achiev'd
> Almost impossible actions – I have heard soldiers
>   say so –
> So I, through frights, and threat'nings, will assay
> This dangerous venture: let old wives report
> I wink'd and chose a husband.
>   (I.i.341–49)

The apostrophe, the amplification of the hostile odds, the abjection of the enemy, the soldierly comparison, the imperative call for historical (if female) witness – all are heroic topoi. They seem to me to preclude the impoverished interpretive option of the 'lustful widow', husbandless and hungry: the tones are martial, not erotic. Instead, the Duchess emphasises her unconventional venture: 'I am going into a wilderness, / Where I shall find nor path, nor friendly clew / To be my guide' (I.i.359–61). A cultural voyager, she arrogates to herself a new role, that of female hero, going knowingly to colonise a new realm of privacy.

It is no news, of course, that men read such self-determination as lust. Pitt-Rivers notes that

> widows are commonly believed ... to be sexually predatory upon the
> young men. ... A woman whose shame is not in the keeping of a man

is sexually aggressive and dangerous. The association reaches its extreme representation in the figure of the witch, the unsubjected female who rides upon a broomstick to subvert the social order.[30]

Such deviants require (or receive, anyway) the discipline of the charivari, a raucous folk shaming of proven relevance to this play, where it dresses the tortures of Act IV in marriage-masque array.[31] But for my point its weight is that this is *Ferdinand's* masque; its ritual structures convict not the married widow but her barren brother – as can be seen when the madness slides from masque to master. Act V makes it clear that no ritual management of disorder has supervened here.

The act of self-defining will that occasions this pseudo-social judgement can usefully be compared to the differently compliant postures of Cariola and Julia, antinomies of definition for the Duchess. Cariola, best of motherly servants, confirms the secret marriage and tends the Duchess at childbed, joining other servants of daring ladies (Juliet, Portia, Desdemona, Beatrice-Joanna) in attesting to a female self-direction that acts within and yet refuses masculine categories of social control. For such women submission to the lady's lord is prefunctory, allegiance in rebellion and evasion with the lady automatic and simple. Indeed, Cariola is an exceptionally focused specimen of the type: she is not given any of the divided loyalties that would accompany the usual suitor of her own (though Delio is structurally available). But neither is there any sign of degradation in her service, of the sense of self-waste that marks characters who are more modern and more problematic. She seems happily to derive almost the whole of her identity from her relational dedication and so to exhibit for purposes of contrast one familiar form of female self-gift for the Duchess to transcend.[32]

This casting, however, must not be seen as merely negative and limited. For in the Renaissance the private company of women often seems to constitute a secret space in the midst of male society, a haven where the normal modes of subjection are cancelled and where a version of traditionally male substantiality is annexed – what we might now hope to call human intimacy. Cariola relates to the Duchess as Kent to Lear (though without the devotional power supposedly conferred by noble rank). She occupies the old mode of identity in service with its hierarchical origins, yet she also embodies the collusive strength that female identity can acquire in an oppressively role-restricted society. But though Cariola unquestioningly aids in the Duchess's self-defining act, she also ends the scene with choric doubt about the potential for such female self-determination in the two-gender world: 'Whether the spirit of greatness, or of woman / Reign most in her, I know not, but it shows / A fearful madness' (I.i.504–6).

Self-giving will of another sort, practised by Julia, deflects the judgemental charge of lasciviousness away from the Duchess. Wife of old Castruchio and mistress of the Cardinal, she acts out the Renaissance court strumpet, male-begot, so that the Duchess can be seen as freeing herself from such male imperatives. Julia contrasts with the Duchess insofar as the Duchess's project does not aim at self-subjecting relational identity but itself founds substantial identity in the normatively masculine sense. Julia reaches out to two sources of power in the play, the Cardinal and Bosola, advertising in departure her husband's superannuated weakness and so catering to a male model of woman as yardstick of masculine worth. She who rejects the ties of marriage attests to the lover's power to draw a woman's heart even against the oppressive double-standard rules of male-dominated society. She demonstrates not her own power of self-determination but his power over her. The courtly adulteress is especially drawn to power, to men who can, by conferring erotic relation, make their women significant or safe. By rejecting her decrepit husband Julia also testifies to her ruthless erotic vigour and so makes herself especially alluring to such men. But her achievement is finally self-wasting: Bosola merely employs her, and the Cardinal tires of her and kills her. When she offers herself as a toy, she initiates her own consumption and disposal. Ironically, the Cardinal murders her for her 'hubristic' attempt to be a peer, a helpmate in a heightened sense, to share in cerebral relation rather than merely physical. Julia's ultimate goals are partly congruent with the Duchess's, since both women seek personal security in a hostile male world, but the means Julia chooses inevitably subject her to men who define her as pastime, as furlough from the business of *negotium* – the terms in which she offers herself to them.

Like Julia, the Duchess is forward in her wooing, but she moves delicately within the proper code of her social superiority to Antonio. As has often been observed, however, she uses this power to cancel itself, stripping herself of superiority in order to invent a private parity that they can occupy together. To see this act as a grave 'moral infraction'[33] is to assent far too easily to a passive conservatism I doubt Webster sought. But it is certainly a social infraction, and Antonio's wariness is, I believe, a response to that fact.

> Ambition, madam, is a great man's madness,
> That is not kept in chains, and close-pent rooms,
> But in fair lightsome lodgings, and is girt
> With the wild noise of prattling visitants,
> Which makes it lunatic, beyond all cure –
> Conceive not I am so stupid but I aim
> Whereto your favors tend: but he's a fool
> That, being a-cold, would thrust his hands i'th'fire
> To warm them.
>
> (I.i.420–8)

The elevation Antonio would reap from this alliance, however disguised, might easily be seen as the goal of *his* ambition, as Delio later thinks (II.iv.80–1). But I think it more likely, in view of the allusions to her tortures in Act IV, that the Duchess's arrogation of masculine sexual self-determination marks *her* aspiring mind, a self-projection very complexly viewed by the playwright.

The Duchess's goal is what we now perceive as a marital norm; as such, it may seem too domestic to count as disruptive social mobility. But such a goal was notably newfangled for the English aristocracy at this time, according to Stone.[34] Issues of female self-determination and mobility across class lines, both social and sexual, had of late come to be commonplace in London. Still, the notion was only slowly comprehended. The Duchess herself must toil to bring her openness into the open, flitting back and forth between attack, intrigue, and renunciation. She criticises high rank as hedging the will, forcing it into allegorical expression (as a tyrant fearfully equivocates, or as one dreams forbidden dreams), and calls on Antonio to awake (I.i.455). With coercive enticement she suggests what a wealthy mine she makes him lord of, and she puts off vain ceremony with a flourish, to appear as a desirous and desirable young widow with only half a blush. Such double, not to say duplicitous, language is necessary (though not sufficient) to capture the wary steward, who has previously been satisfied with fantasies. He must finally be bound by the spy behind the arras, a fitting aristocratic device. But even this forcible conversion of spirit to letter does not secure his free submission to the woman's will: he reluctantly swears but to 'remain the constant sanctuary / Of [her] good name' (I.i.460–1). His fears, not cowardly but conventional, help to justify the Duchess's use of the rhetorical wiles of intrigue, for which she has been condemned – precisely, I think, for their masculine force; more feminine wiles would be more comfortable to many readers. Still, for creating this heretofore unavailable option the Duchess receives what such readers often seem to regard as the just deserts of the mad 'spirit of greatness, or of woman'. She tries to combine male and female modes here, and her world proves just as hostile to the androgyne as to any other sort of monster.

The Duchess's marital inversion, conceptually a liberated move outward into the wilderness, takes the ironic practical form of a secret withdrawal that grows more and more claustrophobic. This effective quarantine encloses her gesture of liberation, which sought to enact the ideal of reciprocity between unequals, so often imputed to the citizens of a supposedly organic hierarchy. Perhaps this ideal originates as an ideology of the nurturant family, in any case, in Jacobean society it serves mainly as an ideological pacifier. The Duchess tries to reclaim it for familial privacy, with her forcible embrace: 'All discord, without this circumference, / Is only to be pitied, and not fear'd' (I.i.469–70). She refers, ironically, to her brothers: she tries to banish old relations from the sphere of the new. But her power is limited, the marriage depressingly short-lived. Though three children are born, they arrive between acts (save for the first child, who vanishes behind the horoscope intrigue). Our sense of husband and wife living in peace together derives chiefly from the scene in which that life ends (III.ii). Their small talk before Ferdinand appears suggests just the sort of deep and fruitful ease so lacking elsewhere in the play. (We do not see the children here; our impression of the nuclear family comes largely from the Duchess's lines about syrup for the son's cold.) But even their boudoir banter addresses (perhaps as usual?) the relationship's foundation in female power, and ironies abound. For instance, Antonio says he rises early after a night with his wife because he is glad his wearisome night's work is over. The affectionate inversion displaces the real reason for early rising: the oppressive need for secrecy, typical of adultery rather than of marriage. Lightheartedness is simultaneously present and painfully absent.

When Ferdinand's eerie appearance disrupts the scene (and allows the Duke a taste of substitution), the Duchess enters a new isolation prefatory to tragedy. Her response to her brother's erect dagger takes a desperately agile variety of forms: she claims that she can die like a prince; she argues rationalistically (and falsely) that she did not set out to make 'any new world, or custom' in marrying; she claims that he is too strict, that her reputation is safe, that she has a right to a future unwidowed. But all her claims fall on deaf, clenched Ferdinand as mere self-justification. Her rational mode of interaction between equals is doomed here, for the urge to parity is the source of the general problem for Ferdinand. When she realises this she flies without further question.

The tenure of her flight is as truncated in dramatic time as the marriage is. But now as then, the Duchess pauses to contemplate the larger significance of her actions, envying the birds of the field, who may marry without restriction; wondering whether her brothers' tyranny is a form of God's will, considering that 'nought made [her] e'er / Go right but heaven's scourge-stick' (III.v.80–1); fearing and yet hoping that she is, like the salmon, higher in value when nearer the fire. These metaphysical manoeuvres are her psychic defence in the face of capture by Bosola: she strives to perceive, and thus absorb and process, her experience *sub specie aeternitatis*, placing her action in a cosmos less inhospitable than her social world. But these defences also contain the kind of speculation familiar from Shakespearean tragedy, where the elevated are crushed as they inaugurate new conceptual options. I think Webster here moves beyond Shakespeare, whose women are insufficiently disillusioned to face the ultimate universal hostilities. The Duchess is the first fully tragic woman in Renaissance drama.

Once trapped, this woman recites a litany from Shakespearean tragic experience. Ironically courtly to the last, she exhibits a 'strange disdain', refusing to grovel and reanimate the ideology she has left behind. She speaks of the thinness of daily life, feeling herself playing a part in tedious theatre. She considers praying but instead curses the stars, calls down plagues on her tyrant lineage, and summons the ultimate and original chaos.[35] Like Job, she refuses to acknowledge sinfulness. Though utterly stripped like the bare, forked galley slave (IV.ii.28), she insists on her founding persona of power, 'Duchess of Malfi still' (IV.ii.142). But in reiterating her freedom's origin (in rank), she inevitably also reminds us of her deep inscription in that system, for she has no independent proper name. Webster insists that she is not Victoria, not Livia, not Lucrezia or Cordelia, but one born to be trapped in rank, however she may struggle in the destructive element.

But this irony escapes her, and she departs defiant, her own deed's creature to the end. She sustains investment only in her children, the bodily fruits of the personal human love that motivated her original action. The only hierarchy she will acknowledge is a residual and absconded heavenly one, utterly unrelated to any supposed earthly representatives. Having detranscendentalised her social world, she sarcastically puts off her last merely feminine attribute, her tediousness, and bids Bosola tell her brothers they can feed in peace. She leaves Cariola behind her, briefly absent from felicity only to mark the limits of the female model her mistress has razed, by biting and scratching and screeching a false and futile claim to the relational sanctuary of engagement to a young gentleman.

II SOCIAL MOBILITY

With Antonio we turn to the issue of upward mobility seen from below. Antonio and Bosola are presented as members of the new class of instrumental men, functional descendants of fifteenth-century retainers who fought the Wars of the Roses for their masters. Under Henry VIII and Elizabeth some of these men came to major power, and many more served in lesser capacities, often as bureaucratic specialists but also as all-purpose henchmen. Wallace MacCaffrey notes that 'the practice of the Elizabethan administration mingled confusedly the notion of a professional, paid public service with that of personal service to the monarch'.[36] These roles interact in Antonio and Bosola – steward and spy, bureaucrat and hit man. Each feels the new obscure insecurity later to be identified and explained by reference to the cash nexus, the shift from role to job. Each feels it differently.

Antonio enters the play as a choric voice, praising French courtly virtues and presenting the dramatis personae in the reified generic terms of the seventeenth-century 'character'. He is thus grounded in our sympathy (and distanced from the action) by his ideological and narrative spokesmanship, an apparently authorial substantiation that Webster immediately undermines by plunging him into political elevation. He loses his distancing footing at once, in part through the very virtues that entitled him to the choric role.

After the choric exposition, we hear of Antonio's first action, his victory in the joust, a traditional arena for aristocratic character contests. But for this achievement Ferdinand has only perfunctory applause: 'Our sister duchess' great master of her household? Give him the jewel: – When shall we leave this sportive action, and fall to action indeed?' (I.i.90–2). Such archaic and sanitised – that is to say, fictional – warfare bores the great Duke. Mobile men like Antonio strive continually to grasp such identity as Ferdinand seems effortlessly to possess (though we know better), but they fail to extract satisfying ratification from its established possessors. This problem is more pressing – and more developed – in Bosola than in Antonio, so I will postpone full discussion of it until the next section. But it is important to see that Antonio's efforts are ill-fated from the start.

We must also see Antonio as one who, like Bosola, is a man in the way of opportunity, a man with a fortune to make. In an early conversation (I.i.224–30) the two servants are superimposed by Ferdinand and the Cardinal, who consider them for a job of spying. As a relatively solid steward, Antonio occupies a more assured position than Bosola, whose tormenting search for secured identity constitutes his role in the play; perhaps for this reason Bosola is judged more apt for spying. But they share the a priori situation of men whose identity is achieved, not ascribed, in a society where such identity has not yet been accepted as fully substantial.

As we have seen, the Duchess's coercive offer animates Antonio's social insecurity. Her steward holds an achieved status of considerable power and security: the skilled estate manager was a Jacobean eminence. For Antonio has arrived at a local pinnacle, and he is satisfied to rest there in honourable service. In part because of this basic satisfaction, he fears the Duchess's adventurous proposal. Despite his erotic fantasies concerning his mistress, he must be coerced into further mobility. Antonio is a 'new man', his position based on new practices of personal self-determination. But his horizon of mobility is clearly circumscribed; beyond its limits he is ill at ease, unprepared for a society open to the top.[37]

Once he enters that turbulent realm his public behaviour becomes apparently more confident and aggressive, more typical of a man on the move. His sparring with Bosola, whose espionage he suspects from the start, takes the form of class insults. He sneers at him as an upstart, publicly adopting the attitude of the class he has secretly entered as the Duchess's consort: 'Saucy slave! I'll pull thee up by the roots' (II.iii.36); 'Are you scarce warm, and do you show your sting?' (II.iii.39). In so doing, he emphasises his own capacity to hire and fire, to make men and break them, ultimately to establish or deny their status; his sneers are combative and self-creative at once.

Such utterances are actually rooted in insecurity. 'This mole does undermine me. ... This fellow will undo me' (II.iii.14, 29). But Antonio's insecurity is less remarkable than its restriction to himself; he does not consider his wife and child in his fear. Barely able to cope with the storms of courtly intrigue to which the Duchess has brought him, he is 'lost in amazement' (II.i.173) when she goes into labour; having presented the cover story, he mutters, 'How do I play the fool with mine own danger!' (II.ii.69). When he hears the threats of Ferdinand's letters, he follows his wife's instructions, however grievingly, and leaves his family to face Ferdinand's murderous rage without him. He fears for his own safety more than for theirs.

Antonio's insecurity also appears expressly in terms of gender roles. He agreed to his wife's coercive marriage proposal with the deference of the subordinate he feels himself to be. Yet he is miserable at one level of this enforced marriage, insofar as it subordinates him to a woman in that private context where both personal and gender will are at issue. When she reassures him that her brothers will not ultimately cause them harm, that 'time will easily / Scatter the tempest' (I.i.471–2), he cannot allow the maternal address to his unmanliness. He asserts that 'These words should be mine, / And all the parts you have spoke, if some part of it / Would not have savour'd flattery' (I.i.472–4). But clearly he would never have spoken such words to her. It was not for him to dismiss her brothers as insignificant until she had done so; only then can he painfully claim, for his own sense of self, that he would have said the words.

A similar compensatory gesture occurs in the boudoir scene. Antonio listens silently in hiding while Ferdinand threatens his wife. Having sworn not to seek Antonio, the Duke leaves; only then does Antonio claim to wish that 'this terrible thing would come again, / That, standing on my guard, I might relate / My warrantable love' (III.ii.147–9). But he had been free just minutes earlier to defy Ferdinand. Then Bosola knocks; Antonio cries in dread, 'How now! who knocks? more earthquakes?' (III.ii.155). During the banter before Ferdinand's arrival Antonio had jested with relative ease about his privately subordinate position. But his elevation, because covert, has not given release from insecurity. He still feels the need to assert his own substance but does so only when he can avoid being held accountable for the assertion.

To rebuke Antonio's petty self-defences would be to miss the point. They should be recognised as unchosen responses to stresses not of his making. Antonio had filled a place where he felt secure and significant. When the Duchess converts his erotic daydreams to reality, they become social nightmares. He is not prepared for life in the seismographic realm of noble intrigue. The Duchess is not insolvent, for instance, as Webster might have arranged, with ample contemporary precedent, if he had desired to probe Antonio as a powerful new man of finance. Antonio is a man of regularities, not an improviser like Bosola. For this reason he is uncomfortable in his private relations with his wife, feeling bound both to the traditional hierarchy of rank, which enjoins his submission, and to the traditional gender hierarchy, which enjoins him to dominate. His culture has not prepared him to be a subordinate husband or to be a princely consort continually at risk. He is finally to be seen, and sympathised with, as a superior's ambitious love. He lives uncomfortably in the courtly world that has enclosed him. Indeed, we might say, the text infects him with ambition: by the time the news of his child reaches Rome he seems ambitious even to his best friend, who fears 'Antonio is betray'd. How fearfully / Shows his ambition now!' (II.iv.80–1). And at his death Antonio speaks of a 'quest of greatness' now his own, retrospectively apparent by its present collapse. This false dream he would spare his son, bidding him fly the courts of princes (a wish in fact ironically ungranted: the son's restoration at the play's end bodes ill for him, whatever it may say for Amalfi). Antonio's final action, the desperately naïve journey to the Cardinal for reconciliation, freezes him for us, as one whose unsought elevation never brought much sense of how to navigate the webs of alliance and enmity.

Like the other characters, Bosola is concerned to govern the grounding of his identity. As an employee he presents one of the most intricate examples of the Renaissance problematic of self-shaping. This representation is initially adumbrated through a dense blend of the predicates of counsellor, malcontent, have-not, henchman, and aesthete, roles all marked by alienation.

Bosola enters on the heels of Antonio's normative set piece on the French court, a model of public service in which the solipsistic vanities of the decorative gentleman are given a final cause in polit-

ical service to the prince. In Bosola's intensified and privatised enactment of Castiglione's courtly counsellor, Webster dissects the internal contradictions of the life to which the nation's ambitious
young men were drawn.

In swift succession Bosola annexes a variety of stances toward
'courtly reward and punishment'. Antonio first labels him 'the only
court-gall' (I.i.23), suggesting the standoffish or outcast malcontent,
almost a specialist Jeremiah. Yet this estimate is at once complicated further:

> his railing
> Is not for simple love of piety;
> Indeed he rails at those things which he wants,
> Would be as lecherous, covetous, or proud,
> Bloody, or envious, as any man,
> If he had means to be so.
>
> (I.i.23–8)

The distanced moralist and the envious parasite coincide in uneasy
dissonance.

Webster also evokes the unrewarded servant: in having Bosola
immediately demand belated reward from the Cardinal for a suborned murder, Webster links him to the social problem of the
veteran soldier, a stranger in his own land, dismissed from desert as
well as from service. Then as now this figure was unprovided for,
and Bosola has not even the minimal fact of service to his country
to cushion his return to social life. He has been a more private
soldier and has taken the fall. He will not rise in the pub or feast his
friends on Saint Crispin's Day. He can only sneer bitterly at his em-
ployers for their relative depravity. Still, he is more than a
Pedringano, much more than a Pistol, for Antonio has 'heard / He's
very valiant: this foul melancholy / Will poison all his goodness'. So
''Tis great pity / He should be thus neglected' (I.i.74–7). The most
complex of Bosola's ills, however, arise not from neglect but from
employment.

For Bosola is preferred, to spy on the Duchess. He is made a
henchman, an agent, an instrument, and so suggests the complicated new problems that arise from the status of *employee*. At this
point in English history, at the beginning of capitalist dominance,
service was undergoing the momentous shift from role to job, and
the ways in which it could ground a sense of self were changing.
Hitherto the prince had been seen as the sacramental source of

identity. Puttenham specifies this relation in a poem about Elizabeth: 'Out of her breast as from an eye, / Issue the rayes incessantly / Of her justice, bountie and might': these rays make 'eche subject clearly see, / What he is bounden for to be / To God his Prince and common wealth, / His neighbour, kindred and to himselfe'.[38] In this view service was simply a mode of assent to the static fact of ascriptive rank. As Stone shows, however, James's sale of honours helped to displace the power to confer identity from God's representative to the money that bought him.[39] As the human origin of rank was gradually revealed, it became clear that the power to confer it was freely available to those who could pull the strings of influence or purse. When ascriptive status emerged as a commodity, the king's sacred role as fount of identity began to decay, and with this shift came a change in the nature of identity itself. It became visible as something achieved, a human product contingent on wealth, connection, and labour. Later, when Marx described it theoretically, the notion could seem a conceptual liberation. As individuals express their life (i.e., as they 'produce their means of subsistence'), so they are. What they are, therefore, coincides with their production, both with what they produce and with how they produce.[40] Here human beings create themselves in the process of work. But in the Renaissance, when this insight began to be visible, it seemed a loss rather than a liberation. The obligation to found identity on one's actions seemed to sever the transindividual bonds that bound the polity together; it left one on one's own, save for the new power of cash, which could buy knighthoods, even titles. Marx of course clearly specifies this historical passage as a demolition: the exchange relation of capitalism, he says, 'has pitilessly torn asunder the motley feudal ties that bound man to his "natural superiors", and has left remaining no other nexus between man and man than naked self-interest, than callous "cash payment"'.[41] For Bosola, an early transitional figure, such clear formulation was not available. I think this nexus seemed to him like a lifeline, weaker perhaps than Elizabeth's nearly divine 'rayes' but still somehow linked to the ontologically solid ground of the ruling aristocracy.[42] In examining Bosola's 'neglect', Webster offers us the first tragic figure whose isolation is formulated in terms of employment by another.

Bosola initially reflects this coincidence of loss and possibility in bitterly deploring his 'miserable age, where only the reward / Of doing well is the doing of it' (I.i.31–2). Webster inverts the proverb to show that virtue is no longer its own reward but has become a commodity, only a means to an end. What formerly conferred a sense of absolute worth based on a collective cultural judgement has now lost its savour and is worthless unless vendible. Bosola is so far modern that he laments not the absence of the old mode but its residual presence. Still, he gets what he seems to want almost at once, within about two hundred lines, when Ferdinand says 'There's gold' (I.i.246). The rest of the play examines (as Bosola dourly inquires) 'what follows'. For the post of intelligencer aggravates his discontent, though it frees him from the material want and shame that dominate his galley life. But such a reward is mere hire and salary; he wants more, is miserable without it. Bosola cannot be said to be merely greedy for gain, a motive that no more explains his actions than it does Ferdinand's (see IV.ii.283–5). But we need to understand what more he wants.

Of course the answer is the same total self-realisation achieved by Cariola and Kent. But the personal service by which Bosola seeks this ultimate goal in fact reduces and dehumanises him. Where Kent's desires were completely coincident with his master's ('What wouldst thou? – Service'), Ferdinand's are withheld from Bosola ('Do not you ask the reason: but be satisfied' [I.i.257]) and so cannot be adopted as purposes. Bosola is specifically alienated from the utility of the 'intelligence' that is his labour's product, and so he creates a reified commodity and a reified self along with it. Marx formulates this action precisely.

> [Alienated] labour is *external* to the worker. ... it is merely a *means* to satisfy needs external to it ... the external character of labour for the worker appears in the fact that it is not his own, but someone else's, that it does not belong to him, that in it he belongs, not to himself, but to another. ... [The worker's activity] ... is the loss of his self.[43]

Instead of founding his identity, Bosola expends it in his work. Hungry for spiritual ratification, Bosola offers up to Ferdinand all he has. He expects this relationship, his relation to his prince, to found him; he expects the cash relation to carry the same kind of life-giving social blood as the earlier circuit of rule and fealty. But instead he merely spends himself and gets paid. Then, of course, he resorts to working harder, presuming he has not yet sufficiently earned his ontological paycheck; and the more he puts himself into his production, the more he loses himself. This sense of his desire helps construe what would otherwise seem a simply 'depraved' ongoing decision to continue doing Ferdinand's dirty work, much in spite, he claims, of his own good nature. Compulsively seeking to be paid, recognized, acknowledged, identified, Bosola expends efforts that intensify his sense of need but prove unequal to the task of filling it. The cash payment is the full exchange value to be got from this employer.

Bosola tries to obliterate this lack of ratification with a device prominent in the English machiavel's career: the aestheticising of intrigue. Noble machiavels may seek this stance in search of Ferdinand's sui generis alienation, but Bosola's purpose is different, even somewhat the reverse. A clue to his practice can be found in Georges Sorel's suggestion that artistic creation anticipates the way perfected work will feel in the society of the future.[44] This kind of activity confers just the unity that alienated labour undercuts. Hence, it may be argued, aestheticising can restore a felt unity or wholeness to actions by decontextualising them, separating them from the context that displays one's fragmentation. In focusing on the aesthetic shape of, say, a suborned act of violence or betrayal, to the exclusion of awareness of the context that marks it *as* suborned violation, alienated labourers can grasp a false sense of integrity by, as it were, alienating themselves from their alienation.[45] Seen in this light, Bosola's aestheticising functions as an evasion, a narcotic that lends a sense of totality while dulling awareness of its falsity. The part seems the whole, for he can devote his whole self (and so reconstitute it for the duration) to the means of the task by ignoring the opacity of its end.

The apricot incident offers a specimen of this technique. Here Bosola observes the Duchess's physical condition in considerable specialist detail (II.i.63–8) and applies a test for pregnancy – the typically alimentary Renaissance device of administering apricots (a laxative and thus labour stimulant). The trick is, he says to himself, 'A pretty one' (II.i.70): Bosola watches not only the Duchess but himself at work, taking pleasure in his professional prying, even setting up private dramatic ironies and sotto voce gloating for his own entertainment (see II.i.112, 117, 140, 145). Lukács offers a theoretical frame. 'The specialised "virtuoso", the vendor of his objectified and reified faculties does not just become the [passive] [sic] observer of society; he also lapses into a contemplative attitude *vis-à-vis* the workings of his own objectified and reified faculties'.[46] Bosola is thoroughly engaged (and thus unifyingly estranged) not only in practising the technicalities of his craft but in appreciating his own stylistic flair.[47]

We can see a similar bifurcation of consciousness in the interrogation scene (in III.ii), where Bosola discovers that Antonio is the Duchess's husband. To unfold it properly we must first examine Bosola's youth, which was characterised by a more ostentatiously aesthetic sense of his actions. For according to Delio, Bosola was

> a fantastical scholar, like such who study to know how many knots was in Hercules' club, of what colour Achilles' beard was, or whether Hector were not troubled with the toothache: he hath studied himself half blear-eyed, to know the true symmetry of Caesar's nose by a shoeing-horn; and this he did to gain the name of a speculative man.
>
> (III.iii.41–7)

Bosola has had the sort of university training that warped his predecessor Flamineo, gave him a sense of ambition, and fitted him for little but mobility. The Lylyan dandy's mode seems not to have worked for Bosola; instead he finally found work with the Cardinal and thus found his way to the galleys. But Delio's gossip shows that the exquisitely intellectual management of reputation is to Bosola a familiar tool, cognate with spying and thuggery; he has only retreated from its more precious manifestations.

Under Bosola's questioning, the Duchess screens her liaison by accusing Antonio of peculation (yet another false financial motive). When Bosola defends him against this accusation and other criticisms from Antonio's former fellows, she replies that Antonio was basely descended. Bosola then explicitly raises the contrast between ascription and achievement that is so central to the play: 'Will you make yourself a mercenary herald, / Rather to examine men's pedigrees than virtues?' (III.ii.259–60). This pointed challenge inspires her to reveal that Antonio is her husband, because it so clearly specifies the terms of her rebellion in choosing him. Bosola's reply says as much about himself as about her.

> No question but many an unbenefic'd scholar
> Shall pray for you for this deed, and rejoice
> That some preferment in the world can yet
> Arise from merit. The virgins of your land
> That have no dowries, shall hope your example
> Will raise them to rich husbands: should you want
> Soldiers, 'twould make the very Turks and Moors

Turn Christians, and serve you for this act.
Last, the neglected poets of your time,
In honour of this trophy of a man,
Rais'd by that curious engine, your white hand,
Shall thank you, in your grave for't; and make that
More reverend than all the cabinets
Of living princes. For Antonio,
His fame shall likewise flow from many a pen,
When heralds shall want coats to sell to men.
(III.ii.283–98)

Her unequal marriage will legitimate many other sorts of deserving mobility: the unemployed graduate will find preferment, the impoverished virgin security with a rich husband. Alien Turks and Moors will flock like Othellos and Ithamores to her side in gratitude for this tolerance of heterodox origin. And this multifoliate action will be eternised by neglected poets happy to get the work. The Duchess has ratified elevation by merit, and Bosola's applause betrays his own authentic experience of the dream – and of the attendant anomie, a blend of the loss of old securities and the lack of new ones.[48]

Many readers accept Bosola's speech as sincere; others presume it to be a ploy designed to unlock the Duchess's tongue. I think it is both: his own sincere response managed in pursuit of his employer's goal. This apparent contradiction is only a particular case of Lukács's reified employee's general deformation: 'His qualities and abilities are no longer an organic part of his personality, they are things which he can "own" or "dispose of" like the various objects of the external world.'[49] Bosola exchanges his authentic emotional stance for the information his master wants. But this self-commoditising exchange manipulation is asymmetrical, for Bosola does not easily revert to the dispassionate stance of the intelligencer. Perhaps the plan for the false pilgrimage is a sarcasm enabling the difficult shift from intimacy to the spy report by positing a ground for an intermediate stage of sneering distance: he can call her a politician, a soft quilted anvil, and so forth and return to his habitual malcontent mode. But even this self-manipulation (if that is what it is) is not fully anaesthetic, for when Bosola *returns* to his commoditised state (the obvious force of the mediate pause of 'What rests, but I reveal / All to my lord?') it is with self-loathing: 'O, this base quality / Of intelligencer!' (III.ii.326–8). A further deflection is needed, a universal projection of the commodity model: 'why, every quality i'th' world / Prefers but gain or commendation: / Now, for this act I am certain to be rais'd, / *And men that paint weeds to the life are prais'd*' (III.ii.328–31). If the Duchess's act was sordid, and his own no lower than any other, Bosola may sedate the sympathy he had for her, at least long enough to file his report.

I will pass more briefly by the well-known torture and murder scene, pausing only to note how it combines the predilections of Ferdinand and his agent. The motive force is of course the brother's, a fact often missed, owing perhaps to his apparent absence. Michael Warren (of the Nuffield Theatre) has suggested that Ferdinand's role in this scene might be made clear by 'having Ferdinand on or above the stage, physically directing the action';[50] I would prefer to have the Duke visible but inactive, frozen in his contemplative mode of alien voyeur. For his part, Bosola steeps himself in procedure, but in the process he is touched by the insistent coherence of his fellow galley slave. She does not reach for external legitimation as he has done but rests in the fact that she is, like Middleton's Beatrice-Joanna, 'the deed's creature', needing no DeFlores to tell her so. And as Bosola lives the parts he plays, his dismissal of earthly values besieges his increasingly stunted goals, even as he pursues ever more grimly the aesthetic anaesthesia of obsession with form. He is finally silent throughout the strangling, returning to life (that is, jerking away from reflection to instrumentality) with the uncharacteristically brutal 'Some other strangle the children' (IV.ii.239). He seems barely under control in the face of the tragedy he has caused, less and less confident of what has now come to seem repayment from Ferdinand.

Instead, of course, Ferdinand rewrites the contract (repudiating debt as Jacobean nobles often did) by pardoning Bosola's *murders*, ironically restoring to his agent the fully humanising capacity of the moral sense. (The 'gift' inverts Lear's denial of Kent's loyal advice about Cordelia.)

> Why didst thou not pity her? what an excellent
> Honest man mightst thou have been
> If thou hadst borne her to some sanctuary!
> Or, bold in a good cause, oppos'd thyself
> With thy advanced sword above thy head,
> Between her innocence and my revenge!
>   (IV.ii.273–8)

Action beyond the employer's instruction is available only to the independent human, not to the tool that cannot think for itself.

When Ferdinand challenges Bosola's humanity, he speaks his own heart too, called out of alienation too late, like Bosola's. But this castigation, meant to deflect his pain, only postpones it. In 'pardoning' his henchman, he schizophrenically enacts revenge and forgiveness at once.

Though the reproach nourishes Bosola's developing rebellion against his reification, he cannot at first abandon his own project. He feverishly opposes legal, moral, rational, and courtly sanctions to Ferdinand's dismissal, demonstrating his service to be in all particulars deserving. This dismissal perverts justice, he says; you shall quake for it; let me know wherefore; 'though I loath'd the evil, yet I lov'd / You that did counsel it; and rather sought / To appear a true servant, than an honest man' (IV.ii.331–3). The parallel with the Duchess's defence in the boudoir is striking; here as there the arguments are incomprehensible to Ferdinand, who again burrows into the dark. And like the Duchess, Bosola must face the ultimate failure of his project, for self-fashioning through employment:

> I stand like one
> That long hath ta'en a sweet and golden dream:
> I am angry with myself, now that I wake
> ...
>   off my painted honour:
> While with vain hopes our faculties we tire,
> We seem to sweat in ice and freeze in fire.
>   (IV.ii.323–5, 336–8)

His dream of ultimate grounding at the hands of another stands revealed as a delusive Petrarchan hope for an absolute beyond earthly grasp.

Faced with this failure, Bosola seeks his ontological grounding anew in a succession of chosen actions that he sees as neither derived from another (as his service was) nor evasively contemplative: 'somewhat I will speedily enact / Worth my dejection' (IV.ii.374–5). Personal vengeance will at least make him his own deed's creature. (This action obscurely coalesces the dual motives of compassion for the Duchess and anger over his own neglect: Ferdinand causes both sufferings.) When we next see Bosola he is accepting employment from the Cardinal with ironic alacrity: 'Give it me in a breath, and let me fly to't: / They that think long, small expedition win, / For musing much o' th' end, cannot begin' (V.ii.118–20). Security, like virtue, rests in the doing, in the subsuming process of unalienated action itself – in the search for a vengeance that he desperately wants to be decisive, constitutive. As Bosola opens himself more and more to the sacramental powers of moral confidence to be got from the act, he turns hopefully to a traditional self-sacrificial idiom: 'O penitence, let me truly taste thy cup, / That throws men down, only to raise them up' (V.ii.348–9). Though he still feels neglect and seeks advancement, he has shifted his ground to the seemingly more reliable realm of the transcendent moral order.

It can only be Webster's comment on this posture that Bosola's next action (reminiscent of Cordelia's death after Albany's 'The gods defend her!') is the unwitting murder of Antonio. His short-lived transcendental stance is utterly disrupted by this monstrous error: 'We are merely the stars' tennis-balls, struck and banded / Which way please them' (V.iv.54–5). The dream of self-substantiation through self-abnegation he now rejects as pointless, swearing 'I will not imitate things glorious, / No more than base: I'll be mine own example' (V.iv.81–2). He denies service to God and to Ferdinand alike as falsely coherent. In being his own example he returns to a stance like the Duchess's unitary 'I am Duchess of Malfi still'. If he cannot realise himself in any cosmic or social terms, he may yet seek identity *par sibi*, and so he grimly carries out a revenge now sheerly his own.

In the play's final action Bosola begins firmly enough, killing the Cardinal's innocent servant to secure the room. But mad Ferdinand comes in as to the wars, finally falling to action in deed, and wounds everyone to the death. Bosola lasts longest, playing his own Horatio for the astounded witnesses:

> Revenge, for the Duchess of Malfi, murdered
> By th' Arragonian brethren; for Antonio,
> Slain by this hand; for lustful Julia,
> Poison'd by this man; and lastly, for myself,
> That was an actor in the main of all
> Much 'gainst mine own good nature, yet i' th' end
> Neglected.
>
> (V.v.81–7)

He casts himself finally and summarily as an agent, a vicarious actor on behalf of all the victims, not least for himself, murderer and murdered at once, haunted throughout by an always pending better self, now definitively neglected. The supposed restorative of revenge has littered the stage, but the body count, though lavish, is sterile. Bosola ends by fixing our eyes on this lack, this gulf, in his final line, about 'another voyage'. For as Lear's undone button invokes nakedness and the heath, Bosola's departure is seaward, to the galleys, to the pathless wilderness from which he entered the play, a castaway looking for solid ground to call his own.

III CONCLUSION

This is the burden felt by all: the shaping of the social self in the abrasive zone between emergent and residual social formations. Webster's play is what Kenneth Burke calls a magical chart, a cognitive decree that names a problematic situation and voices an attitude toward it.[51] Webster's chart insists that the characters' urges and defining gestures are transformations of one another; that they are fundamentally constituted by, 'struck and banded which way please', a net of dimly understood and contradictory social forces; and that these forces shape and limit the kind of actions we habitually regard as individually authentic and chosen (and that carry the responsibilities we associate with tragedy and villainy). Webster provides a social world that constitutes what are clearly not the transcendental subjects of traditional moral inquiry.

Fredric Jameson suggests a more political repossession:

> The cultural monuments and masterworks that have survived tend necessarily to perpetuate only a single voice ... the voice of a hegemonic class. ... They cannot be properly assigned their relational place in a dialogic system without the restoration or artificial reconstruction of the voice to which they were initially opposed, a voice for the most part stifled and reduced to silence, marginalised, its own utterances scattered to the wind, or reappropriated in their turn by the hegemonic culture.[52]

I believe that this play was written, at least in significant part, to dissect the actual workings of the normative ideology set before us at its beginning. Far from providing criteria for the judgement of the heterodox characters (as criticism, seduced by power as order, has often presumed), this ideological frame and those who pose and endorse it are themselves to be judged by the 'heterodox'. Critics' moral judgements directed against the outcast Duchess (as lustful, irresponsible, unwomanly, womanish) emanate from this ideological centre; they are at one with high-minded humanist sneering at sycophants whom the centre in fact invents, summons up for service and ideological approbation. I believe that Webster strives to recover such stifled voices, to bare oppositional gestures unsurprisingly rewritten, both then and often even now, as womanish eccentricity or base-mindedness. My analysis has sought also to reclaim Ferdinand for understanding (if not sympathy) by reading his motives as the absolutised and finally self-destructive core of the nobility's project for dominance. Ferdinand's savage gestures strip to the skin the soothing discourse of reciprocity. To its incantations the play is addressed as a disruptive symbolic act, the reverse of Burkean Prayer – as an Imprecation.

From *PMLA*, 100:2 (1985), 167–81.

NOTES

[Frank Whigham's essay both connects with and departs from feminist readings of Webster's tragedy. By analysing sexuality rather than 'gender' or 'women', class transgression via marriage becomes the central issue of the play. Crucially, also, Whigham emphasises mobility – that is the shifting nature of social and sexual relations in this period. For reasons of space, some of the original notes have had to be cut. A newer version of the essay in revised form can be found in Professor Whigham's *Seizures of the Will* (Cambridge, 1996). The text used is *The Duchess of Malfi*, edited by John Russell Brown (London, 1964). Ed.]

1. For a summary of the debate, see David F. Aberle et al., 'The Incest Taboo and the Mating Patterns of Animals', in Paul Bohannon and John Middleton (eds), *Marriage, Family, and Residence* (Garden City, MI, 1968), pp. 3–19.

2. Jack Goody, 'A Comparative Approach to Incest and Adultery', in Paul Bohannon and John Middleton (eds), *Marriage, Family, and Residence* (Garden City, MI, 1968), pp. 21–46; 32, 35–42.

3. Kenneth Burke, *A Rhetoric of Motives* (Berkeley, CA, 1969), pp. 279–80. However, see Arthur F. Marotti's (Countertransference, the Communication Process, and the Dimensions of Psychoanalytic Criticism', *Critical Inquiry*, 4 [1978], 471–89) approach to this problem, esp. p. 486.

4. Talcott Parsons, 'The Incest Taboo in Relation to Social Structure', in Rose Laub Coser (ed.), *The Family: Its Structures and Functions* (New York, 1974), pp. 13–30; 19.

5. Raymond Firth, *We, the Tikopia: A Sociological Study of Kinship in Primitive Polynesia* (New York, 1936), p. 340.

6. Ibid., p. 304.

7. Parsons, 'The Incest Taboo', p. 18.

8. Lawrence Stone, *The Family, Sex, and Marriage in England, 1500–1800* (London, 1977), pp. 126, 128.

9. Parsons, 'The Incest Taboo', p. 18.

10. Stone, *Family*, 60–1.

11. Baldassare Castiglione, *The Book of the Courtier* (1528), trans. Thomas Hoby (1561) (New York, 1966), p. 29.

12. F. L. Lucas (ed.), *The Complete Works of John Webster*, 4 vols (London, 1927), vol. 2, pp. 23–4.

13. Clifford Leech, *John Webster: A Critical Study* (London, 1951), pp. 100–6.

14. J. R. Mulryne, '*The White Devil* and *The Duchess of Malfi*', in *Jacobean Theatre*, ed. John Russell Brown and Bernard Harris (New York, 1960), pp. 201–25; 223.

15. Ibid., p. 57.

16. Muriel Bradbrook, *John Webster, Citizen and Dramatist* (New York, 1980), p. 144.

17. On the general issue of 'degree' compare John L. Selzner, 'Merit and Degree in Webster's *The Duchess of Malfi*' (*English Literary Renaissance*, 11 [1981], 70–80), a study that overlaps in some ways with my own. On *par sibi* see Hereward T. Price, 'Like Himself', *Review of English Studies*, 16 (1940), 178–81. At this point I should also mention Bob Hodge's interesting article (with David Aers and Gunthers Kress, 'Mine Eyes Dazzle: False Consciousness in Webster's Plays', in *Literature, Language, and Society in England, 1580–1680* [Totowa, NJ, 1981], pp. 100–21) on false consciousness in Webster, which covers much of the same ground this essay addresses.

18. Nicholas Brooke, *Horrid Laughter in Jacobean Tragedy* (New York, 1979), pp. 52, 54, 61.

19. Mark Poster, *Existential Marxism in Postwar France: From Sartre to Althusser* (Princeton, NJ, 1975), p. 13.

20. James Nohrnberg, *The Analogy of 'The Faerie Queene'* (Princeton, NJ, 1976), p. 423.

21. Firth, *We, the Tikopia*, p. 340.

22. Ibid., p. 341.

23. This argument entirely revalues the status of Ferdinand's turbulent response to his sister's marriage as evidence of incest. It reflects similarly

on the formulation that he responds as a cuckold rather than as a wounded brother (proposed by Elizabeth Brennan. 'The Relationship between Brother and Sister in the Plays of John Webster', *Modern Language Review*, 58 [1963], 488–94; 493). Whether these arguments are alternatives I am not sure.

24. Raymond Williams points out that the term 'alienation' could literally mean 'insanity' (as in 'alienation of the faculties') at this time (*Keywords: A Vocabulary of Culture and Society* [New York, 1976], p. 29). See also *OED* 'alienation' 4.

25. I cite Nohrnberg's translation of Comes's Renaissance version from the *Mythologies*, which details the death (see Nohrnberg, *The Analogy*, p. 433n.); for Pausanias, see *Description*, 9.31.7–8.

26. I owe this striking and obviously authorial view of the internal hair to Susan C. Baker, 'The Static Protagonist in *The Duchess of Malfi*', *Texas Studies in Language and Literature*, 22 (1980), 343–57.

27. Alexander Allison observed a vague version of this balanced contrast some two decades ago. Speaking of the 'self-will and erotic bent' that Ferdinand and the Duchess share, he says that 'obverse aspects of the same temperamental excess have brought brother and sister to catastrophe' ('Ethical Themes in *The Duchess of Malfi*', *Studies in English Literature, 1500–1900*, 4 [1964], 263–73; 266).

28. George Puttenham, *The Arte of English Poesie* (1589), ed. Gladys Doidge Willcock and Alice Walker (Cambridge, 1936), p. 106.

29. I think Webster meant to present us with a confusing social problem, not with an occasion for easy and moralistic response. Despite documentary arguments against widows remarrying and for the obligations of state service, it seems unlikely that the audience is supposed to find the Duchess's action antisocial, hubristic, and licentious, as a certain sector of well-known criticism claims (see, for instance, Leech, *Webster*; James L. Calderwood, 'The Duchess of Malfi: Styles of Ceremony', *Essays in Criticism*, 12 [1962], 133–47; and Joyce E. Peterson, *Curs'd Example: 'The Duchess of Malfi' and Commonweal Tragedy* [Columbia, MO, 1978]). Certainly the Duchess's plight is pathetic in personal terms, but I object to seeing her as deservedly punished (nonetheless, as it were), chiefly because the ideology that grounds that judgement – Ferdinand's ideology – is the very ideology the play puts most deeply in question.

30. Julian Pitt-Rivers, 'Honour and Social Status', in J. G. Peristiany (ed.), *Honour and Shame: The Values of Mediterranean Society* (Chicago, 1966).

31. See Inga-Stina Ekebald, 'The "Impure Art" of John Webster', *Review of English Studies*, 9 (1958), 253–67; see also Pitt-Rivers, 'Honour

and Social Status', pp. 47–50; and Keith Thomas, 'The Place of Laughter in Tudor and Stuart England', *TLS*, 21 (January 1977), 77.

32. See Judith M. Bradwick and Elizabeth Douvan, 'Ambivalence: The Socialization of Women', in Vivian Gornick and Barbara K. Moran (eds), *Women in Sexist Society* (New York, 1971), pp. 225–41; p. 231.

33. Calderwood, '*The Duchess of Malfi*', pp. 136–9.

34. Stone, *Family*, pp. 180–91.

35. Leech comments that 'this longing for the first chaos links her with many characters in Elizabethan and Jacobean drama whose ambitions are thwarted and who would in anger overturn the hierarchies of 'degree' (*John Webster*, pp. 76–7).

36. Wallace MacCaffrey, 'Place and Patronage in Elizabethan Politics', *Elizabethan Government and Society*, ed. S. T. Bindoff, Joel Hurstfield, and C. H. Williams (London, 1961), pp. 95–126; p. 104.

37. For discussions that presume Antonio to be ambitious in the wooing scene, see Ralph Berry, *The Art of John Webster* (Oxford, 1972), pp. 108–9; and Michael R. Best, 'A Precarious Balance: Structure in *The Duchess of Malfi*' in Alan Brissenden (ed.), *Shakespeare and Some Others* (Adelaide, 1976), p. 169.

38. Puttenham. *The Arte of English Poesie*, p. 100.

39. Stone, *The Crisis of Aristocracy, 1558–1641* (Oxford, 1965), pp. 65–128.

40. C. J. Arthur (ed.), *The German Ideology* (New York, 1947), p. 42.

41. Lewis S. Feuer (ed.), *The Communist Manifesto: Basic Writings on Politics and Philosophy* (Garden City, MI, 1959), p. 9.

42. Robert Ornstein has adumbrated this idea less technically, suggesting that Bosola 'seeks to give meaning to his life by loyal service' (*The Moral Vision of Jacobean Tragedy* [Madison, WI, 1960], p. 143).

43. Dirk H. Struik (ed.), *Economic and Philosophical Manuscripts of 1844* (New York, 1964), pp. 110–11.

44. Georges Sorel, *Reflections on Violence*, trans. T. E. Hulme (London, 1916), pp. 39, 287.

45. See George Lukács, 'Reification and the Consciousness of the Proletariat', in *History and Class Consciousness*, trans. Rodney Livingstone (Cambridge, 1971), pp. 139–40; and Hans-Robert Jauss, 'The Idealist Embarrassment: Observations on Marxist Aesthetics', *New Literary History*, 7 (1975), 195–200.

46. Lukács, 'Reification', p. 100.

47. For more on the significance of this emphasis on style and manner, see Frank Whigham, *Ambition and Privilege: The Social Tropes of Elizabethan Courtesy Theory* (Berkeley, CA, 1984), pp. 34–9, 88–95.

48. Among those who have made this connection are Best ('A Precarious Balance', p. 173), Selzer ('Merit and Degree', p. 75), and Bradbrook (*John Webster*, p. 159).

49. Lukács, 'Reification', p. 100.

50. Michael Warren, '*The Duchess of Malfi* on the Stage', in Brian Morris (ed.), *John Webster* (London, 1970), p. 66.

51. Kenneth Burke, *The Philosophy of Literary Form: Studies in Symbolic Action* (Berkeley, CA, 1973), pp. 3–8.

52. Fredric Jameson, *The Political Unconscious* (Ithaca, NY, 1981), p. 85.

9

The Moral Design of *The Duchess of Malfi*

R. S. WHITE

Thomas Wilson, a lawyer and literary theorist of the mid sixteenth century,[1] writes of rhetoric moving emotions to stir the conscience or to spur others to moral action. His words are meant for both lawyers and tragic dramatists: 'In moving affections, and stirring the judges to be grieved, the weight of the matter must be so set forth, as though they saw it plain before their eyes' (t 1 v) ... 'Now in moving pity, and stirring men to mercy, the wrong done must first be plainly told: or if the Judges have sustained the like extremity, the best were to will them to remember their own state' (t 1 r). This is the theory behind what I wrote of in *Innocent Victims: Poetic Injustice in Shakespearian Tragedy* as a genre, or inset genre.[2] In each of Shakespeare's tragedies a character is depicted who does not 'deserve' to die, and is innocent, first in the legal sense of 'not guilty', secondly in the moral sense of being virtuous, and thirdly in the scheme of expectations of poetic justice set up in each play. Children in plays like *Richard III* and *Macbeth* are clear examples, as is Cinna the Poet in *Julius Caesar*, torn for his bad verses and nothing else. But the more obvious and fully depicted examples are women such as Ophelia, Lady Macduff, Lucrece, Desdemona, Cordelia, and others. It could be argued that protagonists like Hamlet or even Othello are innocent victims, and also that love tragedy as a genre, particularly *Romeo and Juliet*, is underpinned by the pattern. In Wilson's sense, the virtuous innocents are presented in each particular play as by an advocate 'in moving pity, and stirring men to mercy', so that the audience will be like a jury encouraged to project emotionally into the situation and learn some moral lesson about avoiding cruelty and about avoiding the perpetration of injustice. That this motif was important to audience response in Elizabethan times is evidenced by the fact that one of the very few eye-witness accounts of a Shakespeare play mentions only the pity stirred for Desdemona.

My analysis was written at the time as a conscious contribution to feminist criticism, during the emergence of this movement into Shakespeare studies. The book began to appear in bibliographies of feminist criticism, and influenced (for example) Dympna Callaghan's *Woman and Gender in Renaissance Tragedy: A Study of 'King Lear', 'Othello', 'The Duchess of Malfi' and 'The White Devil'.*[3] Feminist social and literary theory has developed and changed since then, and has broadened into gender studies. Along the way, its earlier emphasis on victimology has been questioned as sentimental, and can now be made to look somewhat dated as feminist critics assert power rather than weakness. At the same time, the generic emphasis on the plight of innocent victims in Renaissance tragedy has found independent support and need not be abandoned. G. K. Hunter in his authoritative volume of the Oxford History of Literature, *English Drama 1586–1642*,[4] has formally created a category of drama which he calls 'Victim Tragedy', although his account mentions only some plays which present the male hero as victim, notably beginning (as I did) with Hieronimo in Kyd's *The Spanish Tragedy*. Some of the female victims, and particularly Webster's Duchess of Malfi, are mentioned in a later section entitled, wrongly in the case of the Duchess, 'Women in Power'.[5] The Duchess may begin with high social station and wealth, but power is something which is insidiously stripped from her. Jonathan Dollimore and Alan Sinfield sketch an argument that she is the victim of society as it is presented in Webster's play.[6] Derek Cohen in *Shakespeare's Culture of Violence*[7] analyses Shakespeare's tragedies with a generally didactic concern in mind, that the plays have a conscious design to sensitise us to the moral framework that allows audiences to condemn, for example, the blinding of Gloucester as well as the fates of the doomed heroines: the same moral and educative emphasis that I argued for in *Innocent Victims*. Harry Keyishian has set up a different framework in *The Shapes of Revenge: Victimisation, Vengeance, and Vindictiveness in Shakespeare*,[8] arguing that what used to be called revenge tragedy turns on the dramatist's alertness to victimisation, not just in moral and ethical dimensions but just as importantly in the psychological sphere. Keyishian stresses 'the potentially redemptive functions of revenge', and once again he takes his bearings from the play that was the most successful on the Elizabethan stage, *The Spanish Tragedy*. All of which encourages me to believe that a chapter on the play that I had signalled as a paradigm case of the tragedy of the innocent victim, Webster's *The Duchess of Malfi*, is still timely.[9]

The Duchess of Malfi is generically unusual, even unique in Elizabethan and Jacobean tragedy. The norm of tragedy was the fall of an initially heroic man or the rise and fall of a great villain. This play is the tragedy of a virtuous woman who achieves heroism through her death. Not only this, she is inescapably a victim of others' evil and of social attitudes, rather than one undermined by inner weakness or overweening ambition. The only comparable works to *The Duchess* are Shakespeare's narrative poem, *The Rape of Lucrece*, Webster's own *The White Devil* (where a woman is at the centre, but this time she is not so innocent) and in a different way *Julius Caesar*, where the centre of the play is not so much one heroic character or villain but rather the issues surrounding the death of Caesar – the causes and then the effects of assassination.

This uniqueness seems to be the main reason why modern critics have had difficulty in dealing with the play. If one reads the Introduction to the most thorough edition, John Russell Brown's Revels text,[10] we find almost strange contortions, carried out apparently without conscious knowledge, to dislodge the Duchess from centre stage: the theatrical history emphasises the fame of the leading male actors, to the extent that Brown can confidently hypothesise that 'In any reconstruction of the first performance of *The Duchess* the female parts will appear less interesting than the roles played by Lowin and Burbage about whom so much is known' (p. xxi). The section on 'Characters' begins with two pages on Bosola, two on Antonio, and only one half-page paragraph on the Duchess, while 'Structure' deals thoroughly with Bosola and Ferdinand. Even more telling is Brown's treatment of the play's 'Viewpoint', where he mentions only critics who dwell on Ferdinand, Antonio or Bosola. Brown is not unusual in his treatment. Rather, he follows what seems to be a well-worn critical formula or orthodoxy dating from T. S. Eliot. In death as in life the Duchess is a victim, this time of critics who understandably go on to find something distorted and even 'muddled' in the play as a whole. All that they can make of it is 'savage farce'. Immediately, scepticism must be expressed about readings of the play which turn it into an indulgence in cruelty for its own sake, an exercise in 'horrid laughter', an amoral and detached presentation of strange psychological states. Instead, since we can be sure that Webster has as part of his intention, and that the play has as part of its design, the creation of a value-system, it is reasonable and virtually necessary to acknowledge its moral terms and the centrality of the Duchess herself, in order to understand the play as a totality. One of those critics who appreciates this point is Dena Goldberg. She argues in *Between Worlds: A study of the plays of John Webster* that the play represents implicit challenges to laws created to regulate sexual behaviour, and that the most fundamental attack is that 'the innate goodness of the Duchess stands as an overwhelming argument against the very basis of law as social necessity', and that her 'impulsive goodness' leads to 'totally anarchistic' (but not chaotic) implications: 'Goodness, Webster shows us, is possible in the world, but it cannot be created by force or rational control'. Equally, Goldberg argues, the play depicts 'the futility of appealing to any law when law is synonymous with power ... '.[11]

In fact, the plot could hardly be more emphatic as an example of the tragedy of the innocent victim. (I should stress once again that 'victim' does not require a lack of assertiveness – far from it, in this case.) The Duchess, a young widow who by inheritance of property has suddenly become a potent commodity in the eyes of her family,[12] falls in love with her steward and marries him, thus arousing the ire of her brothers, who succeed in having her murdered. Like the rival families in *Romeo and Juliet* they suffer remorse and penitence, but unlike Shakespeare's families, they meet their deaths in ways which satisfy poetic justice. A whole society is indicted, and the Duchess's integrity and refusal to accept empty social forms fuel a cause that outlasts her mercenary persecutors. When stated so baldly the narrative is self-evidently ethically instructive, powerful in its manipulation of sympathies, and not at all problematical in its tone, which is designed to arouse anger against the Duchess's family and society at large. We can see clearly why Bertolt Brecht (collaborating with H. R. Hays) would have been sufficiently attracted to the play, as one about economic alienation and class, to rewrite it, ending with the death scene of the Duchess herself.[13] He, at least, was not distracted from the central narrative line.

At the centre of any analysis of *The Duchess of Malfi*, whether moral, aesthetic or thematic, must be the violent and powerful scene of the strangling of the Duchess, in Act IV, scene ii. Here the plot on the Duchess is consummated, the central character is killed, and the action precipitates radical changes in at least two characters, Ferdinand and Bosola. In terms of the moral design, Webster makes it clear by his manner of presentation that the audience is to be shocked into certain recognitions. It may be possible in earlier scenes to see the clandestine relationship between the Duchess and Antonio as dangerously unwise and even foolish. It may be possible early on to blame the indignity of such a furtive and closeted affair on the Duchess's rash choice to fall in love beneath her station (young widows were seen as particularly susceptible to lust), rather than upon her brother's malevolence – in short, to blame her for the consequences. But in this scene it becomes impossible to do so without remaining inhumanly detached from the action.[14] At the beginning of the scene, the Duchess is seen as a quiet, if bewildered, centre of sanity, as the madmen enter. They are, significantly, representatives of respectable professions – a lawyer, a doctor, a priest and an astrologer – as if the apparently respectable occupations of such people have some latent but endemic madness within their very core, just as Ferdinand's lycanthropia is, with the benefit of hindsight, an appropriate significant of his formerly rapacious motives. The madmen take delight in inflicting misery on others. Bosola enters like a grim and ghoulish executioner, willingly doing the bidding of the brothers as a hired assassin. What strikes us throughout the horrifying events that follow is the dignity of the Duchess as she firmly resists any recriminations or pleas for mercy. She is 'Duchess of Malfi still', revealing patience, stoicism and accepting complete responsibility for her actions. It is what happens after her death that clinches the moral dimensions of the play. Even character is subsidiary to morality here, as people seem to step out of their roles under the pressure of the moral pattern, a phenomenon we often find in Brecht, perhaps adding another reason for his decision to rewrite *The Duchess of Malfi*. First, Bosola instantly realises the implications of the 'mists of error' he has been wandering in, and his almost instantaneous repentance shows Webster risking, or even abandoning, any principle of consistent characterisation in favour of pointing a moral. Ferdinand enters:

> [Executioners *strangle* Cariola *and exeunt with her body.*
> *Enter* Ferdinand.]
> **Ferdinand** Is she dead?
> **Bosola** She is what
>   You'll'd have her. But here begin your pity.

> [Bosola *draws the traverse and shows the children strangled.*]
> Alas, how have these offended?
> **Ferdinand**   The death
> Of young wolves is never to be pitied.
> **Bosola**   Fix your eye here.
> **Ferdinand**   Constantly.
> **Bosola**   Do you not weep?
> Other sins only speak; murther shrieks out:
> The element of water moistens the earth,
> But blood flies upwards, and bedews the heavens.
> **Ferdinand**   Cover her face. Mine eyes dazzle: she di'd young.
> **Bosola**   I think not so: her infelicity
> Seem'd to have years too many.
>
> (IV.ii.251–61)

Although unmoved by the sight of the dead children the fact of the Duchess's corpse causes a change in Ferdinand's attitude. He does not exactly repent, but rather he refuses to take any responsibility for the murder he has commissioned. He stresses the Duchess's 'innocence', regrets that Bosola killed her, hates him for it, but promises to pardon him. Bosola's response is indignation at Ferdinand's ingratitude, and a healthy outrage at the pardon, coming from one who has authorised the crime:

> The office of justice is perverted quite
> When one thief hangs another.
>
> (IV.ii.300–1)

Ferdinand's response is psychologically revealing, since his future degeneration into the form of madness of lycanthropia can be seen as a mental refuge from accepting responsibility for his own actions – a way of avoiding conscience and remorse by entering madness. Even the desperate attempts of the maid Cariola to avoid death are presented as rather frenetic and undignified, in contrast to the Duchess's dying moments. Not that we can blame Cariola, of course, for this, but the dramatic contrast is rather set up to enforce a sense of the Duchess's courage and open-eyed maturity. In short, everything in the scene is designed to startle us into a firm and fundamental recognition of the innocence of the Duchess, to make us reassess any suspicion of her own collusion, and to highlight the injustice. Justice and injustice, innocence and guilt, are the central terms of the scene, as of the play as a whole.

I said that this scene forces us to reassess the Duchess's former actions, and here is where I should emphasise that the moral structure of a play is something that has to be proved on the pulses of the audience's experience of the play through a span of time. The moral design of a drama is not something static, an abstract matter of good and bad, rewards and punishments. It is more flexible, drawing us into traps of judging people only to find our judgements shattered in a moral awakening. For there is enough in the Duchess's actions earlier in the play to seduce us into seeing events at least to some extent from the side of Ferdinand and the Cardinal, even if we do not particularly like them. We may judge her in the way that we may blame Cordelia for obstinacy or Desdemona for pliability. We are initially encouraged to wish the Duchess to be less foolhardy, less carnal in her desires, more diplomatic and less provocative in her dealings with her brothers. These feelings come to a head in the scene in which she playfully banters with Antonio. He jokingly leaves her speaking to her mirror, only to reveal inadvertently to Ferdinand the name of her love. The scene is designed at first to make us think that her love is too close to coquettishness and her actions too naïve and immature. But if we do not reconsider, then we are siding with the forces of evil, and the fact that the death scene brutally shatters our earlier preconceptions makes it all the more powerful a moral lesson because we have been initially caught out. Forced to rethink all the preceding action, we must begin to respect the fact that the Duchess has lived her life on a completely different moral and ethical basis from her victimisers. While they have been intent on dragging private and emotional matters into the public world of money and politics, she has asserted her right to keep the private truly private, and she has firmly reserved the choices made by her emotions to herself and her lover. Although these actions are forced upon her by others, they still represent the cardinal rules of love in drama. A comedy is defined by the lovers' resistance to outside pressure (usually from an obstructive father) while tragedy in love occurs invariably when a lover such as Othello or Antony allows emotional life to become confused with public responsibility, or when Romeo commits a very public murder. Furthermore, the Duchess's apparent flightiness and her behaviour with Antonio surely exhibit a woman in love – loyal and playful – protecting the intimacy of the relationship from the callous and brutal world around her. We must recognise the legitimacy of the Duchess's choice of life, as a positive and courageous act. To his credit, Bosola, her murderer, afterwards calls her 'sacred innocence', not wishing her otherwise in some worldly and circumspect way. If she had been more cautious, more diplomatically cagey, then she may have escaped her fate but she would not have been the person she is, 'Duchess of Malfi still'. The victimisation and death of the Duchess allow us to see her former life as valid and even admirable, even if it is not 'the way of the world' in such a destructively manipulative society. There is also the overriding truth that, having fallen in love with a suitor objectionable to her powerful brothers on class terms (as well as posing a threat to their economic calculations for the family fortune), she becomes the victim not of her own desires but of circumstances – necessity as she calls them:

> Necessity makes me suffer constantly.
> And custom makes it easy.
>   (IV.ii.30–1)

More important still, however, she is the victim of others' evil.

We should turn now to her victimisers and ask the reasons for their actions which are imposed upon the Duchess as a form of 'necessity'. We should ask the question of this play and of any other tragedy, *is* there some kind of extra-human destiny at work? Is it a tragedy purely of circumstances, or is the fate of the Duchess the result of human actions committed by malevolent agents? Without much doubt, we have to conclude that in this play the third option is the correct one – neither gods nor impersonal fate cause the events of this play, but human decisions and human actions. We should now look closely at the moral status of the Duchess's persecutors, Bosola, Ferdinand and the Cardinal. To do so is not to apply squeamish twentieth-century moral sensibility to an amoral and decadent play revelling in evil, as many critics who see the play as some kind of 'farce' argue. Instead, such a scrutiny is directly enforced by the moral design, the ideology of the play itself.

In dealing with the Duchess's victimisers, let us begin with the lowest on the social scale and work our way towards the top. Bosola is the one who directly carries out the strangling of the Duchess, and he would appear to be deeply incriminated if only because of this fact. The closer we inspect his role, however, the more interesting and complex it becomes. Just as we found in the climactic scene, so throughout the play, it would seem that Bosola is either a character at the mercy of other people, and in this sense a victim himself, or not really a character at all but a device used by Webster to direct our moral sympathies in this way and that.

Although he is introduced by Antonio as 'The only court-gall', what we see of him immediately is his role as a suitor to the Cardinal, and one who apparently deserves some favour. The Cardinal dismisses him, and this allows Bosola to launch into a condemnation of the Cardinal and his brother Ferdinand which informs us that the two characters are rich, but untrustworthy and treacherous. Delio reveals that Bosola has been in prison for seven years, for a murder commissioned by the Cardinal, and Antonio then praises Bosola for valour, regretting his black melancholy. As the play unfolds, we discover that Bosola's condemnation is indeed a fair moral comment. A little later Ferdinand hints that Bosola is rather ugly (I.ii.160ff), suggesting that this is why he has such a low reputation at court, and Bosola with hurt pride (and an understandable rejection of neoplatonic commonplaces) retorts that the face does not necessarily reveal the character of a man. On the other hand, against his moral acuteness, Bosola is revealed as able to be bought. When Ferdinand gives him gold, he asks cynically but with acquiescence, 'Whose throat must I cut?' Once again, Brecht would have been interested in the way that economic circumstances can underpin compromising moral choices for one who styles himself 'a blunt soldier' (V.ii.169), and who at the end, in his own private tragedy, laments 'We are merely the stars' tennis-balls, struck and banded / Which way they please them' (V.iv.53–4). On hearing that he must 'observe' – or spy upon – the Duchess he has a pang of conscience, calling Ferdinand a corrupter and refusing to be used as an impudent traitor himself. Once again, however, he is bought, this time with a job as provisor of the horse, and declares to Ferdinand with some relish, 'I am your creature'. In doing so, he ironically voices an attitude which will more and more become a sign of the hypocritical court itself.

> Let good men, for good deeds, covet good fame,
> Since place and riches oft are bribes of shame;
> Sometimes the devil doth preach.
> (I.ii.210–12)

Thereafter, we see Bosola in different and even contradictory roles, as confidant to Antonio, as murderer of 'sacred innocence' and as sincere penitent; and as unrepentant murderer of villains. He finally recognises that his own death is plotted as a consequence of his actions, does a good turn for Antonio, and turns into the revenger of the Duchess's death, killing both the Cardinal and Ferdinand in the name of 'what is just'.

How are we to interpret the varying functions of such a confusing character? One answer is to say that he is not conceived as a consistent dramatic character but as a convenient stage device for voicing different points of view at different times, and for adjusting the audience's moral attitudes, just as Brecht regarded all Elizabethan 'characters'. But there is a different explanation, which helps us to interpret the moral design of the play as a whole. Bosola is a character who has no 'place and riches', somebody on the lowest rungs of the courtly society, and in his insecurity he feels driven to carry out whatever duty will bring him either enhanced status or, later in the play, the reward for virtue. He is at the mercy of the characters above him who have power of hiring, firing and even murdering him. We might deplore his acceptance of the charge to spy upon and later murder the Duchess, but we should not be too critical of one who, this time because of his social ostracism and economic dependency, must simply do whatever work he can to gain social acceptance. It may be curious that he ends up as something of a moral spokesman but Webster's point may be that it is almost arbitrary whether a person who is deprived of any standing will do evil or good. *Class* is the central issue, then, Bosola is not so much the victim of circumstances or 'the stars', but of evil people who happen to be higher in the social scale than himself, and who are willing to use him ruthlessly to do their vicious deeds. He is not so much a 'character' with what Hazlitt would call 'mixed motives', but an agent acted upon by others, and constructed upon the basis of social class, exactly as Brecht thought we all are.

That class is an important issue to Webster is signalled in the very unusual statement he makes in his dedication of the play to Baron Berkeley. Normally a dedication would effusively praise the patron for his virtue and his rank, but Webster goes out of his way to say the following:

> I do not altogether look up at your title: The ancientest nobility being but a relic of time past, and that truest honour indeed being for a man to confer honour on himself.
>
> (p. xxxiv)

Of course, Webster means that Berkeley has 'confer[red] honour on himself and demonstrated his virtue. But it is inconceivable that Webster would write this unless his patron was expected to approve of such a derogatory remark about the honours system, especially after James I's sale of honours from 1611 onwards, and the statement must be a cooled message that both men, in the context of the Jacobean court, are critical and sceptical of the integrity of those in great places and those with riches who hide corruption behind a title and a name. It is also a revealing key to the moral design of a play which, when analysed, it itself uniformly critical of men in power.

The two of highest status in the play are the villains, Ferdinand, who is Duke of Calabria, and his brother, the Cardinal. Between them, they represent worldly and ecclesiastical authority. Although their paranoid watchfulness over their sister is only sketchily motivated, it clearly stems from their own class consciousness and, at least in Webster's eyes, has some factual basis in the structure of Jacobean society and the laws of inheritance. Again, they are agents within a class system. Right through the sixteenth century, widows were in a unique legal position in England. They could marry according to their own choice more readily than spinsters, and they could own property and title gained from their husbands. In other words, they were more free of their own family than if they had never married. The three fears that the family would have would be, first, that she could marry somebody the family disapproved of, even a family enemy, or second, she could be forcibly abducted against even her own will without legal protection from her family (and there are several examples of this happening in reality) or third, she could marry beneath her own status and thus, in the eyes of the family, not only deprive them of her inheritance but also demean the family name. These facts are enough, as a contemporary context, to explain the claustrophobic vigilance of the brothers over their sister in the play. Despite the brothers' stated abhorrence of the lust shown through remarriage, their concern, like Bosola's, is really economic. As a widow and a duchess, her status, her rank, is of central and overriding significance to them. And of course the fact that the Duchess does in fact stoop 'beneath' her class, marrying the steward of her own household, would be so shocking and disgraceful to the brothers, so much a realisation of their worst fears, that the fact must be kept secret from them. As she has more children, of course the fact of her marriage becomes more and more difficult to conceal, and the divulgence of the secret leads directly to the banishment of Antonio and the death of the Duchess.

What makes *The Duchess of Malfi* a tragedy centrally concerned with the innocent victim is that Webster does not allow us for a moment to condone the motives or actions of Ferdinand and his hypocritical brother, and instead he presents them as morally perverted, and by the end Ferdinand at least is demented. In short, he is making class consciousness the root cause of their actions, and vehemently exposing these actions as evil. In fact, we find all these preoccupations with corruption in high places, the necessity of secrecy on the part of honest courtiers, and the resulting perversion of justice, stated at the very beginning of the play by Antonio, who is represented as even more a victim than Bosola:

> ... a Prince's court
> Is like a common fountain, whence should flow
> Pure silver drops in general. But if't chance
> Some curs'd example poison't near the head,
> *Death and diseases through the whole land spread.*
> And what is't makes this blessed government,
> But a most provident Council, who dare freely
> Inform him, the corruption of the times?
> Though some o' th' court hold it presumption
> To instruct Princes what they ought to do,
> It is a noble duty to inform them
> What they ought to foresee.
>
> (I.i.11–22)

In the context of the Jacobean court, at the height of James's extravagance, this is an extremely contemporary political intervention, and we should remember that James I did not call a parliament from 1610 to 1621 except in 1614, the year of *The Duchess*. Webster is not accusing the king of anything, for he shows us not a king but a (foreign) aristocracy, but he is warning James of corrupt advisers and ministers, adding that the way to avoid 'diseases' in the state is to rely on a 'provident Council' – in other words a parliament. The advice would not be welcome to the King at a time when his advisers themselves were advocating the dismissal of parliament and rule by direct fiat on behalf of a Catholic faction. Nor is this courageous, pro-parliamentary statement a voice of Webster's opinion from outside the play, loosely attached to the dramatic action. On the contrary, its fundamental suspicion of people in high places, its anti-authoritarianism, its warning of the corruption which flows from the existence of power, is made central to the vision of the play as a whole, the key to its sophisticated and highly crafted moral design.

Webster does not allow the audience to hold any but negative attitudes towards the Cardinal and Ferdinand. We hear in the first
scene that both misuse their wealth and power, that they are surrounded by sycophants and knaves, and that the Cardinal has
already suborned a murder committed by Bosola. In the second
scene, Antonio gives little sketches of each. The Cardinal, he says, is
a 'melancholy churchman' who is jealous of others, lays plots, and
depends on 'flatterers, panders, intelligencers and atheists'
(I.ii.84–5) 'and a thousand such political monsters'. He is also a
bribe-taker. Ferdinand is 'a most perverse and turbulent nature'
who may laugh heartily but only to hide his dishonesty, dooming
men to death by hearsay information. Delio comments

> Then the law to him
> Is like a foul black cobweb to a spider,
> He makes it his dwelling, and a prison
> To entangle those shall feed him
> (I.ii.99–103)

The noteworthy thing about these opinions is that they do not so
much dwell on private weaknesses or personal traits, but entirely on
the two brothers' malicious use of power of the law itself. The
Cardinal hides behind the law and his own vested position which
has been achieved by dishonest means, while Ferdinand, as the law-
maker and law-enforcer, uses it to his own ends, making the law a
dwelling like a cobweb to a spider, trapping others in it. With these
preconceptions, we immediately suspect them both of deviousness
in their badgering of the Duchess over the issue of remarriage, and
even she finds it peculiar that their attack on her is so consistent
that it seems prepared. Indeed, Ferdinand's words are surely to be
interpreted ironically when he warns the Duchess that she is living
in a corrupt, dangerous court and that there are many spies around:

> Now hear me:
> You live in a rank pasture here, i' th' court,
> There is a kind of honey-dew that's deadly:
> 'Twill poison your fame; look to't; be not cunning.
> (I.ii.227–32)

The irony is that Ferdinand himself as head of the court, is the
fountain-head of all the corruption, and as we have seen him
already, virtual head of a police state, set as a spy on the Duchess.

Once again, Webster is making the point that it is the very power wielded by the Cardinal and Ferdinand which explains their human failings – not, as many critics suggest implicitly, that personal failings explain their misuse of power. Evil is not so much irrational as material, and based on self-interested desire for gain. They are seen throughout as men corrupted by power, seeking to maintain their authority even at the cost of their sister's life, and of the well-being of the state.

After the murder of the Duchess, we learn of the 'injustice' (Descara's word) of the violent forfeit of Antonio's lands and money by the Cardinal, confirmation for us that it was essentially property which lay at the root of the brothers' objections to their sister's remarrying, and not solicitude for her welfare. The degeneration of Ferdinand into one who is afraid of his own shadow, and mimics wolves in digging up graves, is a signal that at last, and at least, he is besieged by some kind of conscience about his malicious deeds. There is some part of his personality still independent of the corrupting power of his office and power, which turns upon him destructively. We may not hold pity for him, but we find the retribution from his own feelings, breaking through his dehumanised role of authority, as at least an appropriate result of his actions. Not so the Cardinal, whose one thought is to cover his own tracks, terrified that Ferdinand will, in his illness, spill the beans about the murder:

> Let none upon your lives
> Have conference with the Prince Ferdinand,
> Unless I know it. [*aside*] In this distraction
> He may reveal the murther.
>   (V.ii.222–4)

He kills his mistress Julia in order to eliminate one other possible route for the truth to appear. But as Bosola, the one who knows the true story, says, 'Security some men call the suburbs of hell' and the Cardinal's security, attained only through a combination of killings and subterfuge, is precarious. He has his moment not of remorse but of self-recognition, in seeing 'a thing arm'd with a rake / That seems to strike at me' (V.v.6) when looking into his fishpond, but there is little expression of conscience. Revenge is taken by his own hired killer Bosola, who repeats the word 'Justice'. Bosola dies himself, as he recognises, suffering 'death [and] shame for what is just'. Words like 'justice' and 'truth' so strongly placed must indicate something very fundamental that is happening in the play.

Far from being the 'decadent' tragic-comedy, full of wonderful images but devoid of firm structure, so beloved of critics of the play since its rediscovery by T. S. Eliot, *The Duchess of Malfi* is a strong narrative based on the innocent victim, which would have had great topical concern in 1614 and would have been regarded by contemporaries as closer to the democratic principles and moral austerity of the puritans than the extravagant decadence of a corrupt court.

This essay is a revised version of an unpublished lecture given at the University of Gdansk, Poland, in 1987.

NOTES

[R. S. White's essay might usefully be thought of as the work of a male scholar who has chosen to implement a feminist ethics in relation to Webster's tragedy. This approach enables White to discern for us Webster's own critique of power and court life. The text used is *The Duchess of Malfi*, edited by Elizabeth M. Brennan (London, 1964). Ed.]

1. Thomas Wilson, *The Arte of Rhetorique* (1553), facsimile introduced by Robert Hood Bowers (Gainesville, FL, 1962).

2. R. S. White, *Innocent Victims: Poetic Justice in Shakespearian Tragedy* (Newcastle on Tyne, 1982; 2nd edn London, 1986).

3. Dympna Callaghan, *Woman and Gender in Renaissance Tragedy: A Study of 'King Lear', 'Othello', 'The Duchess of Malfi' and 'The White Devil'* (Hemel Hempstead, 1989).

4. G. K. Hunter, *English Drama 1586–1642* (Oxford, 1997), pp. 69–83.

5. Ibid., pp. 473–8.

6. In their Introduction to an edition of *The Selected Plays of John Webster* (Cambridge, 1983), Jonathan Dollimore and Alan Sinfield stress the play's condemnation of conventional society, but rather frustratingly they do not give detailed analysis. Dollimore provides only a little more commentary in his book *Radical Tragedy: Religion, Ideology and Power in the Drama of Shakespeare and his Contemporaries* (Brighton, 1983).

7. Derek Cohen, *Shakespeare's Culture of Violence* (New Jersey, 1993).

8. Harry Keyishian, *The Shapes of Revenge: Victimization, Vengence, and Vindictiveness in Shakespeare* (New Jersey, 1995).

9. See White, *Innocent Victims*, p. 23.

10. *The Duchess of Malfi*, ed. John Russell Brown (London, 1964).

11. Dena Goldberg, *Between Worlds: A Study of the Plays of John Webster* (Wilfrid Laurier University Press, Ontario, 1987), pp. 94–6 *passim*, p. 107. Another critic who does justice to Webster's heroines is Richard Allen Cave in his *The White Devil and The Duchess of Malfi: Text and Performance* (London, 1988).

12. The position of widows in Renaissance England has stimulated much critical writing: for a succinct summary, see Ann Chance, 'Shakespeare's Widow', in *Shakespeare and the World Elsewhere*, ed. Robin Eaden, Heather Kerr, and Madge Mitton (Adelaide, 1992), pp. 23–35.

13. *Brecht: Collected Plays: 1942–1946*, ed. John Willett and Ralph Mannheim, vol. 7 (London, 1976).

14. See Harriett Hawkins' chapter on *The Duchess of Malfi* in *Poetic Freedom and Poetic Truth* (Oxford, 1976).

Further Reading

EDITIONS

John Russell Brown, *The Duchess of Malfi*, Revels edition (Manchester, 1977). Very helpful annotations to the text.

Jonathan Dollimore and Alan Sinfield (eds), *The Selected Plays of John Webster* (Cambridge, 1983). A cultural materialist edition of the plays. This edition valuably combines textual concerns with issues pertaining to the staging of Webster's plays.

David Gunby, David Carnegie and Antony Hammond (eds), *The Works of John Webster*, Vol. 1: *'The White Devil' and 'The Duchess of Malfi'* (Cambridge, 1995).

Kathleen McLuskie and Jennifer Uglow, *The Duchess of Malfi* (Bristol, 1989). Contains a splendidly detailed introduction on the performance history of the play.

TRAGEDY

While some of the studies listed below are devoted entirely to Webster, many deal with questions of power, gender, and tragedy more generally. Indeed, there has been a critical movement away from reading single plays in isolation in order to account for their ideological import. All of the works below, however, address the politics of gender and theatre with which *The Duchess of Malfi* is so centrally concerned.

Catherine Belsey, *The Subject of Tragedy: Identity and Difference in Renaissance Drama* (New York, 1985). Pathbreaking feminist reading of the genre.

Lee Bliss, *The World's Perspective: John Webster and the Jacobean Drama* (New Brunswick, NJ, 1983). Wonderfully comprehensive and insightful readings of the entire Webster oeuvre.

Harold Bloom (ed.), *John Webster's The Duchess of Malfi* (New York, 1987). Fine anthology of essays on the play.

Dympna Callaghan, *Woman and Gender in Renaissance Tragedy: A Study of 'King Lear', 'Othello', 'The Duchess of Malfi', and 'The White Devil'* (Brighton, 1989). Examines the problem of femininity in 'great man' tragedy.

Jonathan Dollimore, *Radical Tragedy: Religion, Ideology, and Power in the Drama of Shakespeare and His Contemporaries* (Brighton, 1984). This is a landmark cultural materialist study, which reads Jacobean drama as profoundly political rather than as decadent and tending towards sexual depravity.

Dena Goldberg, *Between Worlds: A Study of the Plays of John Webster* (Waterloo, Ontario, 1987). A very useful overview of all of Webster's plays. Each chapter offers an informative reading of a single play.

Lisa Jardine, *Still Harping on Daughters: Women and Drama in the Age of Shakespeare* (1983; New York, 1989). Includes an excellent reading of the economic power of widows in relation to Webster's play.

J. W. Lever, *The Tragedy of State: A Study of Jacobean Drama* (New York, 1987). Lever offers an understanding of tragedy as a political genre – a production of and an intervention in the power relations of its time.

Nicole Loraux, *Tragic Ways of Killing a Woman*, trans. Anthony Forster (Cambridge, 1987). An analysis of the structural predicament of woman in tragedy, which, though it contains no specific reference to Webster, is extremely useful as a way of contextualising the issues of his play.

Sara Jayne Steen, 'The Crime of Marriage: Arabella Stuart and The Duchess of Malfi', *Sixteenth Century Journal*, 21:1 (1991), 60–76. This essay puts Webster's play in the context of the real-life clandestine marriage of Arabella Stuart and tries to gauge how far audiences would have been sympathetic towards the plight of Webster's Duchess.

THE SOCIAL CONDITION OF EARLY MODERN WOMEN

Kate Aughterson (ed.), *Renaissance Woman: Constructions of Femininity in England* (New York, 1995). Splendid anthology of Elizabethan and Jacobean writings on women.

David Cressy, *Birth, Marriage, and Death: Ritual, Religion, and the Life-Cycle in Tudor and Stuart England* (Oxford, 1997). Brilliant and comprehensive account of the social rituals surrounding love and death in early modern England.

Kathleen M. Davies, 'The Sacred Condition of Equality: How original were the Puritan doctrines of marriage?' *Social History*, 5 (1977), 563–78. An important discussion of the social and conceptual upheavals in the state of matrimony caused by the Reformation.

Natalie Zemon Davies, 'Women on Top: Symbolic Sexual Inversion and Political Disorder in Early Modern Europe', in Barbara A. Babcock (ed.), *The Reversible World: Symbolic Inversion in Art and Society* (Ithaca, NY, 1987), 147–90. An historiographical account of the social and symbolic significance of female rule.

Antonia Fraser, *The Weaker Vessel* (New York, 1984). An accessible guide to the condition of women in early modern Europe.

Constance Jordan, *Renaissance Feminism: Literary Texts and Political Models* (Ithaca, NY, 1990). Places literary discourses about women in the context of political discourse, not only in England but in Europe as a whole.

Merry E. Weisner, *Women and Gender in Early Modern Europe* (Cambridge, 1993). A marvellously readable, informative, and up-to-date account of the condition of women. If students need to read one book on women in Europe, this should be it.

Linda Woodbridge, *Women and the English Renaissance: Literature and the Nature of Womankind, 1540–1620* (Chicago, 1984). Forges the connection between the literary representation of women and the actual condition of their lives.

Notes on Contributors

Karin S. Coddon received her PhD from the University of California, San Diego, and was formerly Assistant Professor at Brown University.

Christy Desmet is Associate Professor of English at the University of Georgia. She is the author of *Reading Shakespeare's Characters: Rhetoric, Ethics, and Identity* (Amherst, MA, 1992) and has written widely on Shakespeare and early modern drama.

Andrea Henderson is Assistant Professor of English and Junior Fellow at the University of Michigan, Ann Arbor.

Theodora Jankowski is Assistant Professor of English at Washington State University. She is the author of *Woman in Power in Early Modern Drama* (Urbana, IL, 1993) and has recently completed a book on virginity in Renaissance Drama.

Kathleen McLuskie is Professor of English at the University of Southampton. She is the author of numerous influential articles and books on feminist approaches to Renaissance literature, including *Renaissance Dramatists* (Hemel Hempstead, 1989). She is currently editing *Macbeth* for Arden III.

Mary Beth Rose is Director of the Institute for the Humanities and Professor of English at the University of Illinois at Chicago. Formerly editor of *Renaissance Drama*, her publications include *'The Expense of Spirit': Love and Sexuality in Renaissance Drama* (Ithaca, NY, 1988).

Susan Wells is Professor of English at Temple University. Her books include *Sweet Reason: Rhetoric and the Discourses of Modernity* (Chicago, 1996) and *Out of the Dead House: Nineteenth-Century Women Physicians and the Writing of Medicine* (Wisconsin: forthcoming 2000).

Frank Whigham is Professor of English at the University of Texas at Austin. He has published widely on Renaissance Drama and is the author of *Ambition and Privilege: The Social Tropes of Elizabethan Courtesy* Theory (Berkeley, CA, 1984). His most recent book is *Seizure of the Will in Early Modern English Drama* (Cambridge, 1996).

R. S. White is Professor of English at the University of Western Australia. His many publications on Shakespeare and the Romantics include *Natural Law in English Renaissance Literature* and the New Casebooks on *Twelfth Night* and *The Tempest* (Basingstoke, 1996; 1999).

Index